You call this a

DEMOCRACY?

WHO BENEFITS, WHO PAYS AND WHO REALLY DECIDES

PAUL KIVEL

Illustrations by **ALBERTO LEDESMA**

With a new foreword by JIM HIGHTOWER
and a WORKSHOP/STUDY GUIDE and
AFTERWORD by the author

THE APEX PRESS
NEW YORK

©2004 by Paul Kivel, second printing with new foreword and afterword and workshop/study guide, 2006

Published by The Apex Press, an imprint of the
Council on International and Public Affairs
777 United Nations Plaza, Suite 3C
New York, New York 10017
Telephone/fax: 800-316-APEX (2739)
E-mail: cipany@igc.org
Web Page: www.cipa-apex.org

Library of Congress Cataloging-in-Publication Data

Kivel, Paul.
   You call this a democracy? : who benefits, who pays, who really decides? / Paul Kivel ;
illustrations by Alberto Ledesma
      p. cm.
   Includes bibliographical references and index.
   ISBN 1-891843-27-3 (alk. paper) -- ISBN 1-891843-26-5 (pbk. : alk. paper)
      1. Elite (Social sciences)--United States. 2. Power (Social sciences)--United
States. 3. Equality--United States. I. Title.

   HN90.E4K58 2004
   305.5'2'0973--dc22

                                                                    2004046339

Cover and interior design by Mary Ellen McCourt
Illustrations by Alberto Ledesma
Printed in the United States of America by Thomson-Shore, Inc.,
an employee-owned company.

This book is dedicated to all those
who have lived and died in the struggle,
resisting injustice in thousands of different ways.
May their lives be for a blessing.

And this book is for our children.
May their lives be full of healing, celebration,
compassion, love, and justice. May they build
community from the knowledge that other
worlds are possible.

ACKNOWLEDGMENTS

This book is just a drop in the long-running and swelling river of resistance to the anti-democratic and devastating structural inequities in the U.S. and throughout the world. My primary appreciation is for the creativity, persistence, compassion, and faith that motivates those who contribute to the river of resistance because that river waters the tree of human life.

There are many activists, writers, and researchers from whom I have drawn in putting together this book. They have been relentless in unraveling and exposing how the power elite operate in the United States. Some of them are referenced in the book, and the influence of others is evident in my words.

I am more aware than ever of being embedded in a web of mutual support and interdependency with thousands of people, both in the U.S. and in other countries, who work to provide the food, clothes, products, and services that I daily depend on. I thank them and hope that this book gives something back to the community.

I want to personally thank those who have contributed to sustaining me and my work. Bill Aal, Chris Crass, Allan Creighton, Synthia Green, David Landes, Betsy Leondar-Wright, Micki Luckey, Nell Myhand, Lincoln Pain, Hugh Vasquez, and Shirley Yee read and provided feedback on the book. The Roots group—Allan Creighton, Isoke Femi, Luz Guerra, Nell Myhand, Hugh Vasquez, and Shirley Yee—has provided a fertile place for me to explore the roots of our work in structural inequality. Many other friends and colleagues have participated in their different ways to this work, including Margo Adair, Robert Allen, Bob Boardman, Julia Caplan, Jim Coates, Hari Dillon, Steve Falk, Susan Freundlich, Miriam Grant, Francie Kendall, Terry Kupers, Rachel Lanzerotti, Alberto Ledesma, David Lee, Victor Lewis, Sharon Martinas, Daphne Muse, Rodney Patterson, Suzanne Pharr, Bill Rosenfeld, Penny Rosenwasser, Barry Shapiro, Dara Silverman, Naomi Tucker, Pam Wilhoite, Akaya Windwood, and Tim Wise. Thank you all for your support.

The staff at Apex Press have overseen the production of this book with diligence and thoughtfulness. My appreciation goes to Ward Morehouse, David Dembo, Mary Ellen McCourt, and Judy Rizzi for their dedication to making this and other books they publish available and useful resources in the struggle for social justice.

I want to thank Alberto Ledesma for providing the illustrations for the book. His political clarity, thoughtfulness, artistic creativity, and dedication to the work has been an inspiration to me and a valuable contribution to making the material accessible.

My immediate family, Micki, Ariel, SAM, Ryan, Amanda, Kesa, and Beth nurture and sustain me. They provide the inspiration and support to do the work. I appreciate and love each of you.

CONTENTS

LIST OF ILLUSTRATIONS AND TABLES

FOREWORD

The idea of belonging to something larger than our own egos and bank accounts, the idea of caring, sharing, and participating as a public is the BIG IDEA of America itself. As a boy growing up in Denison, Texas, I was taught this unifying, moral concept by hard-working, Depression-era parents who ran a small business in our small town. They knew from experience and from their hearts what America is all about: "Everybody does better when everybody does better" is how my old Daddy used to put it.

The unforgivable transgression of today's leaders is that they've abandoned this common wisdom of the common good and quit striving for that world of enlightenment and egalitarianism that the founders envisioned and that so many throughout our history have struggled to build. Instead, whether from the top executive suites or from the White House, the people in charge today are aggressively pushing a soulless ethic that shouts: "Everyone on your own, grab all you can, and if you've got enough money, secure yourself in a gated compound."

In this new edition to his path-breaking book, *You Call This a Democracy?*, Paul Kivel has done it again by exploding another myth about our troubled land—the nation that we Americans call "middle class." Instead he shows us how we are ruled by a handful of top dogs and clearly lays out exactly how they operate to accumulate wealth and power under cover of talking about democracy and equal opportunity.

His text and the clear and revealing illustrations by Alberto Ledesma lay bare the way money flows, how decisions are made, and what distractions are thrown up to keep us misinformed. The questions he guides us to use in analyzing political leaders and public policy—Who Benefits? Who Pays? And Who Really Decides? can lead us to clear analysis and effective activism for social justice.

It is time to reclaim democracy, retire the top dogs, and rebuild our economic and political institutions. Paul Kivel's book is an essential citizen's tool for that task.

Jim Hightower, author of *Let's Stop Beating Around the Bush, Thieves in High Places,* and other works of political subversion

PREFACE

I am not a member of the ruling class or of the power elite. But as a 15-year-old I aspired to be. I was quite confident as a young white male with substantial opportunities that it was only a question of judgment, initiative, and perseverance. In my guidance class that year, in answer to the question "Where do you expect to be in six and ten years?" I wrote:

> "In six years I will be in my last year in a business graduate school earning a Master of Business Administration degree at a business college, probably back East. In ten years I will be working for a large corporation as a department manager and be on my way up to the top of the organization. I will then keep climbing until I eventually reach the top. ...I will definitely become one of the most influential men in the business world."

Fortunately, I was more confident than foresighted.

Many things intervened to push my life and work in other directions.

I grew up in an upper-middle-class white Jewish suburb of Los Angeles in the 1950s and early 60s. My grandfather was successful in real estate, and my father as a stock broker. The end result was to increase my family's wealth so that we ended up at the top of the managerial class, and were certainly wealthy by most people's definition.

As a white male in an affluent family with business and entrepreneurial traditions, I was trained to think like a member of the ruling class. I read the *Wall Street Journal* as a teenager, participated in Junior Achievement, watched the stocks my parents gave me. The training involved a set of skills, a set of interests, a set of expectations, and a set of attitudes which my parents and teachers and surrounding culture patiently but persistently instilled in me.

I was taught specific answers to the three questions which frame this book.

Who Decides? I was taught, and came to expect, that I was one of those who would decide. Not only because I was an educated white male, but precisely because I had access to wealth and other resources to back it up.

Who Benefits? I expected that I and my family and community, and by some sort of magical extension, everyone, would benefit from the decisions I made.

Who Pays? Well, I wasn't taught to ask that question. I was taught that since we were all responsible for our own success in life, anyone who paid had only themselves to blame.

It was all very neat and tidy—until I got out in the real world and met real people. I realized that who paid, who benefited, and who decided, were the crucial issues that each of us with even a small amount of privilege (and that includes most of us) has to grapple with.

Who decides what is taught in our schools, where factories are located, who gets paid how much, where toxic waste is disposed of, and who has access to health care—these are life and death issues. We do not live in a democratic, equal-opportunity society because if we did, these issues would not depend on one's gender, skin color, immigrant status, or the jobs that one's parents had. And since these issues do depend on these factors, we live in a class-stratified society. To survive in and change a class-stratified society, we have to know how the ruling class and the power elite operate.

It seems to me that regardless of where we work, what we do, or how we live, without understanding how the ruling class and power elite operate, we and our families, communities, and natural environment will continue to be mercilessly exploited. All of our efforts to build decent lives for ourselves and our communities will be undermined by their agenda, and millions of people will continue to lead impoverished lives, or be exploited, maimed, or killed needlessly.

I have tried to pull together information from many different sources to give an overall picture of how the U.S. ruling class and its representatives in the power elite operate. I am neither an economist nor an historian. I have tried to distill the relevant information so that we can use it to understand what is going on in the U.S. and throughout the world. Each short section of the book is just a glimpse into a larger area that can be explored further through the books and resources beginning on page 177.

There are many very large numbers used in this book. It is hard for me to even contemplate the magnitude of a million dollars, much less a billion, or a trillion. Written out, a trillion dollars is $1,000,000,000,000. How much is that? What is important about the numbers is not necessarily their magnitude, but their flow. Where is the money going? In whose pockets does it end up? And, of course, what could we do with it if it were kept in our communities and used for the public benefit? If you are intimidated or confused by the numbers, just pay attention to whose pockets the money is going and the overall relationships between money, power, and decision-making.

Some of us are also intimidated by any discussion of economics, taxes, stocks, or public policy on these issues. We may have received a lot of miseducation about economics and class; or messages that understanding these issues is just too difficult. We may have emotional barriers stemming from the ways that our families dealt with money, or from negative personal experiences. We may also be responding to social prohibitions about talking about money, or to class, race, or gender-based discouragement we've received from others about our ability to understand these issues.

There are many stories and examples provided throughout the book. These are interesting in their own right, but they are mainly evidence for the general focus of the book—how the ruling class and their representatives in the power elite dominate our society. There is no need to understand all the details—the ruling class has highly trained and highly paid lawyers, accountants, and policy makers to come up with these devices for collecting money. You can skip many of the examples or, if you are interested, explore them in more detail using the resources at the end of the book.

You may feel overwhelmed by the sheer magnitude of the power, wealth, and control that the ruling class has accumulated. Since most of us have little information or opportunity to talk about the class divisions in our society, it can feel hard to take it in, and discouraging to think about the implications of ruling class dominance. It can bring up feelings of hopelessness and despair. You may get to a point in reading this book where it feels useless to do anything to try and make changes. If that happens, stop reading and acknowledge your feelings. You might want to talk with others about your reactions. It might help to remember that the current structure of our society is neither invincible nor inevitable. Ruling classes come and go, power elites are overthrown. Millions of people around the world are resisting and organizing against those in charge of the current U.S. dominated economic and political structures. I take great hope in their efforts.

This book is neither hopeful nor pessimistic. I have strived, instead, for as much accuracy and insight as I could assemble. I do not have answers for you, or simple solutions for our country. I simply hope to broaden our understanding of how wealth and power operate in the U.S., and to support our continuing struggle to build a truly democratic society. I can only provide a framework and information. You have to figure out how best to use it. I hope you will use it to guide your involvement in strategic community action for social change.

My vision is of a society in which every person is cared for and valued regardless of gender, race, cultural background, sexual identity, abilities or disabilities, or access to money. This society would provide adequate shelter, food, education, recreation, health care, security, and well-paying work for all. The land would be respected and sustained, and justice and equal opportunity would prevail. Such a society would value **cooperation** over competition, **community development** over individual achievement, **democratic partici-**

pation over hierarchy and control, and **interdependence** over either dependence or independence. What is your vision?

My vision is broad and long-term. If yours is similar to mine, it will take organized, thoughtful, cooperative, and sustained action throughout our lives. Our action will have to be based on an understanding of the class war we are involved in, or our efforts will end up being subverted rather than subversive, co-opted rather than effective, fragmenting rather than unifying.

Most of us have some intuitive sense that our society is not run in our interests but in the interests of a small, wealthy, and powerful minority. When asked in a poll, "Would you say the government is pretty much run by a few big interests looking out for themselves, or that it is run for the benefit of all the people?" 75 percent of the respondents selected "a few big interests".[1] Most of us know something is drastically wrong with how things work. Hopefully this book will help you understand how and why that is. Then, together, we can focus on how to change a social/political/economic system that does not work in our interests.

Paul Kivel
Oakland, CA
www.paulkivel.com

---

[1] Center on Policy Attitudes, as reported in *The Polling Report,* February 15, 1999 quoted in Dye, *Top Down,* 12.

WHERE ARE YOU IN THE CLASS SYSTEM?

This book is about the ruling class and power elite, but I think it is useful to consider where each of us fall in the economic system. Our class position influences how we understand the system and it helps us all if we talk about how class works in our lives. Otherwise it often becomes a barrier to our living or working together.

Take some time to locate yourself in the wealth pyramid both in terms of your family of origin (when you were growing up) and at the present time. Use the following questions to help you think about the impact of class on your life and life opportunities. (The questions are about the family you grew up in. Go through them a second time and ask them about your current situation.)

These questions are just prompts to help you think about the impact of different economic, class, racial, and gender factors that affect where you and your parents are in the economic pyramid. (See the class chart on page xxii, immediately after this assessment.)

When you have thought through your answers to these questions (and any others that occur to you), talk about your responses with your family, friends, and co-workers. One way the ruling class keeps us divided and fearful is by the social silence over class differences and the illusion that we are all just middle class.

1. Did/do you have enough food to eat? Were there times when you or other family members were hungry? Where did your family shop? What was the basic diet? Did you eat out a lot? At what kind of places? Who cooked your meals? Was there an abundance of foods? Lots of fancy foods? How did other people in the urban/suburban/rural area you lived in eat?

2. What kind of housing did you live in? Did you have a stable home? Were you homeless? Who lived with you—other relatives/another family? Did you rent your home? Did you ever have to move because your family couldn't pay the rent? Did your family own their own home? Did you have your own bedroom? Did your family have a vacation place or second house? Did you feel comfortable in your house, proud of it, embarrassed by it? How much of the

family's budget went towards housing expenses? Where in your area did people with fancier homes live? Where with poorer homes? Was your neighborhood racially diverse or was it segregated? How did that affect the status of the neighborhood?

3. What kind of job(s) did your parent(s) or guardians have? How steady was the work? How safe? How many hours did they work? Were there periods of involuntary unemployment? Was one income adequate for the family? Were two?

   What kind of status was attached to their work? What kind of benefits? What level of income did they bring home? Did the children of the family have to contribute financially to help make ends meet? What could your family not afford on that income? Did your family go on vacations? Where did they go? Did you go to summer camps or special programs? Did your family travel out-of-state? Out of the country?

4. Did your family have any accumulated wealth like stocks and bonds, property, a business, a farm? If so, what opportunities did it provide for the family? How much wealth did the family possess? Did that increase or decrease over your lifetime? Was your family in debt, or constantly worried about paying the bills? Were there educational, employment, or housing opportunities that were not available because your family did not have enough money to take advantage of them?

5. What kind of education or educational opportunities did your parent(s) or other guardians have? How did gender or race affect that? What kinds of jobs did their education (or lack of education) make available to them or exclude them from? How did their race and gender affect that? Were they unable to pursue further education because of financial circumstances? Where did you go to school? What was the class make-up of the school? Of the surrounding schools? How were students tracked by class, race, and/or gender within your school? Where were you tracked? What were the expectations of those around you about what you would do in your life? What were the most visible career paths of those in your immediate family/extended family/neighborhood? Was any higher education paid for by your parents or grandparents? Did you have to work to get through high school and/or college? How much education were you able to get? Did you rely on scholarships? Did you take out student loans to get through school?

6. What were the activities and behaviors that were signs of different classes in your neighborhood? How were class differences in dress, language, values, background, appearance, or behavior manifested in your school? How did they play out in interactions between adults? Between young people? Were you ever embarrassed by your class background? Have you ever embarrassed others, or felt the embarrassment of others because of their class background?

7. How was your class represented on TV and in the movies? How were other classes? Who were "representative" families or characters from different classes in the media?

8. Where did your family shop for food, clothes, and household goods? Did they buy "on-time" or on lay-away? Did they postpone purchases until they could afford them? Did they have to pay attention to budgeting? How was your family treated in stores based on how their class position was perceived? How did their race, gender, and/or immigrant status affect how they were treated? Were they charged more because of their race, gender, or immigrant status? Were there places they were not welcomed, or mistreated? Were there places they could not afford?

9. Was your parent(s) or guardian(s) able to vote for candidates that represented their class interests? Did the local, state, and federal policies that were passed generally support the prosperity and security of your family? Were tax policies, transportation, environmental, educational, and health care policies generally to the advantage or to the disadvantage of your family?

10. Did your family have health care coverage? Was it adequate? Was your family able to have regular medical, dental, and eye checkups? Could your family afford glasses or orthodontic work/braces when needed? Did your family forego or postpone needed medical treatment because they could not afford it? Was your family ever disrespected or treated less well, or treated specially or given special attention because of their class, race, gender, or immigrant status?

11. How did the police treat members of your family based on your family's economic standing? How was that influenced by race, gender, or immigrant status? Did your family look on the police as protecting them? As working in their interests in the community? How was the treatment of your family by other professionals affected by your family's class standing? How did race, gender, or immigrant status affect their treatment?

12. How did you and your family spend their leisure time? Did your parent(s) or guardian(s) have leisure time? Could they afford to buy you toys and games? What kinds of electronic items did you have in your house? What kind did you want but could not afford? Was there money to go out to eat, go to the movies, or to pay for other activities? Did your family go to fancy restaurants or eat out frequently? Could they afford expensive entertainment such as concerts or plays? Did your family go on outings or trips? Did they travel by public transportation, car, or plane? Did they stay overnight? Where did they stay? Did you have to work when going to school? Did you get paid for doing chores or jobs for your parents? Did you receive an allowance? How much was it? What did you spend it on? Were you given money on birthdays or other special occasions?

Class Chart

We can break the wealth pyramid into different parts, each representing a percentage of the population to see how wealth is distributed.

1 percent   ruling class (family income above $373,000 and net financial wealth at least $2,045,000)

19 percent   managerial class (family income between $94,000 and $373,000, average net worth $344,000 including at least $100,000 net financial wealth)

Next 20 percent   middle class (family income between $62,500 and $94,000, average net worth $161,000, primarily in home and savings for education and retirement)

Next 40 percent   working class (family income between $24,000 and $62,500, primary net worth, if any, is in home)

Bottom 20 percent dependent and working poor (family income between $0-$24,000, average net worth minus $8,900).

Income figures are for 2001, net worth figures are for 1998.[1] Keep in mind that these are not hard and fast divisions, just a rough profile. Many people are from mixed class backgrounds, or have changed class during their lifetime. Education, place of residence, number of working adults, dependent adults, children in the family, and other factors influence one's class position. At every level, people of color, and white women have to work longer than white men to earn the same amount because their wages are lower. For example, middle-class African American families work the equivalent of 12 full weeks longer than a white family with the same income,[2] and possess about one-third to one-quarter the wealth of white people at the same income level.[3] On average, women work one full month per year more than men in unpaid child raising and housework.[4]

[1] Mishel, et al., *The State of Working America 2002/2003*, 56,84,281. Net worth, includes residences and personal businesses and is the biggest source of wealth for middle class and managerial class people. Net financial wealth excludes these items and better captures the security, power, influence, and discretionary assets that ruling class people control.
[2] Ibid., 5.
[3] See Richard Shapiro, *The Cost of Being African American*.
[4] See Hochschild, *The Second Shift*.

INTRODUCTION

"In the past, Americans smugly assumed that European societies were more stratified than their own, but it now appears that the United States has surpassed all industrial societies in the extent of its family wealth inequality."
— Lisa Keister, sociologist[1]

"If it's class warfare, my class is winning."
— Warren Buffett, billionaire investor[2]

Do you think the United States has a ruling class—a portion of the population who own tremendous amounts of wealth and who benefit from the way that decisions get made in this country? If you do, you are absolutely right. There is a ruling class in the United States, and it is just as rich and powerful as any ruling class has ever been.

There are an even smaller number of people, the power elite—primarily a few thousand powerful white men, who make many of the decisions that affect our everyday lives. They decide where to invest money, where to build factories or whether to move jobs overseas; they decide what kinds of people get locked up, what's on the evening news, who runs for elections (and who gets to vote), and what is the quality of the food we eat and the water we drink. They decide on the conditions where we work, the state of our neighborhoods, and who has access to health care. Most of the time they decide, they and the ruling class benefit, and we pay. We pay in our wages, our taxes, our health, the quality of our housing, and often with our very lives.

How our society works is not a secret, but neither is it widely known. There are many systems in place to ensure that we are not really clear about what's going on, that we are distracted from noticing the concentration of wealth and power, that when we do notice and do organize to change things, we cannot get very far without running into serious resistance. This book should make clear how our society operates and exactly who it is that decides, how they decide, how they benefit, and how we pay. Then we can decide what we are going to do about it.

This is not a conspiracy theory. The power elite is too large to meet together as a group. They largely operate through normal and visible channels of power and control. There may be small groups of them who meet in secret to plan strategies, or who have more power than others. We may never know for sure. The larger problem is the entire social, political, and economic system that the ruling class and power elite dominate to their advantage.

Brief Definitions

Throughout this book I will use the phrase "ruling class" to describe the top 1 percent of the population in terms of wealth, those with net financial assets over $2,045,000 and average annual incomes above $373,000. I will use the phrase "managerial class" to describe the next 19 percent of the population, those with net financial wealth over $100,000 and average annual incomes above $94,000.[3] I will call these two groups the "owning classes" because this 20 percent of the population own the great majority (around 90 percent) of all the financial wealth of the country.

The term "power elite" refers to the several thousand people, primarily white men, drawn from the ruling and managerial classes, who run the largest and most influential institutions of our country in business, finance, philanthropy, academia, the media, policy formation groups, think tanks, and the government. Members of the power elite act as agents of the ruling class and make decisions which impact the rest of our lives. I will expand on these definitions in sections below.

The ruling class and power elite are two separate but overlapping groups. Membership in the ruling class is determined by wealth, whereas membership in the power elite is determined by participation in, and influence on, economic, political, and cultural decision making. People are members of the power elite because of the institutional power and wealth they direct, not because of their personal assets. They use their institutional power in the interests of the ruling class. The power elite includes many members from the ruling class but also many business and political leaders who are from the managerial class, and even some who grew up in families with few economic resources.

The Impact on the Rest of Us of Having a Ruling Class

When I began to think about writing this book, it was from an abstract understanding of the economic system, and a general awareness of the tremendous inequalities in the distribution of wealth and power in this country. It did not feel personal. Although I was aware of many of the costs of having a ruling class, I did not see all the personal connections to my life and my relationships.

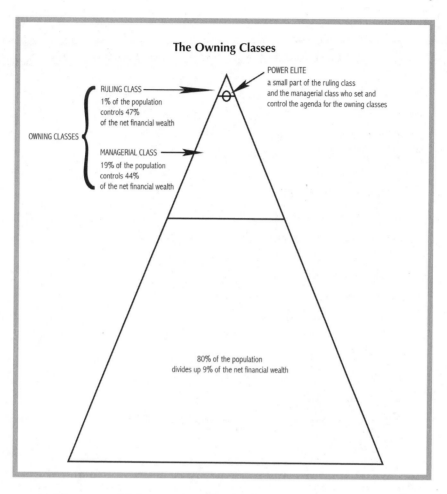

The Owning Classes

POWER ELITE
a small part of the ruling class
and the managerial class who set and
control the agenda for the owning classes

RULING CLASS
1% of the population
controls 47%
of the net financial wealth

OWNING CLASSES

MANAGERIAL CLASS
19% of the population
controls 44%
of the net financial wealth

80% of the population
divides up 9% of the net financial wealth

As I began to think more specifically about some of the people I cared about in my life, I began to see my connections to the root causes of the death and devastation around me. Breast cancer, lung cancer, AIDS, skin cancer, brain cancer, heart attack, family violence, work related "accidents," diabetes, kidney failure, asthma, suicide—I realized that I knew some of the people being killed—family members, friends, colleagues, and neighbors.

The impact of the system became real to me, personal in a chilling way as I realized the close ones I have lost. But precisely because it was so personal it was difficult to see the total impact.

I couldn't tally up all the people killed from inequality, because there are just enough social services provided to keep a lot of people alive, and to make sure that they don't die in the streets. They die alone, or with family, or with

CHECKLIST: Costs of Having a Ruling Class

Do you know anyone, including yourself, or know of anyone ....?

- who currently has, or who has died from, cancer?
- who currently is HIV positive or who has died from AIDS?
- who was seriously injured on their job, has an occupational disability, or was killed on the job?
- who died or was seriously injured fighting for the U.S. military?
- who did not receive prenatal health care when they were pregnant?
- who has health problems or who has died from smoking, or from alcohol or other drug related abuse?
- who died from an illegal abortion?
- who was young and who was murdered in your community, or who has been involved in gang related violence?
- who was not able to complete all the education they wanted?
- who does not have adequate health care coverage?
- who doesn't have enough to eat?
- who has had to move because they could not afford rent?
- who is homeless?
- who is unemployed not by choice?
- who works for less than a living wage?
- who cannot retire at a decent age because they don't have enough money?
- who has to postpone medical, dental, or eye treatment because they cannot afford to pay for it?
- who is a woman and has been battered or sexually assaulted and did not get the help she needed?
- who is a child and has been physically or sexually assaulted or abused and did not get the support they needed?
- who has been a victim of a hate crime?
- who has been locked up for a non-violent offense?

- who is a child and is left alone because their working parents cannot afford childcare or after-school care?

- who cannot apply for or is afraid to apply for medical treatment or other services because they are an immigrant?

- who has had to go into debt for medical expenses, education, clothes, or other basic necessities?

- who was locked up for their political opinions?

- who was denied food, shelter, or work because they are an immigrant?

- who was harassed or deported because they are an immigrant?

- who was seriously injured or killed, or who has to tolerate dangerous working conditions because they are an immigrant?

- who has committed suicide or attempted to kill themselves?

- who was locked up and executed by the state?

- who was locked up and did not receive the medical treatment they needed, the educational opportunities they desired, or the rehabilitation skills they needed?

- who died from severe weather because they could not afford shelter, fuel, or the clothes they needed?

- who has been robbed or beaten?

- who was killed in a car accident?

- who was a victim of police harassment, racial profiling, or police brutality?

- who died from using an unsafe product or vehicle?

- who has a disease or health problems because of toxics or pollutants in our air, water, or food?

- who drinks, uses other drugs, overeats, under-eats, or participates in unsafe or dangerous activities to cover their feelings, or hide their pain?

- who has died unnecessarily because they are homeless, unemployed, hungry, sick, alone, preyed on by others, or attacked by family members?

If you cannot answer yes to at least some of these questions it may be because you live in a wealthy or segregated community and are protected from many of the costs, and information about the costs, that most people have to deal with.

an attendant, one by one, and the cause is never related to the exploitation, violence, and policies of the ruling class and the power elite. They die at home, or in hospitals, nursing homes, and hospices, or in jails and prisons. They die from family violence, unsafe working conditions, homelessness. They die from lack of health care, overwork, child abuse, police brutality, and gang warfare. They die from the production, distribution, and availability of guns and drugs, and from inadequate, unsafe, or non-nutritious food, unsafe products, and environmental toxins. Each death is individual and can be explained, at least partially, by personal factors. These personal factors have social, political, and economic roots, but these are rarely discussed.

It took me a long time to put together the pieces of the puzzle and to be able to see that the concentration of wealth in the current political and economic system is killing us in large numbers, every day. It took me a long time to see that the great majority of individual deaths that don't involve someone dying in peace in old age are probably related to some form of exploitation and inequality, despair and lack of hope,

I mourn the loss of loved ones and grieve with family, friends, and community members for many others. I know some of the casualties. I think that you know some of them too. And everyday, in the newspaper, on the radio, on TV, and over the internet, we hear about many others killed by the effects of the tremendous inequality of wealth and opportunity in this country and abroad.

Not every single personal situation or crisis is the result of social inequality, exploitation, or discrimination, but many are caused by or worsened by these conditions. For example, 18,000 people a year die simply because they lack health insurance.[4] Another 50 to 60,000 die every year from work-related diseases like black lung and asbestosis.[5] Millions of people, those who can find work, perform "work that is faster than ever before, subject to Orwellian control and electronic surveillance, and reduced to limited tasks that are numbingly repetitive, potentially crippling and stripped of any meaningful skills or the chance to develop them."[6] Other effects of the concentration of wealth and power include:

- Severe limits on our democratic rights
- Longer work hours (leading to a lack of time to spend with our children, in social relationships, in democratic activities and in leisure activities)
- A greater threat of violence to ourselves, our families, and friends
- Greater economic insecurity in our lives
- Greater degradation of our physical surroundings
- More discrimination against people of color, Jews, women, lesbians, gays, bisexuals and transgendered people, and people with disabilities
- A false and inadequate understanding of our history and current realities

- Few alternatives to a narrow range of cultural activities
- Wars and terrorism
- Environmental endangerment of human existence.

There is not a single significant issue, relationship, situation, or part of our lives, that is not dramatically affected by the unequal distribution of wealth in our society.

The Impact of the U.S. Ruling Class on the Rest of the World

The devastation caused by the U.S. ruling class is incalculable. Millions of people have been killed directly by war in such countries as Guatemala, Vietnam, Serbia, Somalia, Nicaragua, South Africa, Angola, Mozambique, Cambodia, Laos, Indonesia, and Zaire (formerly the Congo). Tens of millions have died from preventable disease, poverty, hunger, pollution, environmental degradation, land mines, and economic exploitation. In collusion with other developed countries,[7] the U.S. ruling class has plundered vast areas of the earth and left large areas in ruins; unsafe, unhealthy and uninhabitable. Toxic rain, global warming; and large scale degradation of the oceans, rivers, and forests threaten human and all animal existence. There is no person, animal, or place on the earth that is immune to the devastating impact of having such a large concentration of wealth and power under the control of the U.S. ruling class and power elite and its counterparts in other developed countries.

The U.S. power elite has supported dictatorships, undermined democratically elected governments, funded and sold arms to counter-insurgency movements, attacked other countries by force, employed and distributed depleted uranium, land mines, cluster bombs, daisy cutters, defoliating agents such as napalm and agent orange, and used chemical and biological weapons. These actions have had a devastating impact on the rest of the world's population and natural environment.

The U.S. power elite coordinates with the power elite of European countries and that of Japan to maintain control of natural resources and human labor around the world. These power elites work together to safeguard the wealth and power of their country's ruling classes. The U.S. power elite, through its dominance of the economic and military force of the U.S. government, dictates much of the terms of relationships between countries and within countries, directly through U.S. foreign policy, and indirectly through organizations such as the International Monetary Fund (IMF), World Bank, and World Trade Organization (WTO),[8] and through trade "agreements" such as the North American Free Trade Agreement (NAFTA), the General Agreement on Tariffs and Trade (GATT), and the increasing number of bilateral agreements on investment.[9]

A SHORT HISTORY OF THE UNITED STATES RULING CLASS

The United States has had a ruling class since the early colonial period. As analyst of wealth and power, Kevin Phillips, has stated, "…elements of a hereditary upper class have been calcifying and entrenching in Boston, New York, and Philadelphia, at least, over three centuries."[10] This ruling class, although it has often been divided by conflicts of interest and different political perspectives, has always been the dominant force in the political, social, and economic decisions that shaped our country. It has directly controlled between 20 and 50 percent of the national wealth, depending upon the period. But regardless of the percentage of national wealth it controlled in any particular period, and regardless of divisions within it, the ruling class has always come together to maintain and increase its power and control. Individual families rose or fell in fortune, and areas of economic enterprise rose or fell in importance. But throughout our history, a small percentage of the population has continued to be the dominant influence on our political and economic system.

After the first exploratory expeditions to the Atlantic coast, the initial colonies were established by the English crown to be governed by lesser members of the English ruling class. This was part of the expansion of colonialism by European powers which began in the fifteenth century and which continued well into the nineteenth century. This stage of colonialism was initiated by the ruling classes of Spain, Portugal, England, Holland, and France as they divided up nearly all the land and peoples of the world and controlled them for their own enrichment.

The company that claimed most of the early colonial lands from the Atlantic to the Mississippi River and paid for the early ships and settlers who arrived on the eastern and mid-Atlantic coasts (including the Mayflower which the Pilgrims chartered from it), was the East India Company, then the world's largest transnational corporation. Most of the members of the British government and royalty were stockholders in the company, and for nearly 200 years its political and economic power allowed it to control most aspects of life in the colonies.[11]

9

A few people from the English upper class were given large tracts of land in the new colonies. Others were given land in exchange for paying the passage for bond laborers (indentured servants). Some people came to this country and bought land or accumulated land taken from Native Americans and distributed to settlers. Although the colonial ruling class did not have the wealth and power of the English ruling class, the class structure of England, which had been developing and solidifying for centuries, was transplanted to the colonies.

Not every person who became part of the ruling classes of the various colonies was a member of the English ruling class or a representative of the East India Company, but many were, particularly the largest landowners. There quickly developed a landed aristocracy in the colonies that controlled political office and colonial legal, financial, and social policy. Members of the ruling class owned the majority of the land, workers, and access to trade, and maintained extensive communication with their families, friends, and business counterparts in the English ruling class.

By the mid 1600s in Virginia, the largest and most financially successful of the colonies, the ruling class responded to the uprisings of indentured Europeans and enslaved Africans, who were demanding more economic opportunities, by passing laws and organizing militias to protect the status quo. To permanently divide poor Europeans and indentured servants from Africans, they instituted a system of lifetime slavery for workers of African descent, and gave poor whites some racial privileges as compensation for their harsh economic circumstances. For example, workers of European descent were permitted to own land, to beat, and even to own, slaves. Free Blacks were denied the right to vote, hold office, or to testify in court. Intermarriage was punished severely.[12] By the time of Bacon's rebellion in 1676, the landed aristocracy (ruling class) was organized enough to defeat the rebels and institutionalize a system of white supremacy through colonial law to ensure that such rebellions would not be effective in the future.

A century later the ruling class was still completely in charge of the country. In 1760, fewer than 500 men in five colonial cities controlled most of the commerce, banking, mining, and manufacturing on the eastern seaboard, and owned much of the land.[13] The founding fathers were some of the richest white men in the country (although they were not as rich as members of the English ruling class). The American Revolution was led by men from the colonial ruling class who did not want to pay taxes to the British government to further the trading interests of the East India Company.

Many of the debates about the Constitution were about how to protect the local business interests of those with wealth from the ruthless tactics of the Company. The discussions about breaking away from England were focused not on democracy, but on establishing local political control that was more responsive to the economic desires of the colonial ruling class than the English government was. The founding fathers assumed that those who were wealthy should decide policy. They believed that democracy was only for those who, by race, class and gender, deserved it. In writing the Constitution, these men specifically limited the right to vote to white men who owned property, a group who constituted no more than 10 percent of the population at the time. The ruling class was thus solidified on a constitutional foundation of white supremacy and male dominance.

In Colonial times, when the population was small, much of the rule of the colonies was direct. White ruling class men met in state legislatures and

Landowners Create Racial Divisions

Landowners

Before Bacon's rebellion there was little difference between imported labor from Europe and that from Africa. Africans and Europeans worked together, lived together, and intermarried, and protested their harsh living conditions together.

Landowners

European indentured servants and poor whites

Enslaved Africans

After Bacon's rebellion the ruling elite rapidly granted Europeans racial privileges and Africans were consigned to lifelong servitude. Whites and Blacks were prohibited from socializing together and intermarrying, and whites were told they should support slave owners in maintaining Christian values.

chose among themselves who would hold office, who would be the judges, and who would hold other positions of authority. They were the only people who could vote, and they relied on informal networks of communication. During that period, men of the ruling class *were* the power elite.

As the country took land from Native Americans, Spain, Mexico, Russia, and France, the European population increased dramatically. The ruling class needed less direct ways to maintain control of national and local government. In addition, many in the ruling class did not want to or could not be directly involved in decision making, except as voters, and contributors to electoral campaigns. Those who were most involved in business and political activities

Created Equal?

ALL 10% OF US ARE CREATED EQUAL!

WHAT ABOUT US?!

White women, Native Americans, African slaves, white indentured servants, and poor farmers were apparently not created equal.

established ways of communicating among themselves through personal ties, interlocking corporate directorships, policy formation groups, and social clubs.

An interlock occurs when high-level managers or members of the board of directors of one organization sit on the board of another organization which is, in turn, interlocked with other organizations. The interlocks create a web of connections, shared knowledge and values, and political influence. Over time this interlocked network developed into a leadership group or power elite within the ruling class. Most men and nearly all women in the ruling class were supporters of and benefited from the decisions of the power elite, but were not directly involved in running the country and its institutions.

The ruling class found itself dependent on a growing network of professionals as the complexities of running large corporations, government bureaucracies, philanthropic foundations, and other organizations increased. Some of these professionals, who were often part of the next 19 percent of the population in wealth, (the group I call the managerial class, see below) became incorporated into the power elite. This group, almost exclusively white men, consisted of the lawyers, academics, diplomats, researchers, foundation directors, and various other people who provided the technical and professional expertise that the power elite needed to coordinate their efforts.

From the earliest days of the country, some U.S. companies were exploiting land and peoples in other parts of the world including Africa, Central and South America, and Asia. These companies competed directly with companies representing the interests of the ruling classes in European countries. During the same period, the ruling class engaged in the colonization of the continental landmass through the destruction and elimination (genocide) of Native American nations, and the consolidation of a slave-based agricultural economy. The ruling class also used the government to pursue land claimed by Spain, France, Mexico, and Russia. By the end of the nineteenth century, the U.S. power elite was using the U.S. government as a systematic vehicle for colonization and exploitation outside the continent. It began to conquer other countries such as Cuba, Puerto Rico, Hawaii, and the Philippines as colonies, and to use the United States' military force to protect the interests of U.S. business in a regular way in Asia, Latin America, Africa, and West Asia. Until World War II, the U.S. power elite was a part of the international power elite but did not yet play the dominant role it has since come to play.

After World War II, because of its military dominance, the U.S. was best able to take advantage of the postwar reconfiguration of national boundaries and the liberation of many former colonies. Led by the United States, members of the various national power elites met, and developed a more coordinated international system of finances and decision-making.

This system was continuously consolidated during the succeeding decades so that now there is an international power elite with the U.S. power elite as the most dominant force. Multinational corporations have been developed into the primary vehicle for exploitation and profit-making. International agreements such as NAFTA, GATT, bilateral trade agreements, and institutions such as the IMF, the World Bank, and the WTO have become the tools by which the power elite governs the global economy. This system has linked up the ruling classes of all countries, but the primary concentration of power and wealth has remained in the United States, Western Europe, and Japan.

Although the U.S. ruling class has changed in the nature of its wealth, in the forms it uses to control the country, and somewhat in its composition, it has not diminished in its ability to shape central social and economic policy to its benefit. It also remains true that the ruling class and the power elite are overwhelmingly white, and the power elite overwhelmingly male. The institutions they have created are built on early foundations of colonialism, genocide, slavery, white supremacy, and male dominance that continue to divide us along lines of race and gender, and continue to aggressively exploit people of color and white women.[14] Much of the rest of this book is about how members of the ruling class and the power elite operate in today's world to maintain their dominance.

WHAT IS A RULING CLASS?

A class is a segment of society that, through its shared economic position and cultural values, participates in common social, political, and economic interests and specific forms of access or lack of access to power.

A ruling class is the segment that dominates society through its control of power and wealth. It influences and often determines the distribution of and control over resources; who has access to political power; which groups benefit and which do not from social policy; and which groups are central to the life, considerations, and attention of a society, and which are relegated to the margins.

Besides "ruling class," other words used to describe the richest and most powerful segment of society are the elite, the upper class, the haves, the dominant class, the rich and powerful, the decision-makers, the owning class, the money power, and the top of the (economic) pyramid.

A ruling class owns a dominating share of the privately-owned land, the buildings, the stocks and bonds and other financial assets—whatever counts as wealth in a particular society. In other societies wealth might consist of cattle, slaves, minerals, or land. Members of the ruling class are the primary beneficiaries of public policy decisions determining budget allocations, taxes, decisions of war and peace and international trade, environmental policy, health, education, and criminal justice issues.

In every society with a ruling class, the ruling class uses the particular historical, political, and cultural traditions of that society to stay in power, to perpetuate its power through the generations, and to justify why this should be so. In general, a ruling class will use whatever means it can to gain and retain power and wealth. A ruling class chant might sound something like:

What do we want?
Everything!
When do we want it?
Now!
Who do we want it from?
You!

A Ruling Class Is Not...

A ruling class is not a royal family, although a royal family can be part of a ruling class or a front for a ruling class. A ruling class is not the government, although government representatives can represent the interests of the ruling class, or be composed primarily of members of that class. A ruling class is not corporations in general, or transnational or international corporations in particular, although corporations can be run by members of a ruling class, or respond to the interests of its members. A ruling class is not a military dictatorship, although often military dictatorships operate to the benefit of a ruling class.

A ruling class is not a conspiracy. It is not a small group of men sitting around in a room in secret, plotting to take over, or to commit criminal acts. The U.S. ruling class operates publicly, through accepted channels of power such as the government, business, and the courts. There are many members of the ruling class who operate out of a shared understanding of their economic interests but who do not know each other and do not always agree on issues.

WHAT DOES THE ECONOMIC STRUCTURE OF THE U.S. LOOK LIKE?

Who Makes Up the U.S. Ruling Class?

The ruling class in the United States is about 1 percent of the population, or approximately 2.9 million men, women, and children. These families have incomes starting at about $373,000/year (1999) and/or net worth of at least $2,045,000. Most of the ruling class is white and it is predominantly Christian. There are some African Americans, Asian Americans, Latinos/as, and Arab Americans in the ruling class, but they are few and far between and rarely in positions of power. There are practically no Native Americans in the ruling class. There is a higher percentage of Jews in the ruling class than their representation in the general population, but despite the stereotypes, they still constitute a small part of that class.[15]

The ruling class is substantial. But even when you subtract from it children, women, and men who are wealthy but do not participate in making political and economic decisions, the group of predominately white Christian men who constitute the power elite—those who make the decisions that impact all of us—is still large in absolute terms although small in relation to U.S. society as a whole.[16] Obviously they don't all meet in a big room and decide on financial and social policy. There can also be widespread differences of opinion among these decision makers, although these differences generally fall within a narrow range of the political spectrum on economic issues.

Some members of the ruling class are new members who have built up wealth during their lifetime. Others have inherited their wealth and are members of families who have been part of it for decades or even hundreds of years. Some who were previously members are no longer. The styles and values of members of the ruling class change over time, but their access to wealth, power, and influence remains in place. In other words, the class itself continues to dominate over time even as its membership fluctuates somewhat in size and composition.

The Managerial Class

The ruling class makes up only 1 percent of the population and they would be hard pressed to run all the important institutions in our society by themselves. They have set up a system to reward some people with money, education, and other privileges to work for them. (In some sense we all work for them, we just are not rewarded for it and we do not have managerial jobs.) This group consists of the next 19 percent of the population. The managerial class includes families with incomes above $94,000 (average income is

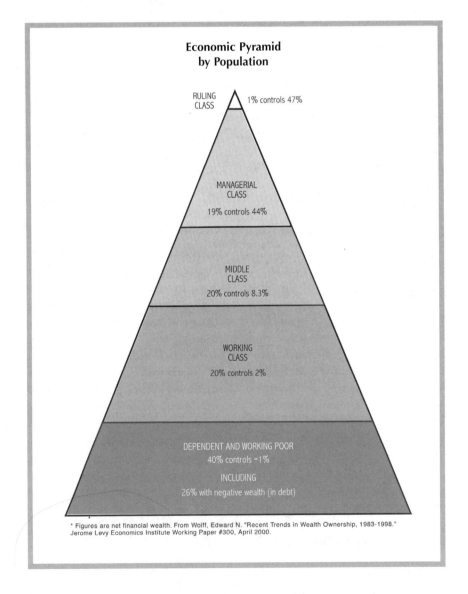

**Economic Pyramid
by Population**

RULING
CLASS — 1% controls 47%

MANAGERIAL
CLASS
19% controls 44%

MIDDLE
CLASS
20% controls 8.3%

WORKING
CLASS
20% controls 2%

DEPENDENT AND WORKING POOR
40% controls −1%
INCLUDING
26% with negative wealth (in debt)

* Figures are net financial wealth. From Wolff, Edward N. "Recent Trends in Wealth Ownership, 1983-1998." Jerome Levy Economics Institute Working Paper #300, April 2000.

$258,000) and net financial worth of at least $100,000.[17] The wealth part of this definition is the important part. People may have a combined family income of $94,000 and might even own their own house, but without financial wealth they don't have the opportunities, resources, and influence that those with wealth do.

I refer to this class as the managerial class because the organizations and people (paid and volunteer) that the ruling class relies on to serve its needs are run (or managed) by members of this class. They are the non-ruling-class

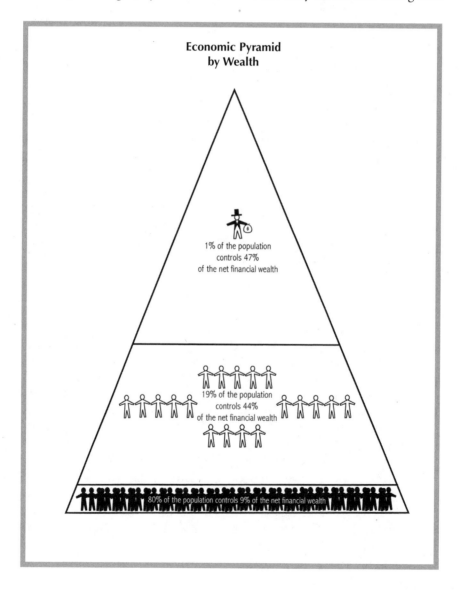

large business owners, corporate managers, foundation directors, corporate lawyers, doctors, architects, elite university professors, diplomats, politicians, and others who are generally paid a lot to carry out policies that benefit the ruling class.

It is not their occupation, but their high income and wealth and access to other resources that define these people and their families as members of the managerial class. In other words, corporate lawyers, but not all lawyers, elite university administrators and professors, but not all university administrators and professors, are members of the managerial class. Some members of the managerial class become so successful that they are able to accumulate enough wealth to enter the ruling class.

Many members of the managerial class are trained in professional programs at specialized graduate schools that provide them with ruling class values and an understanding of ruling class interests. These programs also screen out those who will not be reliable in serving the interests of the ruling class.[18] Other members of the managerial class could be successful small business owners, large independent farmers, consultants, directors of large non-profit organizations, or higher level administrators in local, state, or federal offices.

There are many people who manage or supervise others who are not part of the managerial class because they don't share the high levels of income, wealth, and influence that those in the top 19 percent do. They may be small business owners, school principals, lower- or mid-level administrators or government employees, or management staff of small- or mid-level non-profits.

The top 20 percent or owning classes, (the wealthiest 1 percent and the next 19 percent), consist of about 22 million households, or somewhere around 55 million people. Because of their numbers, and economic, educational, and social advantages, members of the owning classes, with rare exceptions, fill all the top positions in the most influential institutions of our society.

This entire segment is predominately white and Christian, although there are certainly significant minorities of people of color, Jews, fairly recent immigrants, and other groups in the owning classes. Due to housing segregation, job discrimination, glass ceilings, and increasing educational disparities, there is rapidly diminishing economic and educational opportunity for poor, working, and middle class people to join the managerial class at the present.

There are many people in the managerial class who are not managers. They may have a wide variety of jobs, occupations, and lifestyles. Whatever their personal lifestyle and values, the decisions that are made by the ruling class and the power elite usually benefit them economically, politically, and culturally in direct and specific ways. Their work is generally valued, well-paid, and respected. They live in better, less toxic neighborhoods, with better services and infrastructure than most others. They have better educational options for their children than most, and their lives, interests, and points of view are reflected in movies, TV, magazines, and most mainstream culture.

Members of the managerial class may choose to work against their class interests, or to disavow the benefits they have available to them. But just as with members of the ruling class, their choice to do this reflects their privilege.

The Bottom of the Wealth Pyramid

Below the owning classes there is a distribution of white people and people of color, men and women, Christians and Jews, Muslims, and Buddhists, seniors, middle aged, and youth, people with disabilities, heterosexuals and lesbians, gays, bisexuals, and transgendered people. But the people with least power are the people with least wealth. For example, the people at the bottom of the pyramid, those with zero or even negative wealth (they are in debt), are primarily children and seniors, women, men and women of color, people with disabilities, recent immigrants, Native Americans, and the poorest white people.

The Power Elite

In a democracy, the broad majority of people participate in making the major political and economic decisions which affect their lives. That is not true in the United States. We have a social structure in which a relatively small number of people are in unelected positions of vast power, and who act as representatives of the ruling class.

Sociologists C. Wright Mills and G. William Domhoff[19] refer to the members of the ruling and managerial classes who participate in running our society as the power elite. They are the "nonelected, self-selected, self-perpetuating"[20] business, political, social, philanthropic, and cultural leaders who determine how our society operates, and who make decisions that affect us, our families, and our communities on a daily basis.[21]

In one study of 7,314 positions of power and authority in the dominant economic, political, and cultural organizations (5,303 of which were in the largest corporations), nearly all were from the owning classes.[22] The people in these positions controlled "...almost three-quarters of the nation's industrial (nonfinancial) assets, almost two-thirds of all banking assets, and more than three-quarters of all insurance assets, and they directed the nation's largest investment firms. They commanded over half of all assets of private foundations and universities, and controlled the television networks, the national press, and the major newspaper chains. They dominated the nation's top law firms and the most prestigious civic and cultural associations, and they occupied key federal government posts in the executive, legislative, and judicial branches, and the top military commands."[23]

A recent study by researchers Zweigenshaft and Domhoff of the social backgrounds of people in the highest positions of decision making in corporations, the executive branch of the federal government and the military, concluded that this "core group continues to be wealthy white Christian males... [who] have been filtered through a handful of elite schools of law, business, public policy, and international relations."[24]

There are some white women, some white Jewish people, and a few men and women of color among the power elite. They tend to be wealthy themselves and generally share the same values and education that the Christian white men in this group do. Fewer than 1 percent of the CEOs of Fortune 500 companies are women or people of color.[25] Some corporations and gov-

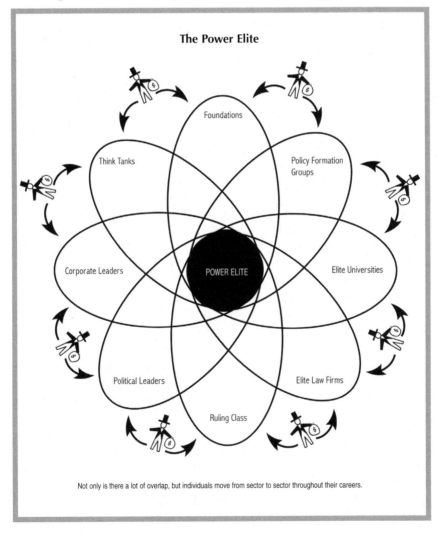

The Power Elite

Foundations

Think Tanks

Policy Formation Groups

Corporate Leaders

POWER ELITE

Elite Universities

Political Leaders

Elite Law Firms

Ruling Class

Not only is there a lot of overlap, but individuals move from sector to sector throughout their careers.

ernment organizations, recognizing the need to look diverse, are selecting more white women and men and women of color to be in the top ranks, but without actually changing their overall culture or practices. One commentator summed up this appearance of diversity by saying "…corporations [are} run by ruling class white boys, some of whom are female and colored…."[26]

Surrounding the power elite are 20–30,000 corporate and other institutional managers and directors who provide the interface with the managerial and ruling classes. They communicate and implement policy, direct operations, supervise mid-level managers, professionals, and consultants, develop strategy, and communicate and advocate for the decisions of the power elite to the media and to the managerial and ruling classes.

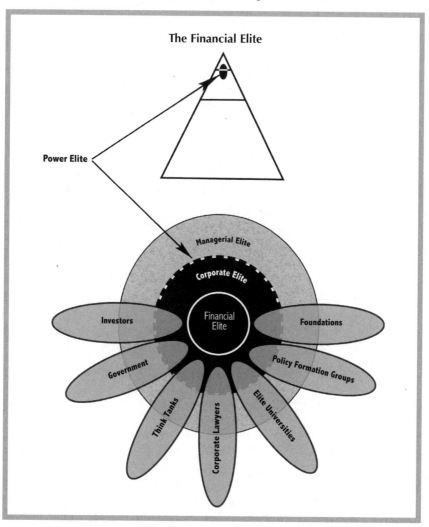

The Financial Elite

The managers and directors of the largest U.S. corporations, who control some of the most extensive financial entities in the world, sit at the center of the power elite. Many of these people command resources equivalent to small or even medium sized countries. Of the 100 largest financial entities in the world, 52 are corporations, not countries. General Motors, Wal-Mart, ExxonMobil, Ford Motor, and DaimlerChrysler each had 1999 sales that were greater than the GDP of 182 nations.[27]

At the center of this circle of corporate elite are the managers and directors of the largest banks, insurance, and other financial companies which are mostly based in New York, Chicago, and California.

Governmental bodies, corporations, and countries need large amounts of financial capital (money for investment) to operate. The largest financial institutions have a pre-eminent place in the corporate and power elite network both nationally and internationally because of their accumulation of capital, their control over large blocks of stock through their trust departments, their extensive information, research, and evaluation capacities, their central place in the extensive corporate board interlocking network, their ability to work together to create loan consortia (group loans)[28] and direct capital flow, their ability to facilitate takeovers and shareholder rebellions, and their ability to influence prices and interest rates, among other factors. Researchers Mintz and Schwartz conclude that, "... a handful of centrally placed financial institutions have dominated capital-investment decision making for decades. They directly control a significant proportion of all stock that changes hands; they lead a majority of lending consortia; and they are involved in almost half of all large financial holdings in major nonfinancial firms."[29]

The financial elite are able to influence short- and long-term capital allocations in the U.S. which, in turn, have tremendous economic and public policy effects on our entire society. Since the 1970s, their ability to yield equally powerful influence internationally through the World Bank, IMF, and WTO give them truly unprecedented power to shape economies and social policy throughout the world.

In the last 20 years, the largest financial corporations have become even more influential members of the power elite because of the increasing volume of national and international speculation which has grown to overshadow any form of productive investment. Not only the traditional banks and insurance companies, but now also pension funds, money market and hedge funds, real estate speculators, and private investors are part of the financial forces which demand high, short-term (and short-sighted) returns from nonfinancial corporate directors and from government policy alike. These transnational financial corporations have become so concentrated that three banks (Citigroup, J.P. Morgan, and Bank of America) control about one-third of all U.S. banking assets; two insurance companies (Prudential and Metropolitan) control one-quarter of all insurance assets; and a handful of large investment firms dominate investment funds.[30]

Finance is well-represented among the largest political contributors, within interlocking corporate circles, on the boards of think tanks, foundations, policy-formation groups, and in philanthropy. Even many of the direc-

Top 100 Economies
(Corporations in Bold Italic)

1	United States	34	Finland	67	*Nissho Iwai*
2	Japan	35	Greece	68	*ING Group*
3	Germany	36	Thailand	69	*AT&T*
4	France	37	*Mitsui*	70	*Philip Morris*
5	United Kingdom	38	*Mitsubishi*	71	*Sony*
6	Italy	39	*Toyota Motor*	72	Pakistan
7	China	40	*General Electric*	73	*Deutsche Bank*
8	Brazil	41	*Itochu*	74	*Boeing*
9	Canada	42	Portugal	75	Peru
10	Spain	43	*Royal Dutch/Shell*	76	Czech Republic
11	Mexico	44	Venezuela	77	*Dai-ichi Mutual Life Ins.*
12	India	45	Iran, Islamic rep.	78	*Honda Motor*
13	Korea, Rep.	46	Israel	79	*Assicurazioni Generali*
14	Australia	47	*Sumimoto*	80	*Nissan Motor*
15	Netherlands	48	*Nippon Tel & Tel*	81	New Zealand
16	Russian Federation	49	Egypt, Arab Republic	82	*E.On*
17	Argentina	50	*Marubeni*	83	*Toshiba*
18	Switzerland	51	Columbia	84	*Bank of America*
19	Belgium	52	*AXA*	85	*Fiat*
20	Sweden	53	*IBM*	86	*Nestle*
21	Austria	54	Signapore	87	*SBC Communications*
22	Turkey	55	Ireland	88	*Credit Suisse*
23	*General Motors*	56	*BP Amoco*	89	Hungary
24	Denmark	57	*Citigroup*	90	*Hewlett-Packard*
25	*Wal-Mart*	58	*Volkswagen*	91	*Fujitsu*
26	*ExxonMobil*	59	*Nippon Life Insurance*	92	Algeria
27	*Ford Motor*	60	Philippines	93	*Metro*
28	*Daimler Chrysler*	61	*Siemens*	94	*Sumimoto Life Insur.*
29	Poland	62	Malaysia	95	Bangladesh
30	Norway	63	*Allianz*	96	*Tokyo Electric Power*
31	Indonesia	64	*Hitachi*	97	*Kroger*
32	South Africa	65	Chile	98	*Total Fina Elf*
33	Saudi Arabia	66	*Matsushita Electric Ind.*	99	*NEC*
				100	*State Farm Insurance*

Source: *Fortune,* July 31, 2000, World Bank, *World Development Report 2000.*

tors and deputy directors of the CIA have come directly from Wall Street firms.[31]

Outside of corporate circles, there are many sub-groupings within the broader power elite based on political, economic, and other differences. There are groups that are Christian Fundamentalist and groups that believe in the separation of church and state, groups that have a world domination agenda and groups that are more internationalist in approach. Groups that favor high tariffs and comparative isolation, and those that advocate for limited trade barriers and an interventionist approach to international affairs.

The power elite (even within corporate circles) is not a simple or harmonious network. There is often sharp conflict stemming from different analyses and agendas between groupings. These conflicts are often negotiated out, or maneuvered around, to reach specific policy decisions. Sometimes they are not worked out, and divisions within the power elite can be leveraged by grassroots movements to effect social change.

On the other hand, there is great mutuality of economic interests and values, and substantial linking of most of the groups within the power elite. Often the power elite can reach broad agreement about general policy issues. The lengthy and sometimes hotly contested process of influencing other members of the power elite and reaching agreement involves the policy-formation groups, foundations, think tanks, and other structures detailed below.

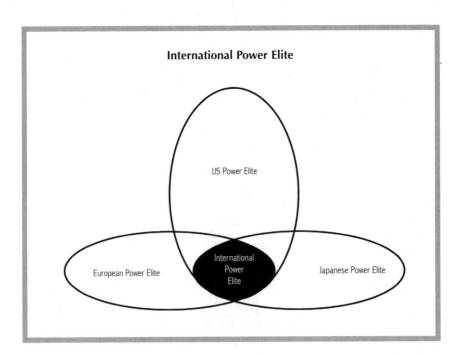

The U.S. Power Elite Is a Primary Component of the International Power Elite

The power elite of the United States has always been closely connected to the power elites and ruling classes of Western European countries, even those who were ostensibly our enemies.[32] Much ruling class wealth is tied to international economic sectors such as oil, arms, finance, technology, chemicals, tobacco, entertainment, banking, communications, and drugs. In addition, most of our largest corporations rely on a significant percentage of international sales, raw materials from other countries, production abroad, foreign employees, and earnings outside of the United States.[33]

On the more personal side, many members of the U.S. ruling class spend a great deal of their time in other countries, especially in Europe. Ruling class institutions such as elite universities, and social gatherings such as weddings, inaugurations, funerals, etc. are also sites where members of the ruling class and power elite form international economic and social ties.

After World War II, the U.S. emerged with a strong, undestroyed economy and with overwhelming military superiority. The foundation of U.S. dominance of the current international money system was established in 1945 with the Breton Woods agreement tying the U.S. dollar to a gold standard. The system was dramatically and unilaterally altered in the 1970s when the U.S. went off the gold standard and reinvigorated the IMF and World Bank.

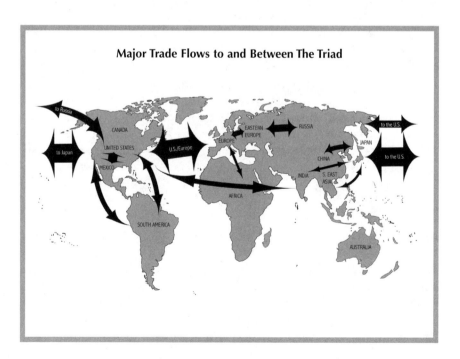

Major Trade Flows to and Between The Triad

Today, the U.S. power elite remains primary because much of the world's wealth is still concentrated in the U.S. With the largest military budget and as the world's greatest military power, the U.S. is able to enforce its policies and defend its economic interests unilaterally when necessary.

The financial system continues to be dominated by U.S. interests, but generally policy is coordinated with the power elites of Japan and Western Europe, often referred to as The Triad.

The economic predominance of The Triad countries is overwhelming. In *Fortune* magazine's 2002 Global 500, of the 25 largest transnational corporations, seven were Japanese, eight were based in the European Union, and 10 were based in the U.S. In terms of market valuation in 1995, for example, of the world's 100 largest corporations the U.S. was home to 43, Japan to 27, Britain to 11, Germany to five, and most of the rest were based in other countries in Western Europe. Russia, China, Canada, Spain, Indonesia, Australia, and Brazil had none.[34]

Most of the trade and financial interchange in the world is between members of The Triad. In addition, each of its members has "gathered under itself a relative handful of poor countries to act as sweatshop, plantation, and mine: The U.S. has Latin America, particularly Mexico; the European Union has Eastern and Southern Europe, and Africa; and Japan, Southeast Asia. In a few cases, two Triad members share a country—Taiwan and Singapore are split between Japan and the U.S.; Argentina, between the U.S. and the EU; and India is shared by all three."[35]

The rest of the world's countries are mostly on the margins of this system. Most of the financial, political and military struggles during the last few hundred years and now into the twenty-first century, including fighting in the Middle East, are really struggles among members of The Triad for control and maintenance of economic colonies around the world, or to subdue resistance from those colonies to their exploitation.

The power elite from The Triad countries have established a network of policy formation groups which help develop international and national financial policies, institutions, and practices. International power elites meet at private conferences such as the Bildenbergs, Davos (World Economic Forum), and Bohemian Grove, and at meetings of the Trilateral Commission, Group of Eight, IMF, WTO, World Business Council for Sustainable Development, International Chamber of Commerce, Council on Foreign Relations, Transatlantic Business Dialogue, and World Bank. The European power elite meet and formulate policy at meetings of the Union of Industrial and Employers' Confederations of Europe, and European Roundtable of Industrialists.[36]

The international power elite promotes an ideology of globalization that calls for the alignment of every national and regional economy into an economic superstructure controlled from the top by The Triad. This centralized and exploitative political and economic system has long been referred to as globalization by its ruling class advocates, and as imperialism by the rest of the world.

With the liberation of most of the world's former colonies, and the development of a sophisticated and integrated international economic structure, the ruling class, and power elite's efforts have shifted from direct colonial political control to indirect international economic control (with military backup), even though the general relationships between imperial powers and subordinated countries remains the same.

In the last two decades, a transnational ruling class has been developing whose allegiance is less and less to the governments and citizens of their countries of origin, and more to their class, and the pursuit of profits at all times, places, and circumstances, regardless of the consequences. This shift toward a supranational world power elite is orchestrated by the executives and owners of transnational corporations, leaders of the global financial network, and the government officials and professionals who work to consolidate their wealth and power further.

The extension of the international economic system so that no region or sector is left unassimilated is a consciously pursued strategy by the transnational ruling class in the current period. But national governments, particularly the U.S., continue to play a leading role in guiding the international economy. As researchers Petras and Veltmeyer conclude, "It is impossible to conceive of the expansion and deepening involvement of multinational banks and corporations without the prior political, military and economic intervention of the nation-state."[37]

The U.S. power elite also shares political and economic interests with the small political, economic, and military elites of the marginal nations, as long as those groups remain in power and can control the economic decisions within their countries. The primary interest of the U.S. power elite is to maintain a small elite in power in each local country or market that will operate its country with the most favorable terms for profit making. When the rulers of a country are unable or unwilling to do so, they are quickly replaced by a group more subservient to U.S. ruling class needs. In the last few decades we have seen this happen in Panama, Vietnam, Granada, Afghanistan, Iraq, Iran, Guatemala, Nicaragua, El Salvador, Brazil, Chile, and Indonesia. These attacks on the territorial sovereignty of other countries are guided primarily by the perceived needs of the U.S. ruling class, and its ability to use the U.S. government and U.S. public opinion to support its goals.

The owning classes internationally (as in the U.S., about 20 percent of the world's population) receive 86 percent of the world's gross product, whereas the working class, the next 60 percent, receive 13 percent, and the poorest 20 percent divide up 1 percent.[38] The class structure of each country is different and the percentages in each class vary by country, but most countries have both a ruling elite on the one hand, and a large majority of the population who have neither living wages nor an adequate and secure quality of life on the other.

In addition to having a ruling elite, many non-triad countries in the world also have a managerial class that benefits from the policies of the ruling elite and provides the markets for the products of national and transnational corporations.

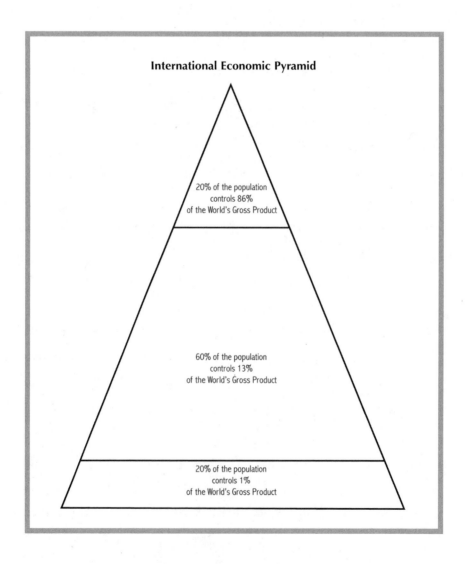

International Economic Pyramid

20% of the population
controls 86%
of the World's Gross Product

60% of the population
controls 13%
of the World's Gross Product

20% of the population
controls 1%
of the World's Gross Product

Just as there are conflicts of interest within sectors of the U.S. power elite, there are also conflicts of interest within the international power elite and within the power elites in individual countries. And just as the U.S. power elite comes together around core issues such as opposition to unions and wage increases, the international power elite comes together on many issues of financial policy, opposition to non-subservient third world governments and leaders, and a rhetoric of "free" trade or "free" markets.

The power elite uses the phrase "free" trade to justify opening up markets in less developed countries to the economic penetration of Triad-based transnational corporations. Protectionist policies within the U.S. such as farm price subsidies, steel import quotas, copyright and trademark protections, and price support mechanisms are not evaluated by the same standards as other country's attempts to protect their economies. In reality, The Triad countries promote a free market for money and speculation, a somewhat free market for goods depending on the interests of the transnational corporations, and a tightly controlled market for labor.[39]

WHY DOES WEALTH MATTER?

Income or Wealth?

Often when we talk about money we tend to talk about income. Since income is all the money that most of us have, this makes a lot of sense. However, income is not the whole picture. It is not even the most important part in understanding the power and control of the ruling class.

Income is the money that comes in every year from work, investments, land, government payments, etc. We are often told about high income individuals—sports stars, performers, lottery winners—who have a sudden steep rise in income. But in 2001, the median income for white people was only $37,800 a year. African Americans received $25,500, and the median income for Latinos was probably similar (recent data have not yet been released for Latinos).[40]

If you have more income than expenses and debt, then you can begin to build your wealth. But for most people, income only serves to pay immediate bills, and they have to try to stay ahead on other expenses. Tens of millions of people in the U.S.—nearly 26 percent of the population—are in debt.

Members of the ruling class have large incomes and a significant amount of it comes from their wealth; the land, stocks, bonds, and buildings that they have accumulated and have had passed on to them. Their income comes from dividends, interest, royalties, profits on investments, rents, and paybacks on loans. For many, they have enough income left over, even though they might spend a great deal, to add to their wealth. In other words, they can use income to increase their wealth.

In 1999, 1 percent of the population pulled in over 50 percent of the total income for that year.[41] In 2000, corporate executives were paid 411 times as much as the average worker,[42] or $10.83 million in total compensation. Looked at differently, in 2001, family incomes for the top 1 percent averaged $1.17 million and even the poorest members of that group received at least $373,000.[43]

Income is important, especially if you have enough of it to increase your wealth. But wealth is the true measure of the ruling class. Wealth (or exceptionally high income, which usually comes from wealth) is what you can use over the years to buy influence, power, security, and the future well-being of your children. Wealth provides for private schools, political influence, investment opportunities, early retirement, overseas vacations, and safe and luxurious houses and vacation dwellings. It also provides for the stability to plan, save for, and create a future for oneself and one's family.

For nearly two-thirds of the population, their monthly income is inadequate to provide security and opportunity. Because of their lack of wealth, their educational and job options are limited and often insecure. Any health crisis, period of joblessness, or family emergency can send them into financial insecurity or poverty. Any shift in the economy, or change in their personal circumstances and they are more likely to go down in income rather than up. In fact, average real wages adjusted for inflation were 22.6 percent lower in 1998 than they were in 1973.[44]

At the same time, people with only income to rely on don't have the money to invest in opportunities for greater stability, advancement, and wealth such as education, retraining, or starting a business. They are always at risk, but they can't afford to take a risk.

On the average (median[45]), white people hold $120,900 in household wealth (assets minus debt), and people of color only $17,100.[46] Most of that wealth is in people's houses. A family cannot sell their house and use that wealth because they would immediately have to use that money to pay for a place to live.

Net financial wealth (household wealth minus housing), is a much better indicator of wealth. By this measure, in 1998, the average (median) white person had $37,000 in wealth, the average African American had $1,200, and the average Latina/o nothing at all. Using 1998 figures again, even adding the value of housing to calculate net worth, 18 percent of the population had negative wealth—they owed more than they owned. Over 27 percent of African Americans, 36.2 percent of Latinos/as, and 14.8 percent of whites had a negative net worth—they were in debt.[47]

The ruling class is rich and powerful because of their wealth. Using 1998, the last year for which accurate figures are available, the top 1 percent of the population controlled 47 percent of the net financial wealth of the country, and the next 19 percent controlled another 44 percent. That left only 9 percent to be divided among 80 percent of the population. Today, members of the ruling class have at least $2.45 million in net worth and most have much, much more than that amount.

Who Owns the United States?

Wealth is about who owns things. Our textbooks and other media would probably say that you and I, "we, the people," own this country. That would be far from the truth. Of course, textbooks and other media are owned by the ruling class so it is not in their interests to inform us accurately about who owns the country.

As of 1998, the ruling class (top 1 percent) owned 67.7 percent of the business equity, 49.4 percent of the stocks, 50.8 percent of the bonds, 35.8 percent of the non-home real estate, and 19.7 percent of pension accounts. The top 10 percent owned 80 percent of all financial wealth including 91.7 percent of all business equity, 84.1 percent of bonds, 85.1 percent of stocks, 74.9 percent of non-home real estate, and nearly 60 percent of all pension accounts.[48]

If we included the amount of these assets that the next 10 percent of the population owns it would combine to cover most of what can be owned in

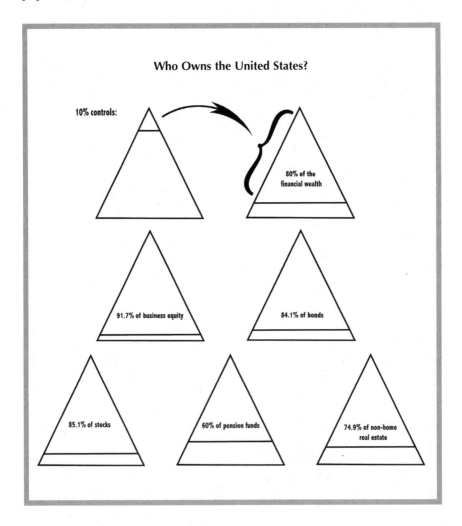

Who Owns the United States?

10% controls:

80% of the financial wealth

91.7% of business equity

84.1% of bonds

85.1% of stocks

60% of pension funds

74.9% of non-home real estate

the United States. For example, again for 1998, the owning classes owned nearly 96 percent of all stock.[49] That is why I use the phrase "owning classes" to describe the ruling and managerial classes. Outside of what the owning classes have accumulated, there is very little of monetary significance for you and me, or even the government, to own.

Where Does Wealth Come From?

Wealth in the most immediate sense comes from owning stocks, bonds, land, businesses, buildings, and other forms of investments. In a more fundamental sense, most wealth comes from exploitation. Wealth is produced from exploiting people's labor, exploiting land, or exploiting other opportunities to gain money.

Specifically, as political analyst and historian Michael Parenti points out, much ruling class wealth comes from, "slave trafficking, bootlegging, gun running, opium trading, falsified land claims, violent acquisition of water and mineral rights, the extermination of indigenous peoples, sales of shoddy and unsafe goods, public funds used for private speculations, crooked deals in government bonds and vouchers, and payoffs for political favors. One finds fortunes built on slave labor, indentured labor, prison labor, immigrant labor, female labor, child labor, and scab labor—backed by the lethal force of gun thugs and militia. "Old money" is often little more than dirty money laundered by several generations of possession."[50] (And, I would add, by charitable acts and contributions.)

People become wealthy through exploitation sanctioned by government policy. If the government required that workers be paid a living wage, and protected their rights to organize themselves into unions, it would be extremely difficult for businesses to exploit workers. If the government protected the land and its timber, mineral, and chemical wealth for the benefit of all present and future residents, it would be difficult for individuals and businesses to exploit the land. However, as we will see in more detail later, the government was set up by members of the ruling class to make it possible for them to exploit people, and the land and its resources so that they could retain and increase their wealth.

Land is the basis of much wealth—land to grow food, land to grow profitable crops like cotton and tobacco, land to harvest timber, land to mine minerals and chemicals, land on which to build factories and cities. All the land in the United States was stolen from the native peoples who lived here. Much of that land went directly to the ruling class. It was given outright, or sold very cheaply to wealthy individuals, to chartered companies, or to businesses such as railroad companies, first by the British and Spanish governments, and then eventually by the U.S. government.

The remaining land, excluding that which was kept by the federal government or given to the states, primarily went to white men for homesteads. By the late nineteenth century over a billion acres of land had been given to private interests.[51] Over 91 million acres was given to the railroads alone. Of the 287 million acres that was allotted for homesteading, it is estimated that 80 to 90 percent went to speculators to be resold for huge profits, and only 11 to 17 percent was actually homesteaded. In almost all cases, this land went to white men because people of color were excluded from access to homesteading, mining, ranching, or other claims, and few white women were able to participate.[52]

In the U.S. and throughout the rest of the world, large corporations continue to devastate government lands and the remaining Native American owned lands by clear-cutting, mining, and pollution. The wealth from land flows to the U.S. ruling class from forests, mines, waterways, and farms around the world, in addition to the exploitation of land within the continental U.S.

Another basis of wealth is the exploitation of people. The difference between the value of what people produce through their work and what they are paid for what they produce, minus the costs of doing business, is the surplus value or profit that is accumulated as wealth by those who can afford to hire workers.

In 1998 it was estimated that, in the United States, an average private sector employee worked a little over two hours for her or himself and almost six hours for the person or business that hired them.[53] A worker who produced $320 worth of goods or services in a day and was making $10/hour would only be paid $80 for her or his work. If it cost another $200 to run the business (including the salaries of the managers), then the other $40 would be profit for their employer. In other words, the employer gained one half the amount the worker did. The more workers, the greater the profit to the employer. Even after subtracting for the costs of doing business, there is tremendous wealth available that is taken from workers and transferred to employers. It does not take very much exploitation to begin a cycle of wealth accumulation.

Up until about 150 years ago, the surplus value of most people who worked for someone else went directly to the individual who employed them. With the rise of large corporate enterprises, the surplus now more often goes to a corporation.

It is often mistakenly assumed that investors produce or create wealth for a corporation by investing their money in stocks. However, buying stocks is like buying used books—it is a secondary market. Just as none of the money from the sale of a used book goes to the author or publisher, none of the money from the sale of stocks goes to the corporation.

The only exception is the money from the sale of new issues of stock. But this is a small fraction of the total amount of stock sales and, when balanced against the amount of stock that corporations buy back from investors each year, the net outflow to investors is many times as great as the money they invest. In 1999 the value of new common stock sold was $106 billion, whereas the value of all shares traded was a mammoth $20.4 trillion. Combining dividends paid to investors and net new equity issues (new issues minus buybacks), in 1998 investors (primarily those in the owning classes) gained, and corporations paid out (workers lost) $505 billion dollars.[54]

Much wealth is created by workers, is concentrated by corporations, and disbursed to investors. The final and major source of wealth is from the unpaid labor of people, primarily women, who raise children, grow food, take care of other adults, and provide a vast infrastructure of support for workers and owners alike. Many women work at paid labor and, in addition, do much unpaid work (sometimes labeled a double or even triple shift). Unpaid women, children who are forced to work, and some men, such as those in prison or those who are sharecroppers, have all of their productive and caretaking labor exploited. Just looking at women's unpaid work, it is estimated that married women with children work, on average, the equiva-

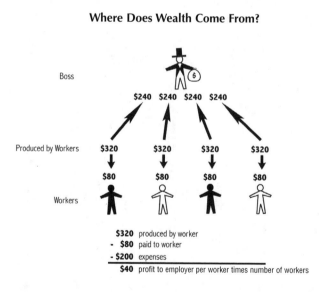

Where Does Wealth Come From?

Boss

$240 $240 $240 $240

Produced by Workers $320 $320 $320 $320

$80 $80 $80 $80

Workers

$320	produced by worker	
- **$80**	paid to worker	
- **$200**	expenses	
$40	profit to employer per worker times number of workers	

If a worker produces $320 for a day of work in the United States, she or he might get to take home about $80 in wages and benefits to live on. The other $240 goes to the boss or owner. The owner's expenses might be $200 (or often less) to run the business, in which case they would make $40 per worker (per day) in profit. The more workers in a company, the more profits for the boss.

lent of one month more a year than their male partners.[55] Employers, and ultimately the ruling class, benefit from the direct labor of workers and from the unpaid labor of women, which provides for the very possibility and support of the paid workforce.

In addition to unpaid labor, the reproduction and raising of children who become workers in economic systems such as slavery, is also unpaid and often exploited labor. After the slave trade was made illegal but when slavery was still part of the economic system in the U.S., slavemasters would use African American women to breed slaves so that they could continue to have a large work force.

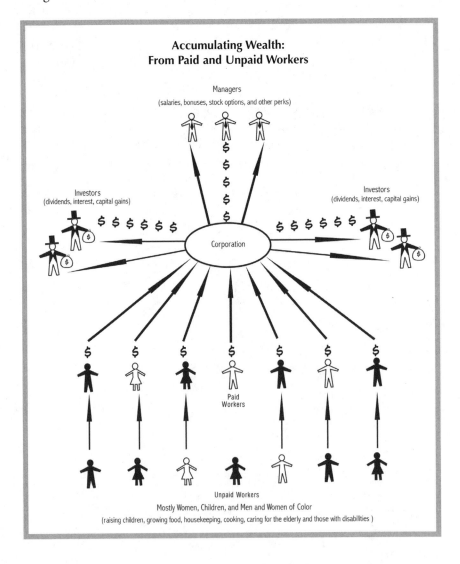

Accumulating Wealth: From Paid and Unpaid Workers

Managers
(salaries, bonuses, stock options, and other perks)

Investors
(dividends, interest, capital gains)

Investors
(dividends, interest, capital gains)

Corporation

Paid Workers

Unpaid Workers
Mostly Women, Children, and Men and Women of Color
(raising children, growing food, housekeeping, cooking, caring for the elderly and those with disabilities)

The accumulation of wealth through the exploitation of paid workers is subsidized by the unpaid labor of women, children, and workers in under-developed countries. The entire economic system would collapse without their work of raising children, producing food through subsistence agricul-ture, scavenging, bartering, taking care of the emotional, psychological, phys-ical, and even sexual needs of workers, as well as the needs of the elderly, of those with disabilities, and of the young.

The accumulation of wealth begins with the appropriation and exploita-tion of the land and its resources. Wealth is produced by paid workers in the United States. Their ability to produce wealth for the ruling class is depend-ent on their being supported by the unpaid and low paid work of women, and men and women of color both in this country and throughout the underdeveloped world. As Economist Maria Mies summarizes, "Women, nature and the people and lands of Africa, Asia and Latin America…formed the invisible underground foundation for this accumulation process."[56]

Speculative Wealth

Speculative wealth is based on buying and selling things on the speculation (hope) that a profit can be made. It is a form of gambling. Financial markets (stock markets, bond markets, commodities markets, etc.) have been created by members of the ruling class in which people can bet on the future prices of stocks, bonds, commodities, precious minerals, and currencies. Very com-plex financial arrangements, such as options, futures, options on futures, indexes, options on indexes, swaps, collars, and swaptions,[57] exist to allow people to bet on prices going up or down today, tomorrow, next week, or next month.

People have long gambled on land prices, gems, sporting events, and temporarily valued things such as tulip bulbs. Now it is possible to speculate on almost anything, and much of the economic activity of capitalism has become trading not only assets, but complex financial claims to future income from assets.

Although worthless to our society as an economic activity because noth-ing is produced, various kinds of gambling and speculation can be highly lucrative to individuals. Speculation favors those who have wealth or access to credit because they can finance their bets. They can buy land, stocks, or futures by putting some money down and borrowing the rest, hoping that prices will go up before their loans are due. Many fortunes have been made (and lost) by speculators, often in times of war, scarcity, or natural disaster.

The net effect of speculation on our society is that prices are driven up by people buying things with the expectation/hope that prices will rise.[58] This can produce wild fluctuations in the price of goods, as speculators try to outwit other speculators by buying low and selling before prices decline from their peak. The lure of greater (and quicker) profits from speculation than from investing money in the production of goods and services distorts the economy and produces great volatility in prices.

Investment in production, which builds an economy and produces long-term profits, is driven out by speculative investment that builds instability, but offers the potential for large short-term gains. Describing the net effect of the diversion of investment from production to speculation (among other factors), economists Bluestone and Harrison wrote, "Left behind are shuttered factories, displaced workers, and a newly emerging group of ghost towns."[59]

There is a tendency for land and housing prices to rise as demand increases due to increased population. The increased population pressure is often from people who have been driven off their land by corporate practices. Those who have the wealth, or have access to credit, are able to buy houses or land in earlier periods and watch the value of their assets increase. Those who did not have wealth, or who were denied access to loans or desirable housing (often men and women of color, and lesbians and gays and single women of all races), were unable to take advantage of increasing housing prices.

In addition to this generally slow, gradual rise in prices, there have been periods in particular areas where land and housing prices have gone up dramatically due to speculation made possible by tax cuts for the wealthy which allow them to keep more cash to invest. This process, sometimes called gentrification[60] in urban areas, has resulted in many poor and working class people, people of color, seniors, single parent families, small businesses, and nonprofit organizations having to leave areas because they could no longer afford to live or operate there. This is another negative consequence of the concentration of wealth that gives some people the ability to speculate on needed resources, and thus drive prices up.

Another kind of speculation occurs when high-level managers are awarded stock options as part of their compensation. Stock options are issued at the current stock price with the hope that prices will rise. A manager can purchase the stock at the current price (let's say it is $2) anytime in the future, even when the price has gone way up. If the price goes to $20 a share, then the stock option holder can borrow money against the current price ($20) to buy the shares at the former price ($2), and then sell the shares at the current price to pay back the borrowed amount and to retain a large profit. Lack of accounting for this kind of financial manipulation and speculation contributed to the collapse of companies like Enron, and to the economic recession of 2000.

An economy based on speculation benefits those few who have the resources to gamble and take the risks, and hurts the many who don't have the resources or desire to gamble, and who cannot afford the risk. In addition, world markets based on speculation make individual countries and regions vulnerable to tremendous fluctuations in their economies based on how speculators/investors evaluate their potential profits.

It is hard to underestimate the magnitude of the speculation in currency by governments, investors, and transnational corporations. Today around $2 trillion *a day* is turned over in international currency markets, under 2 percent of which is for trade and real investment.[61] The collapse of some Asian economies in the late 1990s, the collapse of the Mexican economy in 1994, and that of Russia in 1998 were all at least partly the result of trading by the U.S. and other ruling classes in international stock and currency markets that shifted huge amounts of money out of these economies in very short amounts of time. This collapse in investor confidence produced massive layoffs, bankruptcies, a substantial decrease in wages, and a sharp increase in prices even though the fundamental strengths of those economies remained unchanged.

Wealth comes from direct exploitation of land and people's labor, from the indirect exploitation of people's (primarily women's) unpaid reproductive, service, and subsistence labor, or from speculation, which also contributes to the exploitation of people. Some individuals get richer and most become poorer.

Business owners, corporate managers, and speculators may work very hard at what they do. But they don't work harder than other people, they generally started out with economic, racial, gender,[62] and other advantages, and they don't "deserve" the great wealth they accumulate. Their wealth comes at the expense of the general economy and out of the pockets and hard work of the rest of the population.

The impact of money (or other forms of wealth such as land or slaves) can potentially be multiplied. Money can be borrowed against, used for credit, used for political access, etc. As we will see as we proceed, the economic and political system was set up so that those with wealth can easily maintain and multiply their wealth, while most people have little opportunity to do so. The more one has, the more opportunity one has to increase it. Of course many people lose money, and some are able to turn skills, abilities, experience, hard work, deceit, and luck into economic opportunity. But they face tremendous disadvantages in doing so compared to those who start with some wealth.

There are three stages to the accumulation and consolidation of wealth into a ruling class. The first stage is the exploitation of workers (paid and unpaid, including keeping some people unemployed so that wages can be kept low) and the transfer of wealth from workers to the ruling class. The second stage is investment and speculation—using that wealth to leverage more

Stages of Accumulating Wealth

Stage One: Exploiting Workers

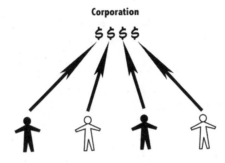

Corporation

Stage Two :   Investment, Speculation, and Consolidation of Power

Stage Three :   Pass it on to children

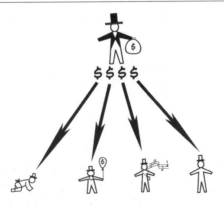

wealth, as well as social, political, and economic power and control. The third and final stage is the transfer of wealth from the present generation to succeeding generations. This book looks at how the ruling class organizes to accumulate wealth at all three stages.

Other Kinds of Wealth

For many of us, besides money and power, there are other things that we count as wealth, such as loving relationships, family, good health, a safe and nurturing community, and a healthy environment. We may have enough of these kinds of wealth that we are not concerned about other people hoarding material wealth. However, the concentration of wealth in the United States by the ruling class dramatically affects the health of our families and communities, and is detrimental to our ability to enjoy nonmaterial kinds of wealth. The concentration of wealth means that many of us lack safety, health, and a healthy environment, and our lives and relationships are limited by the impact of exploitation, discrimination, violence, and pollution.

Wealth and People of Color

White supremacy, the dominance of white people in society and the subordination, exploitation and violence directed at people of color, remains a cornerstone of ruling class power and control.

A substantial amount of the wealth that the ruling class has accumulated is from taking and exploiting the land of indigenous peoples both in the continental United States and elsewhere. Another substantial amount of their wealth is from the exploited labor of people of color. This exploitation has taken many forms, including the enslavement of Native Americans and then of Africans, indentured servitude, tenant farming, underpaid work in the fields, factories and homes, sweat shops, prostitution, and child labor both within the continental U.S. and in other countries. Of course, not only people of color were exploited; most white people, and not-yet-considered-white immigrants such as Italians, Irish, and Jewish people were as well.

People of color as entire populations were exploited systematically over hundreds of years, and that exploitation continues today. Many groups were specifically allowed into this country under restricted conditions such as Chinese workers brought in to work on the railroads, Latinos brought in to work in the fields, and of course, Africans brought in to work on the plantations of the South. People of color still perform much of the most dangerous and least desirable work in the United States, at wages that are significantly below those of most white people.

Much of the financial wealth of the country was based on the exploited labor of people of color. For example, it was not just the entire economy of the south that was based on slavery, but also the economy of the north, which used the cotton produced in the south to fuel profits from the textile industry and international trade.

Not only were people of color exploited; being white itself was a form of property. There was a long series of court decisions that weighed very carefully who was and who was not considered to be white because of the significant material benefits that accrued to those who were deemed to be white. If you were white you could vote, and therefore your vote could be bargained with politicians for economic and social advantages, and your economic interests were reflected in the political decisions that were made. If you were white you were worth more (paid more) as a worker and you were owed more by the government in terms of benefits and consideration. You could own land and turn that into profit. You could have access to loans and credit, allowing you to accumulate wealth. You had credibility in court and therefore could defend yourself, or sue to protect your interests. Your status as a white person gave everything you accomplished more visibility and more reward compared to people of color who accomplished the same things.

People of color were barred in many ways from accumulating wealth, and everything they were involved with was valued less because of white supremacy. Even after slavery was abolished, most people of color were barred from owning land, from homesteading, from receiving credit or loans, from engaging in skilled work, and from gaining higher levels of education. In addition they were charged more than white people for the same goods and services. When they did achieve economic success, white business communities were quick to organize riots to destroy their homes and businesses, such as those that occurred at Rosewood, Florida and Tulsa, Oklahoma.[63]

Given the history outlined above, it is not surprising that people of color, particularly African Americans, Latinos/as, and Native Americans, have accumulated little wealth compared to white people. For example, in 1998, the average black household had a net worth of about 18 percent of the average white household, and twice as many black households as white households had a negative net worth (i.e. they were in debt).[64]

Not all white people shared the same degree of benefits from whiteness, but all white people benefited in specific ways from the fact that they were considered to be white. Not all people of color were exploited to the same degree, but all people of color experienced significant degrees of exploitation. Most of the economic benefits that flowed to white people from the racial exploitation and discrimination experienced by people of color were accrued by businesses such as banks, insurance companies, and retail stores, and therefore these benefits accrued to those who owned the businesses—members of the owning classes. The ruling class was able to develop a system of political and economic domination that was based on racial differences and used to exploit working class white people and to aggressively exploit people of color.

Many of the benefits for women and their children of being white were only for heterosexual women and only as long as they were connected to a white man. They were not entitled to these benefits on their own, but only as they were the property of white men who had access to such perquisites.

Women and Wealth

For much of U.S. history, even white women were not permitted to own or accumulate wealth. Married women (single women were the property of their fathers and whatever they had was his) were not allowed to make out a will because they could not own land or legally control anything else worthy of willing to another person. They could not have legal responsibility for their children, control of their own property, vote, own slaves, buy or sell land, or even obtain an ordinary license. White women could not sue in a court of law except under the limited procedures allowed for the mentally ill and children, and then only when supervised by a man. Enslaved women were the property of their owners, and other women of color suffered the same complete lack of rights that men of color experienced.

Women, in general, were also aggressively exploited by a ruling class based on male dominated values and structures. When they were hired at all, women were paid less for work than men. They were used by men, often without pay or by force, to take care of their social, psychological, and sexual needs, and their unpaid reproductive labor was used to further the ranks of slave and free labor alike.

Women could not generate surplus income to accumulate wealth because so much of what they did was unpaid. The enormous value of women's work in raising children, growing food, doing domestic work, working in the fields, and nurturing men was simply not counted as productive work even though the entire economic system and the accumulation of wealth by the ruling class was dependent on it.[65]

This pattern continues today, because much of women's domestic work; childcare, eldercare, support for those with disabilities, and care for the sick, is still largely unpaid. They are also disproportionately responsible for childcare expenses. In addition, women are paid only about $.76 for every dollar that men are paid. As economic analyst Holly Sklar points out, "The average woman high school graduate who works full time from ages 25 to 65 will earn about $450,000 less than the average male high school graduate. The gap widens to $900,000 for full-time workers with bachelor's degrees [and] men with professional degrees may expect to earn almost $2 million more than their female counterparts over their work-life." [66] Women may make less, but they are charged more. They are seen as higher risk and less credit worthy by lending institutions, and are routinely charged more for retail purchases.

One result of these forms of exploitation and discrimination is that women, in general, don't have the same level of income resources that men have to earn a higher degree, to start a business, or to buy a house. They are not worth as much as men, they don't earn as much as men, and they don't have the same opportunity to accumulate wealth as men.

Personal power over the women in their families was offered to working men as a substitute for power in the work place and in the community. All women, except for some women in the ruling class, were vulnerable to sexual exploitation and to underpaid and dangerous work in fields and factories and in the home, in sweatshops, and in such gender specific areas as prostitution and domestic work.

Women were also commodified by the economic system. Their bodies—size, shape, skin color, facial features, etc.—were turned into products that were sold to men through pornography and prostitution, were used to market products to men through advertising, and were used to market products back to women to pressure them to conform to the commodified image of the perfect woman. All three of these uses of women's bodies and images of women's bodies were sources of irreparable harm to women themselves, and sources of wealth for the ruling class.

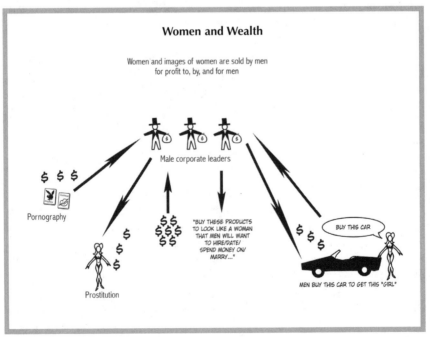

Women and Wealth

Women and images of women are sold by men
for profit to, by, and for men

Male corporate leaders

Pornography

"BUY THESE PRODUCTS
TO LOOK LIKE A WOMAN
THAT MEN WILL WANT
TO HIRE/DATE/
SPEND MONEY ON/
MARRY..."

BUY THIS CAR

MEN BUY THIS CAR TO GET THIS "GIRL"

Prostitution

Being a (white) male was itself a source of wealth. It allowed one to own property, to use the services and labor of women and children, to vote, to represent oneself in court, to take out loans and credit, and to work at the vast array of jobs and trades that women were excluded from. Working class men did not gain as much from these benefits as ruling class men, but the benefits to them were, nevertheless, substantial, including the general protection they had from sexual exploitation and violence, and the cooking, cleaning, childrearing, emotional caretaking, and sexual access they could avail themselves of from women.

Overall, in the early twenty-first century, the hierarchies of race and gender continue to be foundations of our economic system. According to one investigation, "Corporate America has systematically excluded African Americans, Latinos and [white] women from all but a tiny fraction of the millions of stock options that were distributed during a time of unprecedented growth in the economy.... Tell us what pay grade usually receives stock options and we can tell you where the glass ceiling is." Lawyers Mehri and Berk conclude by saying "...the grant of options—and in many cases the subsequent transfers of vast wealth—continues to be a bastion largely reserved for white males."[67] Those white males, that is, who are members of the owning classes.

The ruling class continues to use race and gender to divide people, to exploit some and superexploit others. They claim solidarity with poor, working, and middle-class white people through issues like welfare, affirmative action, and youth crime, to enlist support in their fight to prevent economic and political gains by people of color. They claim solidarity with poor, working, and middle-class men to enlist support in their fight to prevent economic and political gains by women. Because of the global character of the economic system, the U. S. ruling class claims solidarity with all people in the U.S. (and members of other white dominated nations) against the struggles for liberation and an end to exploitation by people in other (nonwhite) countries.

HOW DO THEY RULE? THE CONSTITUTION, CORPORATIONS, AND THE COURTS

Members of the power elite are able to make many decisions themselves through their direct control over land and corporations, foundations, trusts, and other institutions. But their influence over the government and other institutions is often indirect. Although many members of the highest levels of government are from the power elite, many are not. We'll be looking at both the direct and indirect ways that the power elite dominates the political decision-making process in later sections.

The ruling class of the United States has developed three primary ways to retain power (as well as many ways to retain wealth, which we'll also look at later).

The Constitution

The Constitution was set up by members of the colonial ruling class to protect both their wealth (primarily property and slaves) and their influence over government. When the founding fathers wrote "All men are created equal" they were specifically excluding women,[68] as well as all men who were not white, from political participation. By protecting and enhancing the rights of white slave holders, these men were establishing a foundation for their wealth and power in white supremacy and male domination.

The ruling class and the class of skilled artisans and shopkeepers combined made up only about 10 percent of the total population at the time of the American Revolution.[69] As James Madison pointed out to the Constitutional Convention, "the greatest conflict of all in the country was between those who had property and those who had none."[70] He was clear on the role of government in this conflict, writing that it "ought to be so constituted as to protect the minority of the opulent against the majority."[71] The wealthy and those who were successful craftsmen shared an interest in the protection of property rights. Therefore they wrote a constitution that would safeguard their ability to own and develop property, including the ownership of slaves. Besides claiming the exclusive rights to vote and to participate in elected office, those with property further consolidated (and protected) their power by setting up an electoral system that provided for the selection of the president and senators not by direct vote, but by a more easily controllable indirect electoral voting system. They also built into the Constitution other checks on democratic participation such as staggered elections, executive veto, Senate confirmation of judicial appointments and treaties, and an exceedingly difficult process for amending the Constitution.[72]

Because of fears of more working class uprisings such as had just occurred in Massachusetts during Shays Rebellion in 1786-87, the framers of the Constitution created a central government that would hold the union together, establish a strong fiscal and regulatory infrastructure, promote free trade, and protect the interests of the ruling class.

The ruling class at that time wanted the federal government to play a strong role that would facilitate business and ruling class interests but would not interfere in areas over which they wanted to have more regional or local control.

The Constitution protected the property rights (and white supremacy) of the ruling class and lesser property owners in quite specific ways, such as by officially recognizing slavery and establishing the right of return for runaway indentured workers and slaves (Article 4, Sec. 2. [3]). The commerce clause (Article 1, Sec. 8[3]) was included to end protective tariffs that individual states had established to protect local businesses.

The contracts clause (Article 1 Sec. 10[1]) became, perhaps, the most significant protection of the property rights of the ruling class. This clause states that the government cannot interfere in any way in private contracts (private law). This has been the basis of hundreds of court decisions limiting the government's role in regulating business and protecting the rights of citizens because public law has been ruled by the courts to be preempted by private law.[73] The courts have also used the First Amendment to protect property rights by restricting any government effort to limit the free speech rights of corporations.

Corporations

The second tool developed by the ruling class to guard its power was the corporation. The ruling class in Europe had long regulated its affairs and pooled its assets for colonial enterprises by creating trading partnerships, companies, and other forms of chartered business groups. The powerful East India Company, mentioned earlier, is a prime example of the importance of these organizations.

In the United States, by the early nineteenth century, there was already large scale consolidation of banking, insurance, and textile companies, and many business leaders developed links with, or were directors of, several companies. In the early nineteenth century, corporations were companies which were set up with charters from state governments for specific purposes. They provided a particular service to the community, and their charter was for a specific time period, usually between 10 and 30 years. The charter could be revoked if the company did not do what it was chartered for, such as building and providing a toll road between two destinations. These chartered businesses or corporations were tightly monitored and their charters could be, and routinely were revoked by state legislators.

State control over corporations began to erode early on as corporations used their financial and political clout to roll back restrictions on them. In the first of a long series of important pro-corporate, antidemocratic decisions, the Supreme Court held in the Dartmouth decision of 1819 that corporations are protected under the contracts clause of the Constitution.

The ruling class gained even more protection, and opportunity to use the corporate structure from the 1886 Supreme Court Santa Clara decision. The railroads had brought cases to court year after year, spending large sums of money, to establish the right to have a corporation considered to be a "natural" person.

Finally, in 1886, the Supreme Court rendered a decision that was interpreted to mean that a corporation should be considered a natural person, with all the due process rights guaranteed to a person under the Fourteenth Amendment, which had been passed to protect the rights of freed slaves. The decision itself did not grant the status of a person to a corporation. This language was included in the headnotes by a court reporter and became accepted as part of the legal precedent through subsequent rulings.[74]

This decision was used as a precedent to give corporations the right to free speech and the right to due process. Subsequently, courts considered corporations to be on an equal playing field with individuals and communities, even though they had previously been regulated by local governments, and even though they had vastly more resources to defend their interests than either individuals or local governments had. In fact, most individuals at the time, including Native Americans, Blacks, Latinos/as, Asian Americans, and white women had few, if any rights, and virtually no legal standing in the courts at all.

White women had petitioned the court for the right to vote in 1875, also citing the Fourteenth Amendment, but their appeal was denied. They only gained the right to vote in 1920 under the Nineteenth Amendment. Property rights for corporations and their owners were deemed by the courts to be more important than voting rights for women. These rights were also more important than the rights of freed slaves, for whom the Fourteenth Amendment had been passed. In fact, of the 307 Fourteenth Amendment cases brought before the Supreme Court between 1886 and 1910, only 19 dealt with African Americans: 288 were suits brought by corporations seeking the rights of natural persons.[75] The ruling class used corporations to protect and expand its interests and to keep the interests of poor and working class people, women, and men and women of color, subordinate.

By the late nineteenth century, banking, transportation, steel, and other industrial corporations had become huge and complex enterprises in severe competition with each other. Members of the ruling class wanted ways to regulate competition among themselves because they had found that unregulated trade was lowering prices and, consequently, lowering profits. They were also faced with increased pressure from several sectors of the population such as middle-class reformers, populist farmers, and socialists, who were criticizing oligopolistic practices in which business leaders got together to fix prices, divide up markets, and share profits.[76]

There was a wave of government regulatory agencies established in the early twentieth century. Although some corporations fought vigorously against regulation, the largest corporations realized that some form of regulation would divert attention from more drastic efforts to control or dismantle large corporations, would help stabilize markets and regulate competition, would make it harder for smaller competitors to stay in the market, and would be fairly easy to manipulate through political influence. Many specific corporations fought vigorously against attempts at regulating them. But despite the increased regulation, most of the larger corporations were able to use their financial and political influence to continue growing and to increase their domination of state and federal government.

The modern form of corporations arose for a variety of reasons and it had multiple advantages for ruling class power and control. They could use corporations to protect themselves and their families from the financial losses and legal liabilities that this scale of enterprise entailed. As various forms of taxation were introduced, the ruling class used corporations to protect their profits from being taxed, and to pass down wealth to future generations without diluting it.

The corporate structure has allowed members of the ruling class to specialize in running large financial enterprises, enlist the specialized professional help they need, and ensure that they and their families are not liable for the unsafe working conditions, dangerous products, environmental pollution, and even the financial losses of the businesses that produce their wealth. These and many other advantages have continued to be added to and refined over the 120 years since the landmark Santa Clara decision.

For several decades, corporations were national in scope. The largest of them developed markets within the U.S. and consolidated, colluded, and merged with other national corporations while also buying up, taking over, or destroying smaller companies. They had national manufacturing, marketing, and sales strategies.

The growth, mergers, and acquisitions of national corporations through the 1960s and 70s created multinational corporations which had a global reach, and competed against (and cooperated with) the multinational corporations of Europe, Canada, and Japan. Many of these corporations were tied to multinational corporations in other countries through joint ventures, and had extensive networks of subsidiaries throughout the world. They were based, however, in the U.S.

Beginning in the 1980s, with the rise of global financial markets and institutions, multinational corporations became transnational corporations. Economic and political power became even more concentrated in these incredibly huge enterprises. Leveraged buyouts, hostile takeovers, mergers and acquisitions across, as well as within, national boundaries resulted in the rise of corporations which were not only larger than most national economies, but were no longer based in or constricted as much by national governments. Although still nominally based in a country, the allegiance of the transnational corporation is committed more to maintenance of the international financial system and its own profitable role in it, than to a national government. As one senior executive told the *New York Times* in 1991: "The United States does not have an automatic call on our resources. There is no mindset that puts this country first."[77]

Large transnational corporations have now become very powerful. Fifty-two of the 100 largest economic entities in the world are corporations, not countries. (See the chart on p. 25.) The five hundred largest in 1998 had total revenues of $11.5 trillion and employed 40 million people. Their average revenues were $122 billion.[78] Of the Global 500, 191 were U.S. companies. Each of the largest are run by a small group of men who control vast resources, are large financial institutions in their own right[79] even if predominately engaged in nonfinancial production, and have substantial security operations. The nature of the development of these corporations has given the corporate elite a central role in the more extensive power elite both in the U.S. and in the other developed countries.

The Courts

The Dartmouth, Santa Clara, and hundreds of other legal decisions in favor of the ruling class brings us to the third tool they have used to protect their interests—the courts. Although the Constitution set up a system of checks and balances between the branches of government (based on the model of the Iroquois Confederacy),[80] in fact, all three branches were controlled by the ruling class. The checks were on working class power, and the balance was in the variety of governmental tools that the ruling class could use to remain hidden, but in control. The court system was set up to carry on the British legal system which had been established to maintain the rights of the white, male, landed aristocracy. It was given the responsibility of adjudicating in situations where ruling class interests conflicted, or in cases where the government overstepped its boundaries and interfered with ruling class interests by advocating policies that were more advantageous to the general populace. The ruling class bias of the courts was represented very simply by the first chief justice of the United States, John Jay, when he said in 1787, "The people who own the country ought to govern it."

There was always great overlap between lawyers and judges on the one hand, and politicians on the other. In fact, most of our presidents have been lawyers, and many middle and upper-middle-class lawyers have used the practice of corporate law to advance into the ruling class. Presidents, many of whom were from the ruling class, have almost always appointed judges who share their class background, or who they have observed through years of law practice will support the interests of their class. These lawyers graduate primarily from a small number of elite, ruling class law schools, go through a grueling process of reshaping their values to adjust to their future roles, and end up becoming either members of the ruling class themselves (if they weren't born into it), or professional servants of their ruling class peers.

Many people practice law and most are not part of this corporate law system. Only those who are, and who share ruling class values are likely to advance through judgeships into positions of authority within the legal profession. These are the ones who gain positions from which they can influence law school curricula, legal precedent, the American Bar Association, and governmental policy and legislation.

One area in which the ruling class bias of the courts is most evident is in labor-business cases. The courts have consistently aided business interests by prohibiting strikes, boycotts, and picketing, and by issuing injunctions against possible future worker activism and organizing. The courts have been used to sharply curtail the power of unions. They have also colluded in trying and convicting many labor leaders in periods of labor-business conflict. The courts have given the widest possible interpretation to open-shop laws, they have granted free speech rights to employers in union certification elections, they have failed to protect workers' rights to free association and free speech (while protecting the same rights for corporations), and they have ruled that the permanent replacement of strikers is legal. Rarely have they actually protected the legal rights of workers.[81]

The current court system, and the corporate lawyers within it, operate to protect members of the ruling class and their personal and corporate property rights at the expense of ordinary citizens. Although there have been some decisions which penalize corporations for unusually egregious practices, for

the most part the legal system makes it extremely difficult for ordinary citizens to win redress from the harm done to them by corporate actions. The courts, especially the federal court system, are heavily populated with members of the owning classes, and primarily render decisions which protect property rights, not civil and human rights.

To sum up our discussion of these tools, the ruling class created the rules (the Constitution) by which we live, the financial structures that operate to their benefit within those rules (corporations), and then guaranteed that, in any case of conflict, their people would decide the matter (the courts).

HOW DOES THE POWER ELITE COMMUNICATE?

Using the pioneering work of William Domhoff and other sociologists and political scientists we can trace the vehicles that the power elite—decision-making members of the owning classes—use to communicate with each other.

Interlocking Directorships

Over the last two hundred years, business leaders have created a vast, inter-locking system of corporate directorships through which they meet regularly to talk about the business of running business, including all of the policy issues that they need to address.[82] This interlocking directorship has been very stable in its organizational membership for over a hundred years. The largest U.S. banks, insurance companies, and industrial enterprises have been at the center of the network and have the most interlocking directorships. There have been changes as the economy has changed, and certain sectors of the economy, such as computers or railroads, have grown or diminished in importance. These directorships, and the network of board meetings, discussions, and events that members participate in, keep the communication flowing between different sectors of the power elite.

According to political economist Douglas Dowd, the financial sector, always at the center of this network, became even more powerful during the 1980s and 90s because of "...the emerging importance of money, equity, and pension funds; the enormous increase of household, business, and governmental debt; the spread and strengthening of insurance companies (and their mergers with other financial companies); the expansion of individual financial investors; and the spectacular growth of international financial speculation in the vast and explosive derivatives market."[83]

There is slightly more diversity of gender and race in this network than there was 30 years ago, but almost all of its members are from the same ruling class and educational backgrounds as previous members. It is in these corporate gatherings that discussions about economic issues occur, new problems are identified, and the need for new policy articulated. General information about investment policy and opportunity and capital flows is circulated in these networks providing a central place for, "promulgating the variety of values and norms that constitute a corporate culture based on financial hegemony."[84]

About a quarter of these directors sit on two or more boards and have a much more influential and central role than the others.[85] They, and the most influential and connected directors of foundations, policy-formation groups, think tanks, ruling class universities, elite law firms, and the government, comprise the power elite. There is tremendous overlap in membership between corporate directorships and these other networks of organizations. Individuals move smoothly between the various branches of these ruling structures and know, or know of, many of their peers. They meet regularly in clubs, conferences, meetings, and at fund-raising, social, cultural, and political events. They have a shared set of economic values and interests (but a wide range of personal and social ones), a shared information base, and a

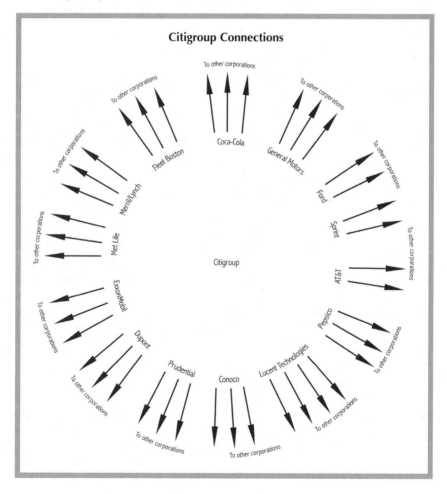

Citigroup Connections

shared sense of their responsibility for defending ruling class interests. They are each actively engaged in some significant way in making, shaping, or influencing important policy decisions made in the U.S.

There is also substantial mobility among this elite, with individuals moving between corporate, foundation, government, consulting, university, and think tank positions. In other words, the interlocking is due both to the interlocking relationships between organizations within the network, and the movement of individuals through different organizations and sectors over time. This mobility factor is a less studied but vital aspect of the way the power elite communicate, and influence political, economic, and cultural organizations.

Most members of the power elite don't have the time or expertise to research and develop policy, much less to get that policy adopted by the government. There is a network of policy-formation groups that do this work for them.

Policy-Formation Groups

As issues, problems, and concerns become identified in formal and informal gatherings of the ruling class and power elite, the policy formation process clarifies the interests at stake among the participants, and sorts out possible (and acceptable) policy alternatives. Policy-formation groups play a crucial role in facilitating and directing the discussions which lead to elite consensus and policy determination and implementation.

Policy-formation groups actually serve several functions. Four of these are internal to the ruling class and three are in relationship to society in general. Internally, these groups provide a setting in which corporate leaders can familiarize themselves with general policy issues, a forum where conflicts between moderate conservatives and ultraconservatives can be resolved, an informal training ground for new leadership, and an informal recruiting ground for determining which academic experts may be best suited for government service. Externally, these groups legitimize their members as experts and as committed to public service; they convey the concerns, goals, and expectations of the ruling class to young experts and professors; and through books, journals, policy statements, press releases, and speakers, these groups influence the climate of opinion in Washington and in the rest of the country.[86]

The first major policy discussion group, the National Civic Federation, was set up by the ruling class around 1900 to respond to labor conflict during the period. The Council on Foreign Relations (CFR) was established in 1921 and has played a leading role in international policy formation (foreign affairs) ever since. Much of the United States' foreign policy has been developed and refined through CFR sponsored dinner meetings and study groups, papers, and its influential journal *Foreign Affairs*. The Council has been instrumental in building elite consensus around specific policies for the last 80 years.

Just looking at the CFR, for example, shows that 37 percent of the top 500 industrial corporations have at least one officer or director who was a member. Of the top 100 companies, 70 percent had at least one member. Twenty of the top 25 banks and 16 of the 25 largest insurance companies had members.[87] Banks have always been very central to this network with the most interlinked directors, and, in the research cited above by Domhoff, J.P. Morgan Bank had 16 members of the CFR, Chase Manhattan Bank had 15, and Citibank (now Citigroup) had 10.

In addition to corporate leaders, former presidents Bush, Carter, Clinton and Ford, numerous secretaries of state and defense, national security advisors, U.S. senators and congresspersons, and most of the recent directors of the CIA have been members. The Council's magazine, *Foreign Affairs*, reflects current thinking on international affairs and is usually an indicator of developing U.S. policy directions.

As a recent article stated, "The importance of the Council stems from its role as the central link that binds the capitalist upper class and its most

Power Elite Mobility
Typical Examples

A.

first   corporate CEO
then   high-level government job
then   foundation director
then   corporate consultant

B.

first   professor—elite university
then   State Dept./foreign affairs official
then   think tank director
then   corporate lobbyist

C.

first   investment banking company principal
then   head of CIA
then   corporate consultant

D.

first   private investor
then   politician or government official
then   foundation director
then   director—policy formation group

important financial and multinational corporations, think tanks, and foundations to academic experts in leading (mainly eastern) universities, and government policy formulation and execution."[88] It is within this elite, private, bipartisan network that much of U.S. foreign policy is shaped and carried out.

Bilderberg is an annual informal gathering of U.S., Canadian, and European business and political leaders, financiers, and cultural leaders which started in 1954 in Bilderberg in the Netherlands. Joint U.S.-Western European economic and political policies (including the development of the European Union) are shaped through the talks at the gatherings and the relationships built through the network. As Joseph Retinger, one of the founders wrote about it:

> Bilderberg does not make policy. Its aim is to reduce differences of opinion and resolve conflicting trends and to further understanding, if not agreement, by hearing and considering various points of view and trying to find a common approach to major problems...the object being to draw the attention of people in responsible positions to Bilderberg's findings.[89]

No statement could better capture the policy formation process by which members of the international power elite meet, discuss, strategize, and come to agreement across differences to further a ruling class agenda.

The Trilateral Commission is an outgrowth of the CFR. CFR chairman David Rockefeller created the commission in 1973 to build consensus on international policy among the elites of Japan, Western Europe, and the United States. The Trilateral Commission sees itself as developing and deciding upon the main components of the global economy and political structure. It has been highly successful in achieving the goals of the ruling classes of The Triad countries, although in the last few years there has developed more concerted anti-globalization resistance to its policy initiatives.

Even more recently, groups such as the Atlantic Council and the Center for Strategic and International Studies have assumed emerging and important roles at the international policy formation level.

The participants in these groups share a common set of ruling class assumptions and represent a very narrow set of interests. They are a very elite group. They are interested in a stable economic environment, concentration of wealth in the developed countries, and a smoothly operating, global, regulated market favorable to their interests. As David Korten comments:

> It is important to note that the Council on Foreign Relations, the Bilderberg, and the Trilateral Commission bring together heads of competing corporations and leaders of competing national political parties for closed-door discussions and consensus-building

processes that the public never sees…it is a closed and exclusive process…. Participants are predominately male, wealthy, from Northern industrial countries, and except for the Japanese on the Trilateral Commission, Caucasian. Other voices are excluded.[90]

There is a similar policy formation process at the national level in the United States. The Brookings Institution still serves as a major domestic policy formation group on a wide variety of issues. For a more narrow range of discussions and policy formation around domestic economic policy, several

Power Elite Members' Multiple Roles
Typical Examples

A.

Member—board of directors
IBM
Standard Oil
American Airlines
American Internet Group
Chevron
Lucent Technology
AOL-Time Warner
Advisor—Center for Strategic and International Studies
Member—U.S. China Business Council
Member—Trilateral Commission
Chairman—Urban Institute
Chairman—American Bar Association Antitrust Section
Secretary—Department of Housing and Urban Development

B.

CEO—Center for Strategic and International Studies
Professor—U.S. Naval Academy
Executive V.P.—Fannie Mae
Various U.S. Department of Treasury jobs
Member—board of directors
Alliance Capital
Jones Intercable
Enron
Aspen Institute
Strategy Group for Policy—Overseas Development Council
Advisor—World Wildlife Fund
Member—Trilateral Commission
Advisor—Goldman Sachs

C.

Member—board of directors
New York Times
IBM
General Dynamics
Manufacturers Trust
Pam American Airlines
Aetna
Trustee:
Mayo Foundation
Japan Society
Public Agenda Foundation
Federal Reserve Bank of New York
Rockefeller Foundation
Secretary of the Army
Secretary of State

groups, such as the National Association of Manufacturers, the Chamber of Commerce, the Conference Board, the Business Council, the Committee for Economic Development, and the RAND Corporation have played important roles. In the last 30 years they have been superceded in importance by the Business Roundtable in influence on specific economic policy issues.[91]

The Business Roundtable has grown quickly to become the most influential group on domestic economic policy in this category of organization. The Roundtable consists of the executive officers of approximately 200 of the nation's largest corporations who lobby for the policies decided on by the membership. The member companies represent a net worth equivalent to nearly half of the Gross National Product (GNP) of the U.S.—an amount greater than the GNP of any other country in the world.[92]

Once its internal discussions are over and the Roundtable reaches agreement on an economic issue, the vast resources of its members are used to mobilize the corporate community to influence policy decisions. In the 1999/2000 election cycle this group poured over $85 million into the campaign through soft money, PACs, and individual contributions. The Business Roundtable has substantial interlocks with such groups as the Conference

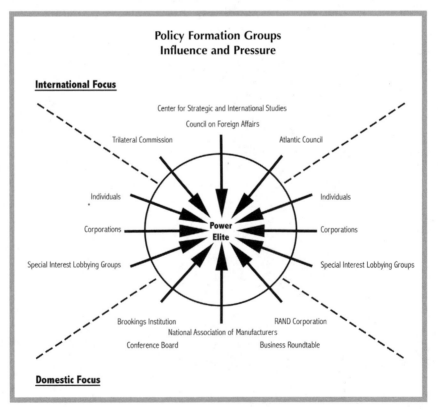

Board, Council on Foreign Relations, National Association of Manufacturers, American Enterprise Institute, Committee for Economic Development, and the Business Council. As Domhoff points out, "The Business Roundtable is at the heart of both the corporate community and the policy-planning network. Its 79 directors for 1997 have 206 directorships with 134 corporations, 32 of which are in the top 50 in size."[93]

Foundations

The discussion, policy papers, reports, and other activities of the policy formation groups become highly influential in creating and promoting power elite policy. These groups are supported, financed, and oftentimes directed by a network of foundations that is also controlled by members of the power elite serving as directors and trustees.

These foundations operate with tremendous assets, placed with them by members of the ruling class to avoid taxes and retain control of the disbursal of the money. The 1998 *Foundation Directory* lists 8,642 large foundations (assets over $2 million) that controlled $247 billion.[94] By 2000, the 10 largest foundations controlled over $101 billion of assets.[95] In a study of the top 50 foundations by size, 85 percent of the directors were men who graduated from elite universities.[96] In one study of the 12 largest foundations, half the trustees were members of the ruling class, and there are many corporate interlocks on the large foundations' boards of directors.

Although the primary function of foundations is funding, many of the ruling class foundations take a leading role in directing research, shaping policy, and developing programming. These foundations may be moderate/conservative such as the Rockefeller, Ford, Mellon, and Rockefeller Brothers Foundations, and the Carnegie Corporation, or ultraconservative like the Bradley, Noble, Scaife, Richardson, Olin, and the Koch family foundations, but they are all tools of segments of the ruling class and are tightly intertwined with the network of policy discussion groups, think tanks, and other groupings of the power elite. For example, the 20 foundations that give over 5 percent of their total grants to public policy groups were closely connected through interlocking directorships with 31 policy discussion groups and think tanks.

The Bradley Foundation is an example of the money and power these foundations wield. With assets over $700 million, the 1998 annual report states that the Bradley Foundation gives out over $30 million a year to groups attacking affirmative action, social security, and all other welfare programs, and to groups promoting deregulation of business and the privatization of education and most other governmental functions. The Foundation funds a wide range of ruling class groups such as the Heritage Foundation, the Madison Center for Educational Affairs, the American Enterprise Institute for Public Policy Research, the Free Congress Research and Education Foundation, the Hoover Institute on War, Revolution, and Peace, and the Ronald Reagan Presidential Foundation. It also funds major conservative publications, such as *The Public Interest, The National Interest,* and *The American Spectator.*

As an investigative report concluded, "Bradley is certainly not the only conservative foundation promoting right-wing causes. It works in concert with a number of others to develop, maintain, and promote a right-wing intelligencia that can play a major role in the manipulation of public opinion and the formulation of public policy. In fact, the Olin, Sarah Scaife, Smith Richardson, and Bradley foundations are often called the 'Four Sisters' for their tendency to fund similar conservative projects, publications, and institutions."[97]

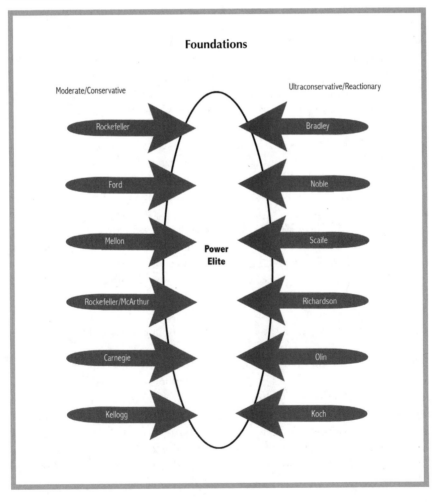

Think Tanks

Think tanks are where the deeper and more thorough research and policy formation gets accomplished. Some are highly specialized and some are connected to academic institutions. Perhaps the three most visible and influential are the Brookings Institution (also listed above as a policy formation group), the American Enterprise Institute, and the Heritage Foundation. Others include the Free Congress Foundation, Empower America, The Center for Strategic and International Studies, and the Hudson Institute. Funding for these think tanks comes from members of the ruling class through the foundations they control, from personal donations, and from the corporations they influence.

Think tanks engage in a much wider range of activities than just research and policy formation. They are also high powered marketing agencies for the policies they want to promote. They produce detailed studies, summary reports, newsletters, articles, op-ed pieces, bumper stickers, radio shows, magazine and TV advertisements, cartoons, pamphlets, video "documentaries," and even displays for public and private libraries. Staff and representatives participate in interviews, public talks, congressional hearings, public policy forums, conferences, and congressional briefings. All of these activities target either the treetops (the power elite) or grassroots constituencies. They also vigorously cultivate and support academics, younger elite leadership, and citizen activists. When they want to get their message out widely on particular issues, they can do so very effectively. For example, Citizens for a Sound Economy sent out more than 3,000,000 pieces of mail in 1996, and the newsletter of the Family Research Council, "Washington Watch," goes out to a quarter of a million people every month.[98]

Some of the issues that the more conservative think tanks have been actively promoting in recent years are school vouchers, charter schools and the privatization of school services, introduction of a flat tax, deregulation of the telecommunications industry, elimination of welfare, reduction or elimination of government regulatory agencies such as the Food and Drug Administration, Environmental Protection Agency, Consumer Protection Agency, and Occupational Safety and Health Administration,[99] maintenance of a low minimum wage, privatization of social security, elimination of estate taxes, limits on the ability of unions to organize, prevention of a national health care plan from being passed, and limits on the ability of nonprofits to engage in public policy debate. The larger work of all of the think tanks, whether they are moderate/conservative or ultraconservative, is maintaining an ideological climate which supports "free" enterprise, privatizes the public sphere, supports ruling class accumulation of wealth and power, produces division, scapegoating, and misinformation in the general population, and which stifles the ability of ordinary citizens to organize themselves and to participate effectively in public policy decisions.

Elite Universities

Some universities also play a substantial role in the policy formation network. There are a handful of very important private institutions such as Harvard, Yale, Princeton, Stanford, and the University of Chicago that play central roles in preparing ruling and managerial class students (and a few scholarship students) to become part of the power elite or to enter the elite professions as members of the managerial class. They are also centers for discussion, research, consulting, advocacy, and policy creation. These schools are largely governed by trustees who are members of the ruling class themselves, and are funded by the same class interests.

Twenty-five of the most important universities for the ruling class hold over 67 percent of all the private endowment funds in the United States. Yale and Harvard hold over $11 billion and $19.3 billion respectively.[100] Prominent members of this section of the academic community provide research and expert testimony for policymakers, teach ruling class values, prepare their students for ruling and managerial class careers in business, phi-

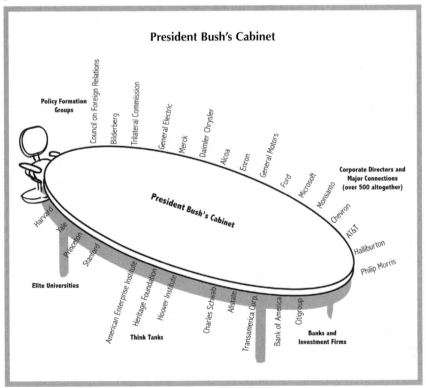

lanthropy, law and the government, and provide legitimation for the policies of the power elite. Some of the highest level administrators and professors of these schools are part of the power elite themselves.

In the broader university system there are also many corporate funded "chairs of free enterprise" which have the explicit purpose of promoting and defending the free enterprise system. St. Mary's University in San Antonio, Texas explains their "chair of Free Enterprise" on their website. "The chair holder presents educational programs for high schools, universities, and the civic community to promote understanding of the conceptual bases of the market system, its functional operations, and its contributions to the economic well being of the individual."[101]

Scientific and social science research conducted at elite universities play multiple roles in supporting ruling class interests. Often that research and the professors who conduct it are directly subsidized by corporations, think tanks, or policy formation groups. For example, after the Exxon Valdez oil tanker disaster, ExxonMobil Corp. hired well-known psychologists, economists, and law and business school faculty to "research" the issue of punitive damages. Soon their articles challenging the competence of juries to set punitive damages were appearing in legal journals. Exxon Mobil cited the articles in its appeals case, and partly on this basis, got its punitive damages reduced from $5.3 to $4 billion.[102] The research and legal opinions have subsequently been cited both by other corporations in their own lawsuits and by judges in cases involving corporate wrongdoing.

Elite Publications

Most of the research documents and policy papers produced by the institutions described above do not have wide circulation. They are meant to be read by members of the power elite so that policies can be formulated, controversies and alternatives sorted out, and strategies devised. There is a network of publications which are used to disseminate both news about the ruling class and its interests, and to guide opinions, economic action, and voting behavior of the owning classes in general. Newspapers and magazines such as *The Wall Street Journal, Barron's, Forbes, Fortune,* and *Business Week,* and for international issues, *Foreign Affairs,* are vehicles that the ruling and managerial classes use to communicate opinions and analysis, current thinking, and planning among themselves.

These sources are very revealing, because members of the power elite are often much more honest about their values and intentions in these publications than in large-circulation daily newspapers such as *The New York Times* and *The Washington Post,* or in the weekly national news magazines such as *Time, Newsweek,* and *U.S. News and World Report.* The primary readers of the elite publications are "politicians, corporate executives of all levels, investors, small business owners, inheritors of wealth, doctors, accountants, investment bankers and so on;" all of them members of the wealthiest 20 percent of the population.[103]

HOW DO THEY STAY IN POWER?

Many presidents, congresspeople, judges, and corporate lawyers are members of the ruling class. For example, 18 of the 19 cabinet appointments that George W. Bush made were millionaires (the other member was "only" worth $680,000), and it is estimated that at least one out of five of all our congressional representatives are millionaires.[104] Forty-three percent of the new members of Congress in 2002 declared holdings in excess of $1 million.[105] Most other decisionmakers are members of the managerial class and are committed to a ruling class agenda. But even though the Constitution, the corporations, and the courts are set up to protect and promote their interests, members of the ruling class have long felt that it was important to control the government.

Through its borrowing, lending, regulating, and spending, the federal government is the only body that could potentially set limits on ruling class interests, regulate corporate practices, and redistribute wealth through taxes and other public policies. The government can also initiate alternative economic structures, shift investment and production into different sectors of the economy, and build educational, political, and cultural projects that strengthen democratic practices. For all these reasons, a government controlled democratically by the majority in the U.S. is dangerous to the ruling class and power elite. As President Woodrow Wilson, himself a member of the ruling class, remarked in 1912, "When the government becomes important, it becomes important to control the government."[106]

Conversely, the ruling class and the power elite use the tools of government to support, maintain, and stabilize the economic system to serve their interests. Through control of the government they can direct the use of force domestically and internationally to protect their profits and quell dissent; they can manipulate the tax and spending functions of the state to their advantage; they can call on the power of national symbols and icons such as the flag, motherhood, apple pie, and democracy to confuse and manipulate people. They can also socialize the costs of their actions and privatize the profits by getting the government and academic institutions to pay for research and development and then reaping the profits themselves.

The ruling class has devised many different tools to insure that the government works in their interest. Some of these tools have shifted over time as citizen's groups have closed loopholes that allowed certain kinds of influence to predominate. The ruling class strives to dominate government policy. They have not been able to control it completely, but on most major policy issues they have prevailed, and on most major policy debates, the issues themselves have been defined within the context of differences between different sectors of the ruling class.

There are conservatives and ultraconservatives in the ruling class on economic issues and on cultural issues. Many members of the ruling class are liberal on some cultural issues such as gay rights or abortion. Even within the power elite, there are both conservative tendencies that push towards a broad pro-business agenda with a right-wing emphasis, and more pragmatic tendencies that emphasize working within the system and maintaining the most effective relationships with all parties to increase their access to policymakers, and ability to influence their decisions. There are conflicts between U.S. based manufacturers and corporations whose operations are mostly in other countries, and between the financial sector and the manufacturing sector, not to mention differing interests within particular economic sectors and between corporations.

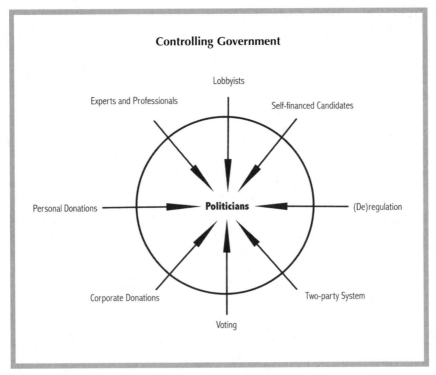

Controlling Government

Lobbyists

Experts and Professionals

Self-financed Candidates

Personal Donations — **Politicians** — (De)regulation

Corporate Donations

Two-party System

Voting

What unites most members of the ruling class and power elite is a primary concern for the protection of their wealth and power by promoting a secure and stable economic framework for economic growth, "free" trade and "free" enterprise, maximal government structure and support but minimal government regulation, low taxes, a stable two-party system to maintain the appearance of choice, and the control of dissent. The rest of us can learn from their ability to put aside their many differences to come together in support of a common ruling class agenda.

Experts and Professionals

Not only are there many members of the ruling class in the top levels of government, but the government relies on experts and professionals for much of its policy-making, and these are supplied by the power elite network of think tanks, policy formation groups, private universities, and foundations described in earlier sections. As Domhoff notes, "most top appointees in both Republican and Democratic administrations are corporate executives and corporate lawyers."[107] A study by the Office of Management and Budget reports that 40 percent of foreign service professionals in the State Department come from eight Ivy League colleges.[108]

Although the Clinton administration included more women, and people of color than previous administrations, those appointed were predominately members of the owning classes with many corporate and policy network connections.[109] More liberal and non-wealthy appointees were in decidedly secondary positions with little influence. The constant flow of people between the corporate world and the government creates a tight network between them, and easy means for policy domination by members of the power elite.

Lobbyists

Lobbyists from corporations, trade groups, law firms, and special interest groups provide another source of "input" representing ruling class interests. Their influence can have a devastating impact on our lives. For example, the U.S. auto industry was able to delay the mandatory introduction of air bags for over 20 years while an estimated 140,000 people died needlessly and even greater numbers sustained serious injury. That same lobbying effort has kept criminal sanctions from being included in the federal auto safety law so that the auto companies are protected from criminal prosecution for killing people through the production of cars that are dangerous.[110]

It is estimated that over 100,000 people work in the Washington, D.C. area lobbying industry, and tens of thousands more in state and local governments. About 75 percent of Washington lobbyists represent corporations, business, trade, and professional organizations, or are lawyers from firms representing these interests.[112] In 1996 it was projected that approximately $8.4

Lobbying Groups

There are general ruling class/corporate lobbying groups such as the Business Roundtable, the Committee for Economic Development, and the Conference Board (they are also policy formation groups) which are highly influential because of the role that corporate CEOs play in them. There are also many powerful industry lobbying groups that work on specific interests, such as the National Association of Manufacturers, the Chemical Manufacturers' Association, American Petroleum Institute, American Mining Congress, Health Insurance Association of America, and the Pharmaceutical Manufacturers Association. Even non-U.S. groups, such as the Foreign Oil Companies Group, a cartel of major petroleum companies doing business in the Caspian, have a well-funded voice on issues of interest to them.[111] Finally, there are powerful managerial class professional organizations, such as the American Bar Association and the American Medical Association, that also contribute large amounts to politicians and wield substantial influence. These groups often work together by creating ad hoc coalitions to work on passage of specific policies such as NAFTA and FTAA, the defeat or limiting of environmental and workplace regulation, the prevention of passage of a national health insurance plan, or the lowering and elimination of various forms of corporate and ruling class taxation.

billion was spent lobbying the federal government, and that amount has increased dramatically since then.[113]

The ruling class is the only group with the money to pay the majority of the bill for this vast array of lobbyists. They face little opposition from other interest groups.[114]

As political scientist Thomas R. Dye describes it, "Lobbying goes well beyond testifying at congressional hearings, contacting government officials, presenting technical information and reports, keeping informed about bills, and following the 'ins and outs' of the legislative process. It includes 'grassroots' mobilization of campaign contributors and voters back home, as well as public relations activities designed to develop and maintain a favorable climate of opinion in the nation. But most important, the special-interest process includes the distribution of campaign funds to elected officials."[115]

As seen in the case of Enron and other energy companies, many times these lobbyists actually write the legislation that affects their businesses. They are also responsible for distributing hundreds of millions of dollars of campaign contributions from special interest groups. Their funding and their professional resources allow them to apply tremendous pressure to politicians who need a constant flow of money to stay elected in today's incredibly expensive election campaigns.

These lobbying groups are very effective. In May 1998, for example, the liquor lobby stopped legislation that would have penalized states that refused to adopt tougher drunk-driving laws. "The death of the proposal to lower the blood-alcohol limit for drunk driving is a classic Washington story of big money, influential lobbyists, and questionable political tactics," observed journalist Michael Kranish.[116]

Most of our federal regulations and policy decisions are not made through publicly discussed legislation, but through the tens of thousands of much less visible administrative decisions and rulings that are implemented by government departments, bureaus, and agencies. It is here that rates are changed, prices altered, taxes raised or lowered, programs started or terminated, eligibility requirements adjusted, environmental, health and safety, and food and drug standards determined. It is in administrative rulings that all congressional legislation is interpreted and implemented. These rulings and regulations have the force of law, and even the courts will seldom challenge them unless the agency has overstepped its regulatory mandate. Here again, it is corporate and private sector lobbyists who pay attention to, and can apply pressure on, the hundreds of committees, offices, hearings, and other processes by which these administrative rulings are decided.

(De)Regulation

There have always been grassroots movements to influence governmental policy. In recent decades there have been consumer, environmental, health care, education, and other movements working to pass legislation favorable to ordinary people. Occasionally successful, most of the time these groups have lost the legislative battle and have been unable to stop deregulation of industry after industry, attacks on worker's rights and safety, the erosion of environmental controls, and the expansion of corporate control.

The push for stricter scrutiny has often come from consumers, workers, and local communities. Especially in times of political unrest, such as during labor uprisings in the 1930s and the Civil Rights movement of the 1950s and 60s, the power elite has been pressured by organized advocacy groups to respond to citizen demands for protection from corporate practices. There have often been differences between groups within the power elite during those periods about how best to mute the criticism without significantly affecting corporate profits.

Although the power elite has resisted many efforts at regulation, some in this group have realized that the appearance of governmental regulation and control is more effective than no regulation at all in allowing them to maintain profits. Thus, the corporate community has acquiesced to such agencies as the USDA, EPA, FDA, and the NLRB as a way to cut off criticism, end conflict, and create the appearance of government supervision.

Usually the more moderate section (often the largest players in a particular industry, who might be considered to be more "liberal") creates policy that appears to address some of the concerns of people in the streets. Such regulation favors the largest corporations because it "limits entry into a market, subsidizes select industries, sets production standards that only big companies can meet, weakens smaller competitors, and encourages monopoly pricing."[117] The agribusiness, telecommunications, energy, oil, drug, rail, trucking, and airline industries are examples of where this has worked.[118]

Written by the industries affected, often regulatory policies are passed, disarmng grassroots movements by the appearance of change. Then, over the next few years the legislation is unenforced, poorly enforced, blocked by the courts, eroded by the courts, or circumvented by various corporate and governmental practices. In many cases these landmark bills are eventually overturned during quieter times, and these industries are deregulated, i.e. government oversight is significantly reduced or eliminated. Government supervised or regulated gains in worker rights, abortion rights, voting rights, consumer and environmental protection, civil rights, and in the provisions of the social safety net have all faced such backlash tactics. The bottom line is that large corporations can thrive with or without regulation because regulation is usually on their terms.

There are more direct ways that the ruling class controls the government, the most blatant being through direct spending to determine candidates, propositions, and public policy issues.

Buying an Office

Many candidates are rich themselves and have used their personal fortunes to finance their campaigns. Investor H. Ross Perot, businessman Michael Bloomberg, actor Arnold Schwarzenegger, and baseball commissioner Peter Ueberroth are only a few among many who have recently followed this route. In the 2000 elections, congressional candidates contributed or loaned $175.9 million to their own campaigns.[119]

Members of the ruling class are not just running for office—some are challenging the integrity of our democratic institutions by manipulating elections and recall campaigns. In 1997, Seattle Seahawks owner, billionaire Paul Allen, reimbursed the city of Seattle $4.2 million to hold a special election to approve a new football stadium—and then spent another $5 million to convince voters to fund the $425 million stadium. In 2003, multimillionaire Darrell Issa spent over $1 million to collect signatures to force a recall election for governor of California. In the ensuing election he ran for governor.

When control by ruling class money is so prevalent and blatant, the credibility of the entire electoral system is diminished.

Members of the ruling class donate millions of dollars to candidates of both parties directly, and through various kinds of fundraising events. In 1996, for example, only 4 percent of the population made a contribution of any size at any level of government, and only .25 percent gave $200 or more. The one-quarter percent who gave $200 or more provided 80 percent of all political money.[120] Bush raised $190 million for his 2000 presidential campaign, and two-thirds of that came from just over seven hundred individuals. Gore raised $133 million, and one-third of that, or $46 million, came from individuals.[121] In 1994, to give another example of the concentration of political donations, the total contributions from just one zip code—10021— on New York City's Upper East Side were larger than the contributions made in 24 states.[122]

Giving at the (Corporate) Office

The ruling class also uses corporations as a major vehicle for political donations through political action committees, again to both parties. In 2002, estimated total corporate contributions from PACs, soft money, and individual donations were over $1 billion.[123] The ruling class also uses "soft money"[124] donations to the Republican and Democratic parties for "party building" which is then channeled to candidates. In 1996, 92 percent of soft money came from business leaders and their corporations to the tune of $263.5 million.[125]

There are many other ways for members of the ruling class to donate to, or otherwise support, political candidates. They can give them corporate stock or property, hire them at exorbitant salaries, provide fellowships and lecture opportunities for them, provide them with free services like legal consultation, offer them investment opportunities, or buy assets from them at inflated prices.

What Does This Money Buy?

Corporations know that their campaign contributions are tremendously profitable investments. In the state of New York, between the years 1999 and 2001, Governor Pataki and state legislators received about $13.6 million in campaign contributions from banks, insurance companies, and other corporations. In return, these businesses reaped a total of $738 million in tax cuts in the 2002/03 fiscal year, and nearly $3 billion over the next five years. This came at a time when the state of New York was facing unprecedented budget deficits because of the recession and the attacks of 9/11.[126] A few other examples (among hundreds) on the national level listed by Kevin Phillips in his book, *Wealth and Democracy*, include:

"The Timber Industry spent $8 million in campaign contributions to preserve the logging road subsidy, worth $458 million... Glaxo Wellcome invested $1.2 million in campaign contributions to get a 19-month patent extension on Zantac worth $1 billion.... The Tobacco Industry spent $30 million in contributions for a tax break worth $50 billion.... For a paltry $5 million in campaign contributions, the Broadcasting Industry was able to secure free digital TV licenses, a give-away of public property worth $70 billion."[127]

Besides specific benefits, large campaign contributions also provide pressure on legislators to lower tax rates for the ruling class, to pass anti-labor legislation, to deregulate industries such as energy, telecommunications and trucking, and to privatize public assets and services such as radio and TV airwaves, welfare, health care, and the internet.

Two-party System

The two political parties give the appearance of competition and the representation of different interests. However, the parties are more like professional football teams owned by the ruling class. Members of the ruling class meet to decide the rules of the game, and the revenue from their network contracts is shared. As long as fans buy tickets, watch on TV, and buy the products advertised by the companies buying airtime, all the owners get richer whether their particular team wins or not. They do earn more if their team wins the Superbowl, just as members of the ruling class gain more if the party they support wins the presidency. But these days most corporations and members of the ruling class contribute to both parties and win big whoever is elected, just as sports team owners have set up revenue sharing plans to divide up media and advertising profits.

The two parties were created not to represent the interests of different classes, but to represent rival interests within the ruling class. In a very simplified way, the Democrats were the party of agrarian wealth, and the Republicans the party of bankers, merchants, and rising industrialists. There have been various attempts to create a third party such as the Populist Party and Green Party, but the control by the ruling class of the two-party system has meant that no third party has been able to gain significant representation.

Third parties have been severely hampered by state and federal laws, coupled with the collusion of the Democratic and Republican parties, which make it difficult for them to get on and remain on the ballot, difficult to raise funds and gain visibility, and impossible to gain equal access to public exposure. The two parties have prevented third party candidates from appearing on public debates at the national and state levels, and have even prevented third party candidates like Ralph Nader, running for president, and Peter Camejo, running for governor of California, from attending, even as audience members, the mainstream candidates' public debates. The end result of these actions is to severely limit the possibility of any third party representing people who don't have ruling class interests.

Voting

In most presidential elections, fewer than 50 percent of the eligible U.S. population votes. Anyone gaining the votes of 26 percent of the electorate wins these races. In nonpresidential and other off-year balloting, turnout can fall to 25 to 30 percent.

The lack of alternatives to ruling class candidates has systematically discouraged ordinary people from voting. When there was a vibrant Populist Party one hundred years ago, voting percentages were 70 to 80 percent of the eligible population.

But today, even if you want to vote you may not be able to, and your vote may not count because of ruling class resistance to allowing registration and voting to be easy, systematic, accessible, and free of harassment. The U.S. Commission on Civil Rights estimated that during the 2000 presidential election in Florida, nearly 200,000 votes were lost because of faulty voting machines and ballots, voter intimidation, and confused poll workers. Racism is certainly a factor, because the Commission goes on to report that Black voters in that state were 10 times more likely than non-Black voters to have their ballots rejected. Nationally, the Massachusetts Institute of Technology estimated that four to six million votes were "lost" because of voting foul-ups.[128]

Potential voters are also discouraged because at-large elections, off-year elections, winner-take-all elections, and the lack of proportional representation, mean that their vote may count for very little. In addition, because of the collusion between the two parties, most districts are drawn so that one party or the other will nearly always be the winner. The two parties, representing one ruling class, have gone ahead and decided which party will win most districts. Since these districts rarely vary from election to election, the candidates are completely beholden to the parties for staying in office.

There have always been restrictions, such as poll taxes, property requirements, age, gender and racial conditions, literacy tests, and grandfather clauses used to keep people from voting. In many states convicted felons cannot vote, and in some, anyone convicted of a felony cannot vote for the rest of their life. In the 2000 election in Florida alone, more than 400,000 ex-felons, about half of them black, were denied the right to vote.[129] Also in that election, there were documented instances of police and INS intimidation of voters, manipulation of the polls, illegal purging of names from voting roles, and inferior, less reliable voting equipment in lower income precincts. There is also growing concern among many citizens about the new electronic voting methods. Without a paper record, the results from electronic voting are completely unverifiable and could provide another way for the ruling class to disenfranchise the rest of the electorate.

The owning classes are not that large in absolute numbers, but a large percentage of their members vote because they know their vote will count, and that the candidates they vote for will work in their interests.

Many countries use different systems to represent the interests of poor and working-class people, and people who have particular concerns. They rely on proportional representation, instant runoffs, government funding of campaigns, election-day registration, nonpartisan redistricting, and other practices. In many of these countries 75 to 85 percent of the eligible population votes, they have multiple parties, and a much wider array of interests is represented in the electoral process than is represented in ours.

Not all politicians are members of the ruling class or even share all of their values. Many who become officials are not from the owning classes. However, all elected officials in positions of significant leadership are dependent on the ruling class for the funds and other support necessary to be elected to office. Once in office, they are dependent on the expertise and professional skills of members of the power elite, and professionals trained at elite universities. They are faced with constant pressure from lobbyists ($1.4 billion spent in 1999)[130] that business interests provide, and because they need the media in order to remain in office, they are beholden to the corporations that control it. It is no wonder that in the current political system, the power elite remains the dominant player, and the ruling class as a whole, the primary beneficiary of the entire process.

HOW DO MEMBERS OF
THE RULING CLASS INCREASE
THEIR WEALTH?

The ruling class has developed many different mechanisms for preserving and increasing their wealth. They have made extensive use of the federal government to provide a strong, secure, and regulated infrastructure for doing business. The power elite has directed governmental policies at the local, state, and national level to feed money directly and indirectly into the accounts of the ruling class.

Corporate Welfare

The amount of corporate welfare—government policies that directly subsidize big business—was estimated at $195 billion dollars a year in 2000.[131] Corporate welfare takes the form of direct subsidies such as farm subsidies,

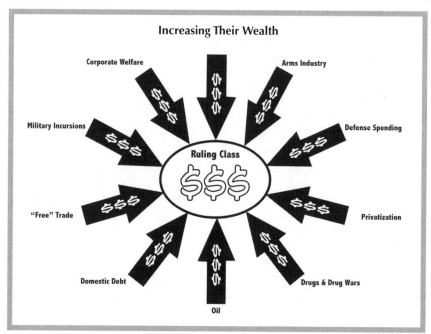

reduced prices; such as low cost leases of public mining and timber rights, paid government infrastructure such as roads for logging companies on public lands (a $140 million expenditure in one recent year[132]), and sewers and roads for new developments, subsidized research, tariffs on foreign imports, various tax breaks (including lower taxes on overseas business operations than on domestic ones), exemptions, depletion allowances, and domestic and foreign tax shelters and tax havens. Giving away public resources such as the airwaves, and mineral and logging rights for practically nothing is also part of corporate welfare.

Military Incursions

"War is a continuation of business by other means"—Bertold Brecht

Another substantial way that the ruling class benefits from government support is through the amount spent on military invasions and incursions in non-European countries, which go to protect U.S. companies' investments. Much of our foreign policy is determined by the goal of protecting the profits of companies doing business—acquiring raw materials, manufacturing goods, or selling finished products. There has never been a clearer statement of the benefits to the ruling class of U.S. military interventions then the following by one of the most celebrated leaders of the U.S. Marines, General Smedley Butler. After he retired and had reconsidered his career he wrote:

> I spent 33 years and 4 months in active military service…and during that period I spent most of my time as a high-class muscle man for big business, for Wall Street and the bankers. In short, I was a racketeer, a gangster for capitalism.

> Thus, I helped make Mexico and especially Tampico safe for American oil interests in 1914. I helped make Haiti and Cuba a decent place for the National City Bank boys to collect revenues in. I helped in the raping of half a dozen Central American republics for the benefit of Wall Street.

> I helped purify Nicaragua for the international banking house of Brown Brothers in 1902-1912. I brought light to the Dominican Republic for American sugar interests in 1916. I helped make Honduras right for American fruit companies in 1903. In China in 1927, I helped see to it that Standard Oil went on its way unmolested.[133]

The long-term political and economic benefits from these wars flow to the United States (and other Triad countries), and the damage is done to the local people, culture, and economies. For example, the military invasions of Vietnam and Cambodia, the bombing of urban areas of Panama City, the bombing of Serbia, Afghanistan, and the bombing/embargo/sanctions/invasion of Iraq have left shattered countries in their wake. Although written in 1902 with the Belgian attack on the Congo in mind, Joseph Conrad in his novel "Heart of Darkness" could be accurately describing the 2001 invasion of Afghanistan, or the 2003 invasion of Iraq.

> They were conquerors, and for that you only want brute force.... They grabbed what they could get for the sake of what was to be got. It was robbery with violence, aggravated murder on a great scale, and men going at it blind.... The conquest of the earth, which mostly means the taking it away from those who have a different complexion or slightly flatter noses than ourselves, is not a pretty thing when you look into it too much.[134]

International Debt

In addition to the profits from the exploitation of natural resources in Asia, the Middle East, South America, and Africa, the ruling class is reaping enormous profits from the debt that has accumulated in many less-developed countries. Rising oil prices, much of which is fueled by international oil cartels, massive corruption by western supported dictators, and IMF and World Bank mandated loans (many of them for development projects such as dams and industrialized agriculture that have had a devastating impact on the residents of those countries), have pushed many poor countries into debt to multinational banks. Some of these countries have had to borrow additional money just to pay the interest on their debt. Between 1980 and 1996, nearly two-thirds of IMF member countries experienced some sort of credit disaster.[135] Each crisis, while of concern to the major financial institutions, ends up leaving them even more able to set stringent, self-serving conditions for fiscal policy than before (structural adjustment policies), and able to collect additional money on the high-interest debts.

By the year 2000, the transfer of money from impoverished countries to ruling class owned banks in the U.S., Europe, and Japan reached $50 billion a year. Developing countries owed more than $2 trillion. African countries alone are paying $162 billion more than they receive in new loans every year.[136] During the 1990s, Latin American countries transferred over $600 billion to Western banks.[137]

Often, countries were economically or militarily coerced or threatened into taking out the original loans. In other countries, the money was borrowed and then embezzled by dictators or military governments such as in Zaire, where Mobutu Sese Seko made off with an estimated $5 billion from his years as a U.S. supported dictator.[138] International loans and subsequent debt repayment provides one mechanism for the power elite of The Triad countries to reward (or punish) members of the ruling classes of poor countries.

The crushing burden of this debt, the undemocratic control by external financial corporations, and the unfair and unreasonable transfer of this money to Western countries are some of the reasons why there is a growing international movement for relief from the burden of these debts.[139]

The transfer of wealth from the rest of the world to the overdeveloped countries has been so massive in recent decades that a former World Bank executive has said, "Not since the Conquistadores plundered Latin America has the world experienced a flow in the direction we see today."[140]

Arms and Armaments

The arms industry is a major source of profit to the ruling class, and this industry is heavily subsidized by the U.S. government. U.S. based companies sold nearly $50 billion of conventional weapons to other countries during

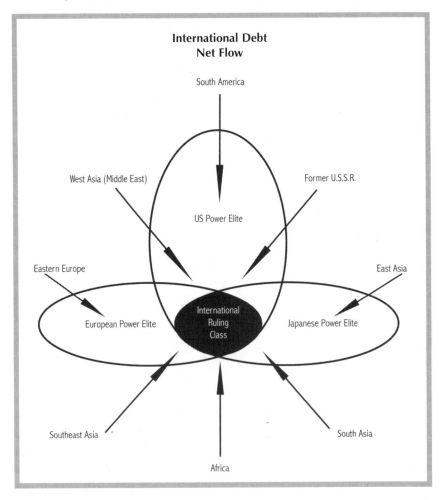

the period between 1996 and 2000—this was just under half of all world-wide legal arms sales during this period.[141] The government's vast expenditures on defense, constant military involvement, and huge direct and indirect subsidies of arms sales to other countries, provide the military industrial complex with growing markets and little risk in its investments.

These arms sales include information and technology for making nuclear, biological, and chemical weapons. These have been sold to many countries directly, or by proxy through intermediary countries whose governments we supported. There is no concern for how these weapons are used as long as they are directed at non-Westerners (people of color). The only time we challenge the possession of these weapons (and then only very selectively) is when they might be directed back at us or our allies.

This industry does not provide large benefits to the taxpayers of the United States because of high government subsidies, huge tax breaks, export credits, research and development costs, and offsets (deals in which the U.S. agrees to purchase goods from another country to offset some of the costs of weapons). According to the World Policy Institute, more than half of all U.S. weapons sales are financed by U.S. taxpayers rather than by the foreign governments purchasing the arms. During 1996, the U.S. government spent more than $7.9 billion to help companies secure just over $12 billion in new international arms sales.[142] However great the cost to the government (passed on to us as taxes), that $12 billion represents tremendous profits for members of the ruling class.

Defense Spending

Just as with the arms trade, domestic defense spending is a tremendous source of profits for ruling class investments in a wide array of industries. These expenditures cost the United States public billions of dollars every year in unnecessary military spending and corporate subsidies, and they divert money from education, health care, and other social services. Extravagant and unnecessary defense strategies such as star wars keep profits flowing even in times of relative peace.

As political analyst Noam Chomsky states, "Internationally, the Pentagon was an intervention force, but domestically it was a method by which the government could coordinate the private economy, provide welfare to major corporations, subsidize them, arrange the flow of taxpayer money to research and development, provide a state-guaranteed market for excess production, target advanced industries for development, etc."[143] A recent reflection of the importance of defense spending for fueling corporate and therefore ruling class profits was the rapid growth of custom software firms (and eventually the internet) during the 1970s and 1980s based on demand from the federal government that was largely a defense department demand.[144]

Privatization

The privatization of public resources such as our national forests, federally owned mineral deposits, the postal service, and telecommunications, provides the ruling class with publicly developed resources at little cost, that they can turn into new sources of expansion and exploitation. For just one example, the value of the assets, such as cable channels, privatized by the Telecommunications Act of 1996 (a bill that broadcast lobbyists helped shape) was estimated by one analyst to be $70 billion.[145] That is not a bad return on the investment of $53 million that was spent by communications and electronic interests in lobbying for the legislation.[146] Public services such as education and health care are also being privatized at a rapid rate with disastrous results. When a public service such as education is privatized (public schools being handed over to private corporations to run), quality usually decreases, costs rise, safety, educational, and health standards often decline, and the public is ultimately left to clean up the mess. Nothing is off limits in the ruling class search for profits. There is even talk today of privatizing air traffic controllers and letting corporations squeeze the most profits they can out of supervising our airways and flight patterns.

Internationally, the demand on poor and less developed countries by the IMF and World Bank for the privatization of publicly owned assets such as utility companies, natural resources such as water, mineral and timber rights, and electronic and transportation assets, has led to the state sale of national assets at ridiculously low prices. This has led to the further concentration of ownership in the hands of transnational corporations, and increased profits flowing to the U.S., Europe, and Japan.

Oil

Oil has become the fuel of the world economy and a crucial resource for the U.S. economy. But it took a lot of work (and generated a lot of profits) for the power elite to develop the U.S. economy in ways that required huge amounts of oil. The Rockefeller oil companies, working with Ford Motor Company and Goodyear Tire and Rubber, bought up the very efficient local transportation systems across the country and closed them down, while promoting the road building and gasoline consuming car culture that replaced them.[147]

After World War II, U.S. oil companies wrested control of the international oil trade from British companies. Since then these oil companies, some of the largest and most powerful corporations in the world, have monopolized oil production, refining, distribution, and sales, while at the same time blocking the development of alternative energy sources.

Today, much U.S. foreign policy is about controlling or protecting access to oil in such countries as Afghanistan, Iraq, Saudi Arabia, Columbia, Venezuela, Indonesia, Iran, and Panama. John Lehman, former Secretary of the Navy, has said that the U.S. government spends $40 billion a year in oil-related military expenditures in the Gulf.[148] Peter Hain, Foreign Minister of the UK, has said that protecting Middle East oil supplies costs between $15 and $25 per barrel of oil, with most of the expense being paid by the U.S.[149]Much of this is a form of subsidy to the oil companies and a source of tremendous profits to the ruling class.[150]

Drugs and Drug Wars

There are two kinds of drug markets, and they are both highly lucrative for the ruling class.[151] The first is legal drugs either developed directly by government-sponsored academic research or by tax-deductible corporate research. Pharmaceutical companies are then given unrestricted license to sell these drugs for whatever the market will bear, creating a highly profitable and expanding $400 billion-a-year industry.[152] Although they employ over 90,000 drug representatives and spend $8 billion in the U.S. marketing their drugs, pushing drugs is highly profitable. The nine largest multinational drug companies made $191 billion between 1991 and 2000, a 40.9 percent return on investment.[153]

The illegal drug market is also highly profitable both directly and indirectly. The trade in illegal drugs is estimated to be bigger than the legal drug industry and oil industry, and is second only to the world arms trade. In 1998 it was probably worth somewhere between $500 billion and $1 trillion a year. Over half of that flows through U.S. banks.[154] Investigative journalist and author, Alain Labrousse, has estimated that, "80 percent of the profits from drug trafficking ends up in the banks of the wealthy countries or their branches in the underdeveloped countries."[155]

Much of the money from illegal drug operations finds its way directly into the pockets of the ruling class through tax havens, money laundering, legal "services," and the provision of chemicals used in the growing and manufacturing of drugs. Indirect profits from the war on drugs, including increased military expenditures, purchase of drug fighting equipment, and the growth of the prison-industrial complex, are also important sources of profits related to drugs. Eighty percent of federal prisoners are locked up on nonviolent, drug-related charges, fueling a prison-industrial complex which presently incarcerates 2 million people in the United States, over half of whom are people of color.

International wars against "narco-terrorists," and the domestic war on drugs provide further sources of profit to the ruling class, and specific means for the surveillance and control of local communities of color and overseas communities in developing countries. These drug wars have become an effective way for the ruling class to increase military and police control as a supplement to the extensive levels of financial control that it already employs.

As a condition of aid, loans, and investment funds, many countries are forced to open up all levels of their national security to U.S. monitoring and control to certify their compliance with U.S. drug-control restrictions. Extensively documented U.S. government involvement in the domestic and international drug trade in heroin and cocaine has devastated communities of color, has pacified and co-opted dissent, and has been used to channel funds into covert CIA operations.[156]

The ruling class is able to make tremendous profits from the promotion, distribution, and sale of legal and illegal drugs. It then uses widespread drug use to justify extensive surveillance and control of low-income communities and communities of color by the criminal justice system in this country and through counter-insurgency and counter-terrorism programs in countries such as Columbia.

Oil, Drugs, and Arms

The oil, drug, and arms industries are very often intertwined. In Vietnam, the U.S. set up heroin production to fund the arms provided to local tribes fighting against the Vietcong.[157] In Iran, the U.S. illegally sold arms for drugs to maintain access to oil in the Middle East, and to protect U.S. investments in Central America.[158] In Afghanistan, the U.S. developed the opium trade to allow the Afghanis to fund arms purchases to fight the Russians. This was expected to open up U.S. access to the oil fields of Central Asia.[159] In Colombia, the U.S. has used the excuse of combating drugs, to supply arms and other military aid to the Columbian government's counterinsurgency program in order to maintain U.S. access to Columbia's substantial oil deposits.[160]

Over the years the U.S. economy has become increasingly dependent on petrodollars, the amount of money reinvested in the U.S. economy by oil-producing countries, and narco-dollars, the amount invested from the laundering of drug money. Our foreign policy continues to be driven by the need to control sources of oil and to finance military and foreign policy initiatives with money from drug trafficking.

"Free" Trade and "Free" Markets

A different kind of corporate welfare involves the lowering of trade barriers for investment in poor and developing countries while protecting and subsidizing sectors of the U.S. economy. Under the rhetoric of free trade and free markets (even though U.S. markets are, and have always been, highly regulated by tariffs, subsidies, import duties and other structures), IMF and World Bank policies and GATT, NAFTA, and other trade agreements force open markets in less-developed countries, require the privatization of public resources, and push highly inappropriate models of development with huge capital-intensive projects in developing countries. At the same time, the most competitive U.S. economic sectors, internationally, are those that are highly subsidized by the U.S. government, such as arms, pharmaceuticals, oil, agriculture, and computers. In addition, very tight protection on copyrights, patents, and trademarks is another source of trade restriction and provides substantial advantage to Triad-based corporations. Many areas of trade are highly protected, and regulated, and subsidized within developed countries, while international agencies demand that developing countries operate completely without barriers to transnational corporate investment. This trade is better labeled free (and unfair) access than free trade.

Domestic Debt

Various forms of federal, state, and local and consumer debt are ways to transfer money to the ruling class from the majority of taxpayers. For example, when a state or local government needs money to build schools, dams, or prisons, it could simply tax those with money, as is done in many countries. Instead, our governments often issue bonds, which is a way of borrowing money from the rich and then paying them interest for the credit. The interest on many of these bonds is tax-free, producing an additional benefit (see below under taxes).

When the federal government runs a budget deficit, this debt is also financed by bonds, in this case treasury bonds. The owning classes, both in the U.S. and in other countries, hold the majority of these bonds, and it is the general U.S. population that pays for this borrowing. Each time that the federal government or a state or local government borrows money, they are subject to the conditions placed on the loans by the financial sector. Every time that a city, state, or the federal government has a debt crisis, those conditions become even more onerous and the financial markets assume even greater control—able to dictate harsher public policy so that they can insure greater profits on their loans.

Do you owe money to the ruling class? Are you paying off housing, student, car, or credit card loans?

The other form of debt is consumer debt. When the ruling class and the power elite keep wages so low that ordinary people cannot get by on what they earn, when people have to borrow to buy housing, cars, or to pay for major health expenses or to go to college, and when people's desire for consumer goods is pumped up by massive amounts of advertising, they often use loans and credit card debt to pay the bills for what they need or want. This currently huge level of common debt is borrowed at high interest rates. The debt is accumulated by large financial corporations and then packaged into bonds, bond and stock funds, and other financial instruments, and the money is paid out to those in the ruling class who invest and/or speculate in them.

As economist Henwood points out, there are additional advantages to the ruling class from a high level of consumer debt. It reduces pressure for higher wages by allowing people to buy goods they couldn't otherwise afford. It helps to nourish both the appearance and reality of a middle-class standard of living in a time of great inequalities of wealth and power, and it constrains people's ability to take political risks through social action when they have high mortgage, student loan, or credit card payments.[161] Student loan-based debt, in particular, can have a substantial impact on the work options and risk-taking activism of young adults.

A tremendous amount of money is funneled to the ruling class by these various forms of domestic debt because, in general, the more money that is concentrated by the ruling class, the more the rest of us have to borrow from them in order to get by. Each form of debt also carries with it either direct or indirect forms of control, or at least limits on the activities and choices of those who borrow. The terrible irony of this system is that all of us who owe money on housing, student, car, credit card debt, or other forms of consumer

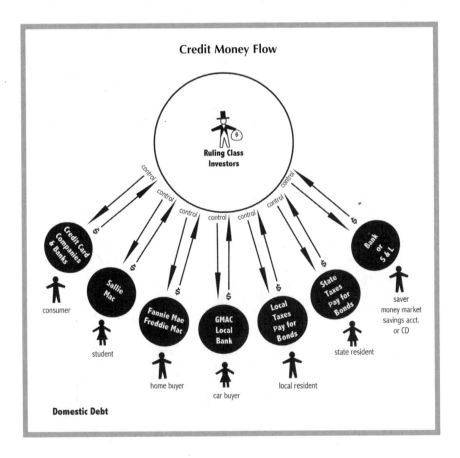

debt, end up owing money (and paying lots of interest) to the ruling class, even though they already own most of the wealth of the country!

Federal Reserve Bank

The U.S. Federal Reserve bank sets interest rates which have a major impact on the U.S. economy in such areas as employment, investment, personal and institutional debt, and money flow. Although the majority of its members are appointed by the president, they are mostly bankers, members of other large financial institutions, and/or presidents of reserve banks; i.e. direct representatives of ruling class interests. The system is also self-financing through its portfolio of U.S. government treasury bonds, making it further immune to governmental oversight. The Fed is a primary instrument used by the power elite to keep unemployment and inflation within acceptable (to those with wealth) limits. Through their manipulation of interest rates they guarantee that millions of people will remain unemployed or underemployed, and that the financial interests of those who own bonds and stocks will be protected.[162]

Corporate Crime

The period at the end of the nineteenth century when corporations gained dominance politically and economically was not called the age of robber barons by accident. Unethical, immoral, illegal, ruthless, corrupt, and socially and environmentally destructive practices are hallmarks of a privately owned corporate economy. While most of the activities described in the previous section are legal or quasi-legal, members of the ruling and managerial classes are also not above just stealing money. There are many current examples of corporate executives at Enron, WorldCom, Tyco, Arthur Anderson, and Adelphia, engaged in illegal activities costing our country billions of dollars.

While our attention in the evening news is more often focused on street crime, corporate crooks are siphoning trainloads of money into private accounts, over 46 times what street crime costs us. The FBI estimates that while street crime costs U.S. taxpayers about $3.8 billion a year, white collar crime costs U.S. taxpayers more than $200 billion a year and does irreparable harm to the individuals and communities who end up losing jobs, losing savings, and paying higher taxes to cover the costs.[163] Rarely are these crimes prosecuted. Even when they are, penalties are light and sentences are lighter still. We have over two million people in prisons in the United States, but in the last ten years the Securities and Exchange Commission has jailed only 87 executives for corporate wrongdoing.[164]

PRESERVING THEIR WEALTH

Beyond corporate welfare, there are also a variety of ways that individuals and families in the ruling class preserve and increase their wealth through government tax policies.

Capital Gains Taxes

Profit from the sale of property, stocks, and bonds held longer than one year is taxed at a special low capital gains rate, now at 15 percent, rather than at a normal income tax bracket rate. Because they own the majority of the stocks and bonds and property, the ruling class receives 62 percent of all cap-

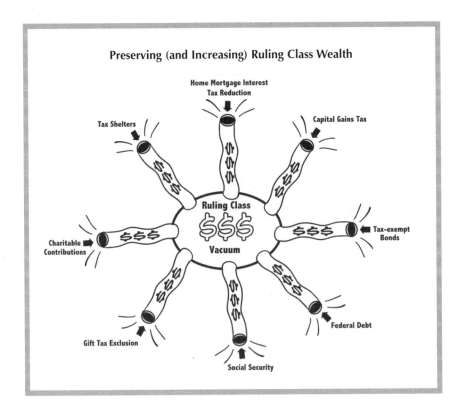

Preserving (and Increasing) Ruling Class Wealth

ital gains. The total gained by the owning classes is approximately $90 billion a year.[165] The managerial class receives most of the rest.

Tax-exempt Bonds

Some investments are treated even more favorably by the tax laws. Interest payments on bonds issued by municipal authorities such as cities and water, utility, and school districts, are tax exempt. A tax-free $44.3 billion was paid out this way in 1991, most of it to the top 20 percent, who had the wealth to buy the bonds in the first place. By 1995, the cost to the federal government in lost taxes was over $20 billion a year. About two-thirds of this subsidy went to state and local governments and the other one-third to wealthy bondholders.[166]

The Federal Debt

The federal debt itself is another vehicle the ruling class uses to accumulate wealth. The short-, medium-, and long-term bonds that finance the debt are a safe and steady source of income for many. It is estimated that during the 1990s around $2 trillion in interest payments on the national debt will primarily benefit those at the top of the economic pyramid.[167] Primary causes of federal debt are low taxes, tax cuts, and tax breaks for high wealth individuals and corporations. Members of the ruling class can then take their extra wealth and buy the bonds that the government has to sell to cover its debts—they gain a double bonus from this cycle.

Home Mortgage Interest Tax Deduction

The interest that a homeowner pays on a home mortgage is tax deductible. Because there is such a high limit on the amount that can be deducted, members of the ruling class can deduct large amounts of money that ordinary homeowners and renters cannot. In 2001, for example, if the home mortgage deduction had been capped at $300,000 a year, the government would have collected another $4.7 billion. If it had been capped at $100,000, it would have generated $40 billion.[168]

Tax Shelters

Corporate tax shelters provide the ruling class with methods of avoiding taxes on their income and wealth. Many personal options exist for sheltering money, including individual retirement plans, oil and gas investment partnerships, various forms of trusts and limited liability companies, offshore tax havens, foreign banking accounts, and "chains of electronic concealment," the highly complex and sophisticated ways that members of the ruling class and their financial institutions have for hiding income and assets through pass-through accounts and front companies.[169] Although many of these structures are theoretically available to anyone, in reality only those with wealth can enjoy the economic advantages of using them.

Charitable Deductions

Ordinary people give away a larger percentage of their money than those with wealth do. But the amount that non-wealthy people can claim as a tax deduction is very small. Members of the ruling class do make charitable donations in substantial amounts but, as noted earlier, this allows them to retain control over their money and to fund organizations that serve their interests. Charitable contributions can also substantially reduce the impact of estate taxes and allow inheritances to be passed on to heirs through foundations, keeping control within the family.

Social Security

Because there is no means test for social security, those with high incomes can collect benefits even if they do not need them. Since social security contributions are capped at $87,000, workers subsidize a half million members of the owning classes to the tune of more than $6.6 billion a year (1993).[170]

PASSING ON THEIR WEALTH

The essence of a ruling class is not just its wealth, but its ability to preserve and protect that wealth through the generations, so that it remains in power.

Estate Tax Reductions

Members of the ruling class can pass on $1.5 million to their descendants tax free before the estate tax kicks in. The estate tax itself has been progressively lowered down to its current level of just under 50 percent on estates of over a million dollars.

Gift Tax Exclusion

Although money passed to heirs before one dies is taxed at the estate tax rate, some of it can be passed on tax free. Members of the ruling class (and anyone else who has the wealth) can give up to $11,000 a year to as many individuals as they like, including their children or grandchildren, completely tax free. A couple with three children could give $22,000 to each one for a total of $66,000 a year free of inheritance tax liability.

There are many vehicles that the ruling class has developed so that its members can protect their wealth. The ones mentioned above are only a few of them. But it should be clear that they have a significant impact not only on protecting wealth but on keeping money out of the public domain.

The essence of a ruling class is intergenerational permanence, the ability to pass on its wealth to succeeding generations. The U.S. ruling class has developed several prominent ways to do this.

Inheritance

The most direct way to pass on wealth traditionally has been through inheritance. The U.S. ruling class is no exception. They have fought continuously to reduce inheritance taxes and most recently, to eliminate them entirely. Economist Lester Thurow estimates that between 50 and 70 percent of all wealth is inherited.[171]

To put this into perspective, as of 1998, 92 percent of the population had never received an inheritance. Of the remaining 8 percent, half had inherited less than $25,000. Just 1.6 percent had received as much as

$100,000.[172] The recently passed bill to gradually eliminate the inheritance tax, if made permanent, would guarantee that the children of the ruling class would be the most powerful members of our society in perpetuity (or until overthrown).

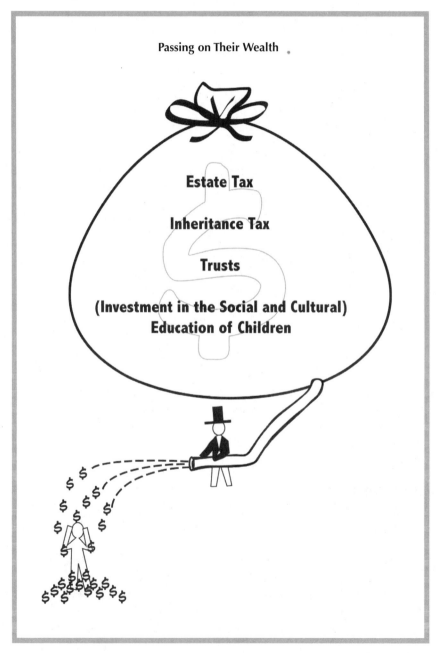

Trusts

Another way to circumvent the tax system, both in the present and across generations, is the complex system of trusts that the ruling class and its legislators and lawyers have devised to pass on control of its wealth so that it isn't diluted or taxed. A trust allows a family to divide up an estate among heirs without having to divide the actual property. Each individual receives a share of the income from the trust, but the property is managed as a unit. Often this management is handled by a bank, trust company, family office, holding company, or investment partnership.

A family office, for example, is a ruling class family's private management business. The assets are held in common by the family's descendants and managed as a unit, with each family member receiving earnings from the investments. In a *Forbes* magazine article, "Achieving Immortality via the Family Office," there is a description of how the Burden family keeps the $500 million fortune of Cornelius Vanderbilt growing, 150 years after he died, through the use of a family office.[173]

Trusts provide significant tax advantages. Members of the ruling class are continually trying to establish longer time periods for trusts to remain in operation. Recently a number of states have allowed the creation of a new trust to circumvent some of the time limit restrictions developed by the government in the past. The new trust is called a "dynasty" trust. "This type of trust offers significant long-term flexibility and advantages to individuals who want to establish a truly perpetual, tax-favored source of income and capital for future generations."[174] Dynasty trusts can preserve assets forever by protecting assets from claims of trust beneficiaries' creditors or ex-spouses, or from lawsuits against trust beneficiaries.

Trust assets are not subject to estate taxes and in some cases, state income taxes. They can also shield assets from gift and generation-skipping-transfer taxes.[175] The motto of Bessemer Trust, which operates many ruling class family trusts, is "Enhancing private wealth for generations."[176]

Education

Another way to ensure the longevity of the ruling class is to ensure that its children have such an educational advantage that they are the best qualified to hold positions of power in society. In a society like ours, in which only about 25 percent of all people complete a college degree, post high school education is the key to higher paying jobs, connections, and the ability to accumulate wealth. The ruling class has developed a network of private preschools, day schools, boarding schools, and elite colleges and universities especially geared to educating ruling class children.

People with wealth know the importance of this educational network in giving their children and grandchildren substantial advantages in life. In one study of people with over a million dollars in net worth, one-third paid for their adult children's graduate school tuition, and 43 percent funded their grandchildren's private school fees. This study concluded, "The most frequent and valued gift that millionaires received from their parents was tuition."[177]

Even with these economic and social advantages there are lots of talented and smart people who are not members of the ruling class who could compete with ruling class children. To preserve plenty of room for ruling class children, private schools, colleges, and universities have instituted affirmative action programs such as sibling preferences in private schools, legacy admissions (special quotas for the children of alumni), and special exceptions for large donors in colleges and universities. More ruling class youths are admitted under legacy admission guidelines or because of parental donations (15 to 25 percent in some elite universities) than minority youth are admitted under affirmative action programs covering race and gender.

According to sociologists Perrucci and Wysong, there are about 50 elite colleges and universities in the U.S. (20 universities and 30 liberal arts colleges). Children of the managerial class, often having attended well-endowed, predominately white suburban high schools, compete with children from the ruling class from the elite prep schools, to get into these colleges and universities. Graduating from one of these schools then leads them to the elite graduate and professional schools (about 15) in law, medicine, business, or engineering, or directly into positions in major corporations.

A small number of working-class high school students and students of color are selected to compete with the children of the rich. A few of the most assimilated make it all the way through the system into lucrative careers.[178] Karl Marx noted, "The more a ruling class is able to assimilate the most prominent men [and women] of the dominated classes, the more stable and dangerous its rule."[179] To take advantage of this population, the private educational system is geared to both accept and assimilate some of the brightest working- and middle-class youth into ruling class culture. They are able to "cream" the most creative and talented, and integrate them into the ruling and managerial classes. One working-class student describes the process as mining the working class. He goes on to write:

> Our scholarships were attempts by our elite benefactors not only to be generous but also to mine us for what they often condescendingly praised us for—our "freshness" and "vitality," our "passion" and "original thinking"—and then to train us and even trap us with loans and enormous debts into serving their institutions.

> We usually made their lives richer rather than enriching those of our own people, whose sacrifices had gotten us as far as they could.[180]

Whatever their class origins, what students learn in this educational process is also important to the ruling class and the power elite. Those who will become managers must have values and attitudes that allow them to work independently without challenging the status quo, and to manage the educational, health, defense, criminal justice, charitable, cultural, and other

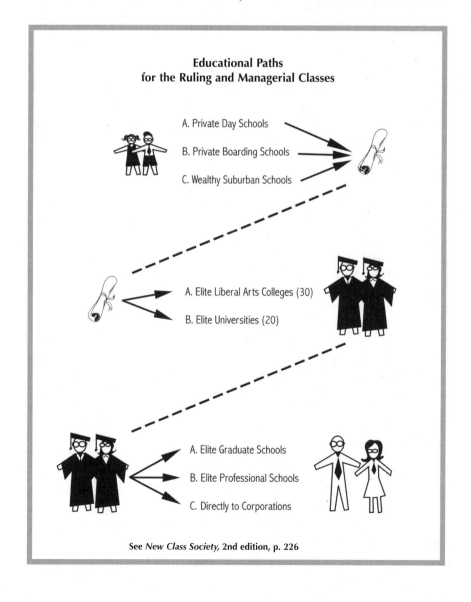

**Educational Paths
for the Ruling and Managerial Classes**

A. Private Day Schools

B. Private Boarding Schools

C. Wealthy Suburban Schools

A. Elite Liberal Arts Colleges (30)

B. Elite Universities (20)

A. Elite Graduate Schools

B. Elite Professional Schools

C. Directly to Corporations

See *New Class Society,* 2nd edition, p. 226

programs, organizations, and institutions they are charged with. Even more than their skills and expertise, these individuals are groomed for their " 'professional attitude'—[to be] confident and assertive individuals who exude the feeling that they are very much at home playing by the rules and that there is no pressing need to question the social structure in which they do their work."[181]

The resulting professional is uncritical of, and subordinate to, the interests of members of the ruling class who employ him or her. This educational system produces a person whom the ruling class "can trust to experiment, theorize, innovate and create, safely within the confines of an assigned ideology."[182]

Children

In addition to education, there are other ways for owning class families to pass on advantages to their children that enhance their ability to stay at the top of the economic pyramid. A study by researchers Stanley and Danko found that 59 percent of the respondents (all millionaires) helped their adult children purchase a house (17 percent even helped out with mortgage payments), 61 percent loaned them money without expecting to be repaid, 17 percent transferred securities, and 15 percent transferred all or part of a family business to them.[183] Parents can also provide substantial cash gifts (up to $11,000 a year is tax free), give cars, cosign loans, and connect their children to internships, summer jobs, post-graduate jobs, and valuable professional, political, and economic contacts. Ruling class women, in particular, spend a lot of their time ensuring that their children attend the right pre-schools and private schools, socialize with other ruling class children, have opportunities to join clubs, sororities, and fraternities, and are able to participate in charitable balls as debutantes and escorts.[184]

These various kinds of support, some financial, some educational and cultural, add up to substantial advantages. While they are undeniably tremendous assets, such advantages may or may not lead to a successful or satisfying life for the adult children. This support may undermine independence, good economic judgment, or even ambition or achievement. Receiving such gifts without an awareness of the privilege they entail may lead to a false sense of having worked hard and earned one's money or achievements.

Because they grow up with money and with the expectation that they'll have access to the best things in life, children of wealth often develop a tremendous sense of entitlement. If they are white and/or male, without knowing about all the forms of affirmative action they have been the beneficiaries of, they may also conclude that they deserve what they have, and that others do not.[185]

Marriage

To preserve the values, connections, and wealth of the ruling class, its members have been very concerned about their children marrying within the class. They can't control this completely, of course, but the comparative isolation of ruling class families, the social networks that they are a part of, and the class values they hold in common guarantee that their children will primarily partner with others of their class. Debutante balls and other charity events, sororities and fraternities, and an extensive system of ruling class women's social and philanthrophic clubs all contribute to the likelihood of intraclass dating and marriage.

There are also upscale dating services available throughout the country to promote these premarital connections. The following is an ad from one such service: "Join the Ivy League of Dating. Graduates and faculty of the Ivies, Seven Sisters, Johns Hopkins, M.I.T., Stanford, U. of Chicago, CAL Tech, Duke, U.C. Berkeley, Northwestern, meet alumni and academics. The Right Stuff."[186] The following ad from an upscale magazine is a more direct appeal to class values: "Pretty Professional Blonde, upper-class, non-smoker, seeks refined, upper-class or upper-middle-class gentleman, 30-42, with six-digit income, well-educated Protestant...for marriage and children."[187]

Some middle and managerial class people marry into the ruling class—usually marrying someone they met while attending an elite college or university. Often they are introduced to the values and behavioral codes of the ruling class through mentoring by older, richer, or longer-term members of the ruling class (including by mothers- and fathers-in-law). In the majority of cases, they are assimilated into ruling class values and won over by its wealth and opportunity, thus contributing to the preservation of the ruling class over time.

Integrating New Members into the Ruling Class

Some people from the managerial class, and even a few from lower economic levels, accumulate enough money to move into the ruling class. Fortunes are made on new technologies, lucrative government contracts, innovative marketing ideas, new products and services, illegal activities, government subsidies, and straightforward exploitation of workers. Old fortunes generally don't fade away, but there is a gradual expansion of the ruling class as the population grows. New members and their families are incorporated into the ruling class in two stages.

The first stage occurs as the economic success of a person (usually a man) gives them connections to the local and national power elite through business contracts and contacts, through political contributions, and through participation in charitable activities. They may have opportunities to join clubs, live in more restricted neighborhoods, send their children to elite schools and universities, and be invited to exclusive events in which they are socialized into the culture, expectations, and inner circles of money and power. Some people who accumulate first generation wealth avoid these processes, live comparatively simply given their means, and it is only their children who are acculturated into the ruling class socially.

The second stage occurs as the next generation comes of age having grown up with the material, educational, and cultural benefits of being a member of a ruling class family. Their expectations and opportunities are developed within a network of schools, camps, special programs, and travel opportunities which allow them to circulate easily in ruling class company and to share ruling class values. One indication of this acculturation process is that while only 29 percent of corporate presidents went to Ivy League colleges, 70 percent of their sons and daughters did so.[188]

There are certainly exceptions to these patterns. Some children of the ruling class of every generation, both from old and new wealth, reject ruling class values and live outside ruling class networks. Some give away most or all of their money to charitable causes and reject their privilege. Others work for social justice throughout their lives. The general patterns described above prevail in most cases, but individual members of the ruling class make decisions about their values and how they want to live their lives. The assimilation of new wealth and new generations does not work perfectly.[189]

PROTECTING THEMSELVES AND THEIR FAMILIES FINANCIALLY

I have mentioned how the corporate structure itself was created as a way to protect individuals and families of the ruling class from personal liability for the harmful decisions they make in the pursuit of profit. Limited Liability Companies, Limited Partnerships, and other related kinds of investment structures also offer protection from liability. The regulations and legal precedents that corporations operate under also make it very difficult for the public to hold the stockholders and directors liable for the harmful practices of a corporation. Limiting liability is one of the purposes of a corporation.

Offshore Financial Havens

Lax international financial controls, secret accounts, offshore tax havens, private banks, and shelf corporations allow members of the ruling class to control assets, launder illegal arms and drug money, and avoid U.S. taxes (to the tune of $70 billion a year).[190] The Organization for Economic Cooperation and Development estimated in 1998 that wealthy individuals may control as much as $15.5 trillion in assets this way.[191] Through correspondent banks, large U.S. banks, and other financial institutions (such as Merrill Lynch, Citigroup, Bank of America, Bank of New York, Chase Manhattan, J.P. Morgan Chase, Morgan Stanley, Goldman Sachs, and Wachovia) gain more than $150 billion a year in income from these unregulated and untaxed assets.[192] Most of this private banking, in the specialty known as "asset protection," is protected through International Business Companies (IBCs) which often conduct no actual business but are simply a series of shells through which money is passed and protected. There is even a glossy magazine, *Offshore Finance USA,* which provides a how-to guide for hiding money abroad.[193]

Besides allowing members of the ruling class to avoid taxes, lawsuits, creditors, and even divorce and child custody payments, offshore tax havens, secret accounts, trusts, shell banks, and chains of electronic concealment also make it difficult to establish ownership of assets and therefore liability when reckless or illegal activities are engaged in.

Bailouts

Government bailouts are another way in which members of the ruling class protect their investments from the effects of corporate corruption, misguided financial policies, the devastating impact of structural readjustment policies, and the vagaries of the global marketplace. A bailout can take several different forms. After 9/11, Congress allocated $15 billion to bail out the airline companies. This money was not for the tens of thousands of workers who were laid off, but for the investors who might lose their money, and for the corporate management who would lose their jobs if the companies went bankrupt. The U.S. government has routinely bailed out large companies such as Chrysler Corp. ($1.2 billion in loan guarantees), and Conrail ($5 billion loss), Lockheed, and Continental Illinois ($7.5 billion) in defiance of the principles of the "free market," simply to protect investors' money.

The largest U.S. bailout was the Savings and Loan scandal, in which members of the ruling class looted hundreds of billions of unrecovered dol-

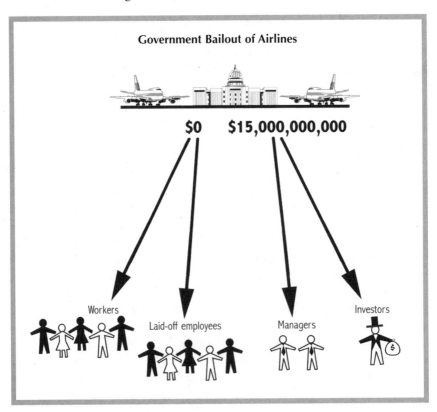

Government Bailout of Airlines

$0 $15,000,000,000

Workers

Laid-off employees

Managers

Investors

lars from Savings and Loans with the federal government picking up most of the liability and passing it on to taxpayers.

There were several causes for the collapse of the Savings and Loan Industry, but deregulation of the industry was a major one. Deregulation led to fraud and corruption,[194] self-dealing (directors lending money to themselves), and high-risk loans—at the same time that the government raised the levels that it guaranteed deposits through the Federal Deposit Insurance Corporation (FDIC). The ruling class made off with billions of dollars leaving U.S. taxpayers to hold the bag. This bailout has been estimated to cost U.S. taxpayers between $300 and $500 billion. It won't be until around the year 2020 that we will have paid off all of the debt from it.[195]

On the international level, massive bailouts were initiated through the IMF after the collapse of the economies of Mexico ($50 billion) and countries in Southeast Asia ($120 billion) to protect U.S. and other investors from potential losses due to currency devaluations, large scale bankruptcies, and loss of confidence and instability in the international economy caused by the currency speculation of many of these same investors.

Insurance

The insurance industry is set up explicitly to guarantee that ruling class members don't experience financial losses, and to protect them from financial and personal liability. Director's insurance, umbrella insurance, and various forms of liability insurance make personal wealth virtually impregnable from those damaged by the practices used to create that wealth. Fire, theft, and disaster insurance protect personal and corporate property. Various forms of life insurance are primarily used by the rich to pass on wealth by lessening inheritance taxes.

Corporate risk insurance is another kind of insurance that uses public funds to guarantee ruling class profits. For example, the Overseas Private Investment Corporation of the U.S. State Department, the Multilateral Investment Guarantee Agency, and the International Finance Corporation of the World Bank, provide billions of dollars worth of insurance against restrictions on currency and repatriation of profits, on risks of expropriation, and on political risks ranging from war, coups, revolution, and terrorism, to strikes, distribution problems, and bureaucratic delays.[196]

PROTECTING THEIR POWER

Dealing with Resistance in the U.S.

In response to the constant resistance by ordinary people to their policies and practices, the power elite has developed some very specific ways of responding to dissent in order to maintain control. As discussed below in the section on the buffer zone, jobs that control people and maintain the status quo are primarily carried out by men operating in military or paramilitary organizations, either overtly or covertly. When people organize on a broad scale such as in strikes, marches, demonstrations, rallies, pickets and boycotts, the police, state militias, or units of the National Guard have been called on. At the same time, the CIA, FBI, and other federal and state agents have attempted to hamper the legal activities of organizations by tapping phones, monitoring communications, or closing down, burning down, or destroying, offices and equipment. The Internal Revenue Service (IRS), the Immigration and Naturalization Service (INS), the Bureau of Alcohol, Tobacco and Firearms, Department of Housing, the Drug Enforcement Agency (DEA), and many other federal and state agencies have been used to harass individuals and organizations. In addition, provocateurs have been planted in meetings and on staff to try and stir up violence and promote conflict within organizations.

Individuals and organizations have been targeted with expensive lawsuits, have been arrested, harassed, intimidated, detained, threatened, subjected to grand juries, falsely imprisoned, and some people have been murdered. Individuals such as Karen Silkwood, Martin Luther King, Jr., Fred Hampton, Judi Bari and Darryl Cherney, and the Rosenbergs, among scores of others, have been killed or have had attempts made on their lives. Members of such groups as the American Indian Movement, MOVE, and the Black Panthers were systematically targeted for disruption and murder under the U.S. government's COINTELPRO. MOVE was a political organization of African American families living together in several houses in a neighborhood in Philadelphia. After a confrontation with police in 1985, one of their homes was bombed from the air by the authorities, and the ensuing fire destroyed 61 houses and killed 11 people, including five children. COINTELPRO (Counter Intelligence Program) was an FBI operation during the 1960s through the 1980s which engaged in many illegal activities to spy on, harass, disrupt, and destroy legitimate organizations and organizing efforts.[197] There is evidence that this program is currently being reactivated.

Since September 2001 we have experienced a wave of illegal detention, deportation, arrests, harassment, and physical attacks on Muslims, Arabs and Arab-Americans, and immigrants, that has been fostered by the efforts of the police, the FBI, the INS, and private security companies.

The power elite has also used private foundation and government grants to fund dissident groups and movements and to steer organizations toward more mainstream activities that are consistent with the status quo. Non-profit sector jobs have also co-opted some grassroots community leaders into

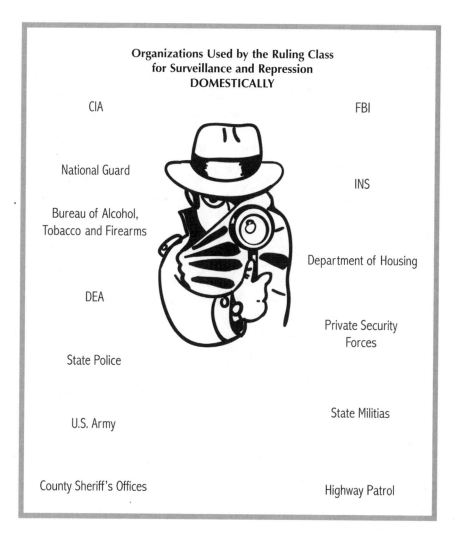

**Organizations Used by the Ruling Class
for Surveillance and Repression
DOMESTICALLY**

CIA

FBI

National Guard

INS

Bureau of Alcohol,
Tobacco and Firearms

Department of Housing

DEA

Private Security
Forces

State Police

U.S. Army

State Militias

County Sheriff's Offices

Highway Patrol

becoming part of the buffer zone (see below), disconnected from their communities.

In addition to the direct violence and the economic co-optation, the power elite has used the legislature to make many kinds of strikes, boycotts, marches, rallies, and pickets illegal, and then relied on the courts to pass injunctions preventing protest activities from taking place.

Dealing with Resistance in Other Countries

The policies of the U.S. power elite, working in conjunction with the ruling elites of Western Europe and Japan, have had an even more devastating impact on people outside the U.S. than within it. While the resistance in many countries has been relentless and well organized, the methods used by the power elite in retaliation have been brutal. The U.S. is simply the most recent in a long line of imperial powers that have employed any means necessary to retain power and concentrate wealth.

The most noticeable actions of the U.S. power elite have been direct invasions and bombings of countries trying to win their independence, protect their sovereignty, or protect their economy from plunder, such as Vietnam, Laos, Cambodia, Serbia, Afghanistan, Iraq, and Somalia. No less devastating has been the impact of counterinsurgency operations, low-intensity warfare, and dictatorial, colonial, or occupying governments in Guatemala, Nicaragua, El Salvador, Indonesia, East Timor, Angola, the Congo, South Africa, Zimbabwe, Saudi Arabia, Israel, and Iran.

Some of the additional tactics that the power elite has used to protect its interests in other countries are: assassinations and attempts on the lives of political leaders; trade embargoes; funding oppositional parties; co-opting labor unions; training police, military, and paramilitary groups; chemical and biological warfare to destabilize economies; manipulation, threat and intimidation by international financial agencies; attacks on currencies; capital flight; and the abduction, harassment, threat, and intimidation of individuals and organizations. To achieve its goals the power elite uses the CIA, the U.S. military, private security companies, corporate networks of information, agents, and security, the military and paramilitary forces of other governments, international drug cartels, and individual local agents.

HOW DO MEMBERS
OF THE RULING CLASS FEEL
ABOUT BEING RICH?

Most people in the ruling class do not refer to themselves as ruling class, and many would deny that there is such a thing or that they are in it. There are always people with much more money they can point to. No one looks or feels rich when compared to the wealth of Bill Gates ($43 billion), Warren Buffet ($36 billion), and Paul Allen ($21 billion).[198] Others see the affluent lifestyles presented in the media and think that most people have as much as they do. Many in the ruling class might feel discomfited or embarrassed by being included. Others, of course, are proud of their heritage, or oblivious of its implications. Often, ruling class family members don't know the full history of how their family's wealth was accumulated.

Comparatively few members of the ruling class, only 7,000 to 10,000, are members of the power elite—directly involved in high levels of corporate, political, and cultural decision making. The rest benefit from their decisions but may be largely ignorant of how their class operates to their benefit. Because of their geographic, cultural, racial, and economic isolation, they may also be very ignorant of how most people in the rest of society live. Often, their primary contact with working people and with people of color is with those who are employees, or who provide some service for them.

This isolation and feeling of entitlement, coupled with a sense that others have vastly larger amounts of wealth than they do, are also common among members of the managerial class. With high consumption levels and pressures to spend money to maintain their standard of living, members of this class often have virtually no sense of the enormous wealth and privilege they possess, and may have a very distorted view of the reality of most of the rest of the population. High levels of consumption may make some feel very insecure financially and not at all wealthy.

Many members of the owning classes share the view that they have earned what they have and that less privileged people could be successful, if they simply worked harder, got more education, spoke English better, acted right, etc.

Most members of these classes do work hard (although no harder than others) and are quite unaware that their hard work was coupled with many class, racial, and gender preferences in jobs, connections, educational opportunities, housing and business loans, government infrastructure, and general credibility, to give them substantial advantages over others. Because they spend most of their time in exclusive communities and institutions, they are unlikely to question why people who are different from them do not participate in their clubs, schools, and other organizations. There are always "objective" criteria to mask discrimination and other barriers so that members of the ruling class can assume that they are qualified and others are not, no matter how biased those criteria are. For example, most students at elite prep schools, colleges, and universities are not likely to question the absence of other students who do not meet their school's admissions criteria.[199]

Members of the owning classes often share the view that they have the experience to analyze and judge other people's situations and the answers to other people's problems. The feelings of superiority, entitlement, and judgment that are reinforced throughout their lives by their wealth, their peers, their education, by the media, and by learned racism and patriarchal values are very hard (but not impossible) to resist. F. Scott Fitzgerald, in his novel *The Great Gatsby*, written in 1928, perhaps best summed up the sense of entitlement pervasive among members of the ruling class when he wrote, "They were careless people…they smashed up things and creatures [and countries] and then retreated back into their money or their vast carelessness, or whatever it was that kept them together, and let other people clean up the mess they had made."[200]

In general, members of the ruling class are not careless in the personal sense that F. Scott Fitzgerald used the word. Many are well-intentioned, caring, and generous to those around them. But in terms of the economic and governmental policies they support, they tend to be careless, ungenerous or even mean and callous about their impact on those outside their circle of care. They can vote for decisions about sending troops overseas, which have a devastating impact on the lives of poor and working-class people and their communities, knowing that their own investments will prosper and their children will not have to die as soldiers. They often support mean-spirited public policies such as reductions in welfare, increased criminalization policies, lower spending on public schools, and other services, because they can afford to pay for their needs.

Even in a personal sense, people with wealth can assume that they can rely on their money, power, and connections to bail them out when they or their children are involved in accidents, criminal activity, dangerous practices, high-risk behavior, careless actions, or personal harm to others.

Many people without wealth learn to defer to the attitudes and values of those with wealth either as a survival skill or as the internalized messages that those with money, because they have money, must be smarter, more together, more valuable, or better people than other people. This deference, in turn, reinforces feelings of entitlement in members of the ruling class.

Are Members of the Ruling Class Good or Bad, Happy or Sad?

There are all kinds of rich people who are members of the ruling class. There are honest people and thieves; people who are old and young, charitable and greedy. There are introverts and extroverts, able-bodied people and those with disabilities. There are child molesters, and also those who help feed the hungry. They are gay, straight, bisexual, and transgendered. Nor are people without great wealth particularly virtuous or particularly anything else. There are good people and jerks among every class. Some members of the ruling class work to defend their power and privilege, many of them leave that up to the power elite, and a few have even worked to change the current economic structure. This book is about the operations of a class of people as an institution that has great power and influence over our lives. It is not a comment on the integrity or values of its individual members.

Members of the ruling class are not necessarily happy because they have so much wealth, nor are they necessarily unhappy. Happiness and unhappiness are not related to how much wealth one has. Some members of the ruling class may feel uneasy, guilty, embarrassed, or ashamed of their wealth. Others may feel proud, comfortable, satisfied, superior, valuable, or virtuous because of their wealth. Still others may deny they have much wealth, complain about how hard they have it in life, or try to ignore issues of class altogether.

Having great wealth and being a member of the ruling class allow for great variety of feelings about it for individuals. But the ruling class (and the power elite) as a whole, acts on the assumption that great inequalities of wealth and power are normal, unremarkable, justified, and should not be challenged. Many people with wealth fear popular participation in political and economic decision making, and distrust the government because it is the one arena in which ordinary people can potentially hold enough leverage to place limits on ruling class operations. Most are also vehemently against labor in general and unions in particular because of their potential ability to organize enough workers to challenge ruling class control.

WHY DON'T WE SEE THEM?

"The way our ruling class keeps out of sight is one of the greatest stunts in the political history of any country." — Gore Vidal[201]

The ruling class and the operations of the power elite are mostly invisible to the general population. If you were a member of a group that controlled so much wealth and power in a country that styled itself a democracy, you probably would not want to be too visible either. People can be more easily misled about the source of their problems if the ruling class is physically out of sight. They don't need to use public transportation, public parks, public libraries, or public hospitals because they can afford private services. Many of them live in gated communities and most of those with jobs work in secure office buildings. They send their children to private schools or select suburban public schools, and they usually vacation in less accessible or heavily controlled resorts in this country and abroad.

Members of the ruling class want to socialize with each other because they share values, activities, and the task of raising their children to the values that they care about. In addition, misinformation about others, elitist values, and racist attitudes lead many of them not to want to associate with their "inferiors."

Not all members of the ruling class live a lifestyle of great wealth. Some live very modestly in middle-class neighborhoods. But there are certain broad patterns of living, socialization, and activity that not only mark most members of the ruling class, but enable them to pass on their values and maintain their privileges. Some of these patterns of living and values change over time as new generations of achievers and inheritors of wealth emerge. There are trends in what goes on one's walls, where one vacations, how conspicuously or extravagantly (or not) one spends one's money.* But there are some general patterns that remain relatively unchanged over time.

Living Privately

Much of the ruling class lives unobtrusively and privately in secluded and often heavily guarded areas. These areas, such as Beverly Hills, Tiburon, Scarsborough, Plano, Upper Manhattan—some thirty zip codes across the country[202]—are well-known, although no less exclusive because of that. Increasingly, members of the managerial class also live in gated communities, the fastest growing kind of community association.

In 1998 there were 30,000 gated communities with more than 3 million houses for 8.4 million primarily white and affluent people.[203] A brochure for The Reserve at Tampa Palms in Tampa, Florida, an exclusive enclave with its own championship golf course and lakes, says it offers "a sense of unequalled privacy and security [that] is enhanced by a tall, elegantly landscaped brick wall, creating a distinctive approach leading to the gatehouse entrance, which is staffed around the clock for your peace of mind."[204]

There is another level of slightly less exclusive housing in projects that are physically separate and governed by homeowner associations. There are over 200,000 of these, usually paid for by membership fees, with mandatory membership for those who live in them. In 1999, 42 million people in the

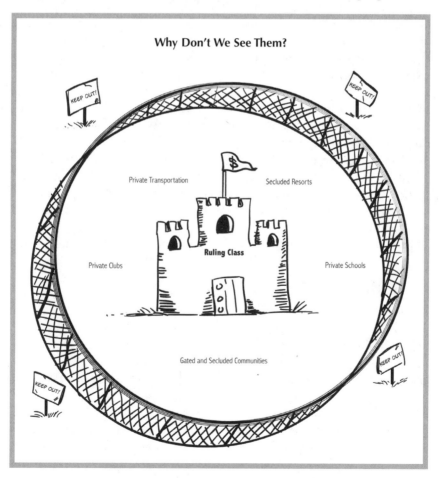

Why Don't We See Them?

Private Transportation

Secluded Resorts

Ruling Class

Private Clubs

Private Schools

Gated and Secluded Communities

KEEP OUT!

U.S. were living in planned developments governed by associations. This was approximately 15 percent of the population.[205] These associations come complete with contracts that specify (and enforce) codes, covenants, and restrictions regarding property use, maintenance, and services. They may also provide security guards, trash collection, and other services.[206]

Members of the owning classes have the means to vacation in resorts to which the rest of us do not have access. They may also have vacation homes in communities that allow them to continue to socialize among their class.

Some people with wealth live very modestly and some take simple vacations. Although much is made of their example, it does not necessarily reflect more general patterns of exclusion and consumption.

Education of Children

Children of the ruling class, in general, go to private day care, to private day schools and often, at least for a while, to a private boarding school. In the United States only about 1 percent of teenagers go to an independent private high school of an upper-class nature. (Obviously not all private schools serve the upper class, although many do; the rest primarily serve the children of the managerial class, with private religious schools being somewhat of an exception to this pattern). This school network is supplemented by special classes, tutors, summer camps, vacations, and special travel opportunities. A majority of the male graduates, and increasingly the female graduates, of this educational and social progression pursue careers in business, finance, or corporate law. A great many of the rest follow other professional careers.

In addition to the segregated culture of education described above, and contrary to popular opinion, there is still an extensive network of debutante balls and coming out parties, as well as the numerous ruling class sororities and fraternities, which provide opportunities for ruling class young adults to meet and socialize with others of their class (as well as providing the opportunity for important future business and social contacts and networks).

Social Clubs

While the children are being socialized through their educational opportunities, adults from the ruling class may be socializing at social clubs ranging from the family-oriented country clubs and downtown lunch and dinner clubs, to highly specialized clubs catering to a variety of interests, often around sports activities such as yachting, tennis, golf, horseback riding, or hunting. Often families belong to several clubs, and these may be in different cities, contributing to a network of social interactions and communication. Some clubs are national, or even international in character, such as the yearly gathering at Bohemian Grove, about which much has been written.

Many of these clubs are exclusively white, and some are exclusively male (or exclusively female). In all cases, membership is highly screened. One can only become a member if recommended by other members and approved by the board of directors. These clubs provide opportunities and settings for special events such as coming out/debutante parties, bachelor parties, and weddings. In the midst of socializing, these clubs and events also provide informal opportunities for members of the ruling class and power elite to discuss business, cultural, and social developments, to build family, political, and economic alliances, to further careers, and to advocate for issues and policies in exclusive and private settings.

There are other ways that members of the ruling class socialize among themselves that involve private parties, social and cultural events, government functions, resorts, and elaborate fundraising events. This broad network of youth and adult activities provides recreational and social opportunities for all members of ruling class families in privacy and luxury. It also educates the young in the values of the class, allows them to meet and socialize with their class peers, and prepares them for the careers and intimate relationships that perpetuate the ruling class.

THE RULING CLASS AND
THE BUFFER ZONE

Over the years the ruling class has created a series of jobs and occupations for people who will help them maintain their power and wealth. We refer to this as a buffer zone because it acts as a buffer between those at the top of the pyramid and those at the bottom. The buffer zone is not an economic position indicating income or wealth; it is a role that some people perform through their work that helps the system run smoothly and without change. The function of the buffer zone is threefold.

Taking Care of People

There is so much concentration of wealth by the ruling class that there is not enough to go around for the rest of the population, especially those who are poorest. Millions are hungry, homeless, without health care, decent jobs, or opportunities for education. Every year hundreds of thousands of people die from the effects of poverty, racism, sexism, and homophobia. If these people died in the streets, there would be constant mass uprisings.

If most people receive minimal levels of care and those who die do so in hospitals, at home, in rest homes, or in prisons, it is less likely that people will add up the total impact of the concentration of wealth. So there are many jobs for people to take care of those at the bottom of the pyramid: nurses, attendants, social workers, teachers, youth workers, child care workers, counselors—poorly paid jobs that are primarily done by women and that provide minimal services to those in need.

Taking care of those in need is valuable and honorable work, and most people do it with generosity and good intentions. But in our society, it is also unsupported, low-paid, exploitative work. It serves to mask the inadequate distribution of jobs, food, and housing, and to hide the full impact of the concentration of wealth.

Besides those who work in nonprofits and government jobs to help those in need, a tremendous number of people voluntarily serve in food and shelter programs, visit the sick, tutor the less educated, and comfort the needy. Such individual efforts are important for sustaining the fabric of our community life. But when temporary shelter becomes a substitute for permanent housing, emergency food a substitute for a decent job, tutoring a substitute for adequate public schools, and free clinics a substitute for universal health care, we have shifted our attention from the redistribution of wealth to the temporary provision of social services to keep people alive.

As sociologist Janet Poppendieck comments in her study of the emergency food system:

> ...this massive charitable endeavor serves to relieve pressure for more fundamental solutions. It works pervasively on the cultural level by serving as a sort of 'moral safety valve'; it reduces the discomfort evoked by visible destitution in our midst by creating the illusion of effective action and offering us myriad ways of participating in it. It creates a culture of charity that normalizes destitu-

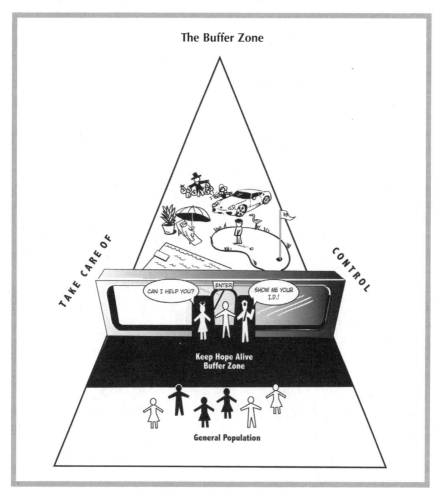

tion and legitimates personal generosity as a response to major social and economic dislocation. It works at the political level as well, by making it easier for government to shed its responsibility for the poor… it makes private programs appear cheaper and more cost effective than their public counterparts… and their [food program's] maintenance absorbs the attention and energy of many of the people most concerned about the poor, distracting them from the larger issues of distributional politics.[207]

Keeping Hope Alive

In addition to (barely) surviving, people must have some hope that their (or their children's) situation will get better, or they will have nothing to lose in challenging the power structure. Another role of people in the buffer zone is to keep hope alive by distributing opportunities for a few people to gain access to jobs, housing, health care, or educational opportunities so that it seems like there is opportunity for all.

Many people in the buffer zone are in jobs where they decide who gains access to the meager benefits available. These "success" stories are widely publicized (and used to justify further funding) and anyone who doesn't succeed is judged to be deficient and unworthy of assistance. Students are told that if they stay in school and work hard they will get ahead. Workers are told that if they follow the rules and work hard they will get ahead. Ordinary people are told that if they follow the rules and work hard they will be successful.

Working hard usually does make a difference in one's life. But it makes a crucial difference where one starts and what educational, cultural, social, political, and economic resources a person has available to them. Most people cannot get very far just by working hard. And in the last 30 years, many people who have worked very hard indeed have actually seen their income and quality of life decrease.

With so much wealth and opportunity held by the owning classes there is very little left for those at the bottom of the pyramid to fight over. But people only continue to fight to get ahead if they believe they have a chance. Thus the need for people in the buffer zone to dole out opportunities to move up the ladder. These opportunities take the form of special testing, tracking, financial, and academic programs to select those with the abilities and personal qualities to move into higher economic levels.

The process of creaming—selecting the most talented and ambitious members of the working and middle classes to move up the economic ladder—also has the additional benefit to the ruling class of adding new ideas, energy, and perspectives to the power elite. This effectively co-opts leadership in the working and middle classes and leaves those selected to advance, isolated and alienated from their communities.

Programs to provide educational, job, and housing opportunities for those who lack resources were hard fought for and are necessary to provide more opportunity. But without a more serious leveling of the playing field between the owning classes and the rest of the population, the gap in opportunity to succeed in this country will continue to grow larger. And those with the least opportunities will continue to have to compete with each other in a society with a shortage of affordable housing, too few jobs and job training programs, and diminishing educational opportunities. On top of that, without addressing race and gender based discrimination in these areas, people of color and working-class white women will continue to face serious disadvantages in competing with working-class white men for unnecessarily scarce resources.

Controlling People

People at the bottom have always gotten together and organized to change the system into one that is more fair and democratic. First white men, then men of color, and then all women, and most recently young adults between 18 and 21 have gained the right to vote through organized struggle. The abolition movement, civil rights movement, women's liberation movement, disability rights movement, lesbian and gay liberation movements have all fought for greater inclusion and participation in society.

The struggle against injustice in all forms is continuous. The ruling class has, therefore, needed people to control those at the bottom. Some of the male-dominated occupations are police, security guards, prison wardens, immigration officials, deans and administrators, soldiers, members of the National Guard and state militias, and, of course, the father of the family as the disciplinarian. Most boys are trained for occupations that will help control people and maintain the system for the ruling class. The power elite has used government troops and state militias to control workers; police and prison guards to control communities of color; immigration officials and border guards to control immigrants; soldiers to control other countries; security guards to control petty theft and access to personal and business property; and the FBI and the CIA to control dissidents here and in other countries. A significant number of men are employed in jobs that are explicitly enforcement roles. Before September 11, 2001, employment at the FBI stood at 27,000; the Drug Enforcement Administration at 10,000; Bureau of Alcohol, Tobacco and Firearms at 4,000; Secret Service at 6,000; Border Patrol at 10,000; Customs Service at 12,000; and Immigration and Naturalization Service at 34,000. Local police forces, security guards, and prison wardens add hundreds of thousands more. The federal government has recently added 28,000 baggage screeners to this work force.[208]

Taking care of those at the bottom, keeping hope alive, and controlling those who rebel are the primary functions of those who have jobs in the buffer zone. The division in roles is not absolute. There is a lot of control built in to the "helping" professions, and there are always attempts to put a kinder face on controlling work (i.e. community policing).

Many in the buffer zone are white although, because of the gains won through the civil rights and women's liberation movement era, there are small but increasing numbers of people of color working there. Racial and gender job stratification typically means that white men control or manage men of color, and white women control or manage women of color in private, public, and nonprofit sector jobs. Men are taught to expect to control women in both work and interpersonal spheres.

For those of us in the buffer zone, the challenge is how to do our jobs subversively. How can we take the meager funds we receive for direct services and use our resources to educate people about the issues, empower them to make changes in their own lives, and help them organize with others to demand change in the system.

One way to do this is to de-professionalize our work, and assume that battered women, homeless people, school dropouts, and the unemployed can do the work that we do if given the information, skills, and opportunity. Another part of being subversive is giving people information from the inside of agencies and institutions about what is really going on. Who makes decisions? Where does most of the money go? Who really benefits from these programs? Instead of advocating for people's interests we can help them learn

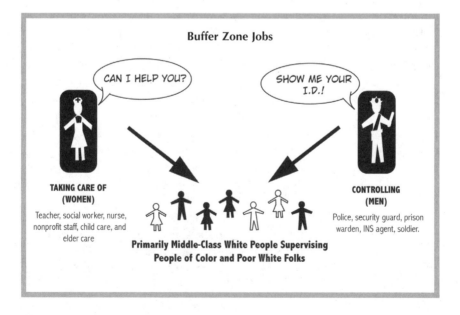

how to advocate for themselves. We can focus on leadership skills just as much as survival skills, social change just as much as social service. There are numerous ways to work subversively from within the buffer zone when we think less about how to help some individuals get ahead, and more about how to help the community get together.

Managing the Buffer Zone

At the top of the buffer zone are members of the managerial class. They set the standards and norms for their professions. Members of the managerial class determine policy and curricula at the main training and educational institutions, and they run the professional associations. They may have connections with funders from the ruling class and with members of the power elite. They determine who moves up in their professions, what are acceptable practices, and they make sure that those carrying out buffer zone jobs do so in ways that contain and control those at the bottom of the pyramid rather than support and empower them.

Even in fields in which women predominate, such as teaching, counseling, therapy, and social work, many of those in higher levels of management and training positions are white men. Some have been screened and trained by elite universities and professional schools. Many of the others have come through professional or vocational training programs which rely on curricula developed primarily by men from the managerial class at elite universities and professional schools. In either case, they are exposed to attitudes and values that support the hierarchical structures of society.

Most people enter the helping professions from a heartfelt desire to help people succeed and thrive. Many feel a strong conflict with the professional "best" practices in their field. They can see that, although some people may succeed in the system, many more will fail. They may feel that their work has been structured to be only minimally effective in helping people or changing things. There is much resistance from them towards the managers and administrators they encounter. There is a constant struggle between those practitioners who are trying to undermine the rigid hierarchies of our society and the managers and administrators who are trying to maintain them.

It is the job of the members of the managerial class to promote those workers, programs, and organizations in the buffer zone who accept and comply with the system, and screen out, render ineffective, or get rid of those who challenge it. They usually have no choice because they are accountable to their funders. Sometimes the funder is a governmental agency, sometimes (and increasingly) a corporation, but in most cases, it is likely to involve at least some funding from a foundation. Today, buffer zone work is likely to be funded by a combination of government and private funding.

PHILANTHROPY

"Although private wealth is the basis of the hegemony of this group, philanthropy is essential to the maintenance and perpetuation of the upper class in the United States."[209]

A primary way that leaders in the owning classes control the work in the buffer zone, avoid taxes, and influence policy is through philanthropy and the nonprofit sector.[210] Most of the "taking care of" and "keeping hope alive" functions of the buffer zone are provided by nonprofits which are funded by corporate donations, individual donors, ruling class controlled foundations, or the government, through contracts with nonprofits.

There are huge economic benefits from the tax deductions for charitable giving that go directly to the wealthy. Perhaps just as importantly, the largest share of charitable giving by members of the ruling class or their trust funds—$19 billion a year out of $366.24 billion in assets—goes to endowed foundations that have members of the ruling class as trustees who decide how to spend it, often to further ruling class interests. Many of these trustees are very well paid. One study found that the 238 foundations surveyed paid out nearly $45 million on "trustee fees" in a single year.[211]

Independent or family foundations accounted for 84 percent of all foundation assets and 76 percent of all giving. Corporate foundations gave $2.89 billion and community foundations $2.15 billion.[212] Through this process, members of the ruling class avoid income and estate taxes while retaining control of their wealth.

Much of the money goes to ruling class think tanks and foundations, to ruling class cultural institutions such as art museums, opera, and the theater, or to hospitals, ruling class universities, and other public charities. Sociologist Teresa Odendahl writes, "The vast majority of nonprofit agencies and programs do not primarily serve the needy.... [the richest Americans] contribute disproportionately to private universities, the arts, and culture, rather than to community health clinics, legal aid programs, or other projects for the poor."[213] Rather than this money going to the public through taxes, to be invested and controlled by the public, it is given to foundations that have no public supervision.

Professor of political science Joan Roelofs describes how control over the nonprofit sector is control over decisions about the use of the vast amount of land, buildings, financial investments, human resources, public access, and influence that churches, hospitals, private schools and universities, museums, trusts, United Ways, and the many other types of nonprofit agencies have accumulated.[214]

In 2000, nonprofits controlled over $1.59 trillion in financial assets and had revenue of over $822 billion.[215] Nonprofits also control significant amounts of federal and state monies through contracts for the provision of public services such as health care, education, housing, employment training, and jobs. The ruling class, through the nonprofit sector, controls billions of dollars of private and government money ostensibly earmarked for the public good, but subject to practically no public control.

Although these organizations appear to have an independent, nongovernmental voice, most of the largest nonprofits and nongovernmental organizations (NGOs) have on their boards of directors members of the power elite—corporate directors, members of elite academic, media and policy groups and wealthy donors—all representing the interests of the ruling class. In addition, most substantial nonprofits "are linked to each other and to the major corporations by their funding, their invested assets, technical assistance, interlocking directorates, and central organizations such as the Independent Sector, and Council on Foundations."[216]

There are many public policy and foreign policy implications of ruling class funding for nonprofits and their equivalent on the international level, nongovernmental organizations (NGOs). These organizations can provide a cover for direct control of issues and perspectives by members of the ruling class who use them to fund projects in their own interest or for the interests of the U.S. government and the ruling class in general. George Soros' funding and guidance of the Open Society Institute and Human Rights Watch to further the interests of U.S. foreign policy is a well-documented example of this kind of practice.[217]

The Rockefeller, Carnegie, and Ford Foundations have a long history of funding projects of direct benefit to the U.S. government and specifically the CIA. The Council on Foreign Relations was originally largely a front for J.P. Morgan and Company, although the other big three moderate/conservative foundations gave it substantial funding in the early 1950s. The Ford and Rand Foundations became major players in domestic and foreign policy after World War II, and the interlocks between these major foundations were numerous.[218]

The Ford and Rockefeller Foundations also furthered ruling class policies by sometimes funding moderate community organizations and steering public policy towards the provision of individual services rather than towards structural change. This has been most well documented during the sixties when these foundations lavished funding on more conservative civil rights groups to limit protest movements, and to co-opt[219] leadership and redefine issues in the Black community. Poor white, Latina/o, and Native American communities were similarly targeted by this funding.[220]

On the international level, philanthropic foundations have been involved throughout the world funding "sustainable" development, supporting conservative political parties and unions, helping write constitutions, revising civil laws and university curricula, and developing nonprofit sectors in various countries to replace charitable, cultural, social, and educational functions that were formerly government responsibilities (privatization).[221] McGeorge Bundy, president of the Ford Foundation, and later scholar-in-residence at the Carnegie Corporation (Foundation) said that he "agreed that everything the [Ford] Foundation did could be regarded as 'making the world safe for capitalism'—reducing social tensions by helping to comfort the afflicted, provide safety valves for the angry, and improve the functioning of government."[222] The major foundations have an insider's understanding of the functioning of government because many of their officers are part of the power elite and often become members of government. In particular, over the years, many secretaries of state have been foundation officers, including Dean Rusk, John Foster Dulles, Edward Stettinius Jr., Henry L. Stimson, Frank B. Kellogg, and Charles Evans Hughes.[223]

By providing the funding and policy framework that many concerned and dedicated people work within in the nonprofit sector, the ruling class is able to co-opt leadership from grassroots communities, is able to keep nonprofit work focused on the provision of a narrow range of social services, and is able to make the funding, accounting, and evaluation components of the work so time consuming and onerous that social justice work is virtually impossible under these conditions. This provides the perfect training ground for workers in the buffer zone described above.

Finally, philanthropy has the further benefit of associating members of the ruling class with good works—doing things to benefit the community. Even though their money came through the exploitation of workers and the degradation of our communities and of the environment, this fact gets cleaned up or laundered by the charitable contributions of people like Carnegie, Rockefeller, Vanderbilt, Stanford, Cornell, Rhodes, and more recently by the charity of Ted Turner, George Soros, and Bill Gates. This reputation laundering is one reason why we often don't pay attention to how the ruling class operates.

The public has benefited from the libraries built by Carnegie's ill-gotten gains. George Soros' wealth, built through global speculation which helped devastate entire economies, funds some useful reports from Human Rights Watch. The Ford Foundation funds some dedicated community programs.

It is not a commentary on the work of particular groups funded by the ruling class to question the larger social, political, and economic impact of ruling class philanthropy. On the other hand, neither can we presume that

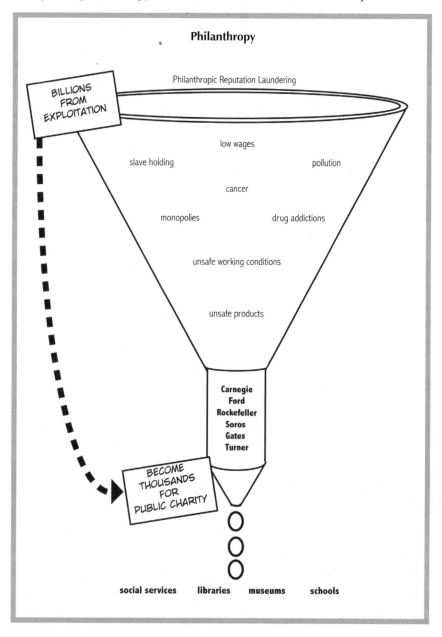

projects funded by these foundations are unaffected by the sources of their funding. We need to examine the impact of the work of particular groups, the impact of the entire system of philanthropy, and the nondemocratic structures of power and wealth which leave decision making in the hands of the power elite.

WHY WE DON'T FOCUS OUR ATTENTION ON THE RULING CLASS: THE ROLE OF THE MASS MEDIA

"It is arguable that the success of business propaganda in persuading us, for so long, that we are free from propaganda is one of the most significant propaganda achievements of the twentieth century."[224] — Alex Carey

Media Ownership

The mass media in the United States has become increasingly consolidated in recent years. A handful of corporations now controls a large percentage of TV, video, radio, music, internet access, cable, movies, and magazine and book publishing. Time Warner, Disney, Bertelsmann, Viacom, News Corporation, Sony, Vivendi, G.E., and a few other companies determine to a large extent what we read, what we see, what we hear, and where and when it is available to us. They are major political donors in their own right, and they are controlled by members of the power elite. Their primary purpose is to make money through selling advertising. Their primary function is to define what problems are, to create issues and concerns in the public mind, and to prepare people for public policy solutions. They also serve to distract attention from ruling class domination and to create the fear which will justify power elite policy decisions.

Media Bias

As political analyst Michael Parenti notes, the media is not neutral, it reflects a clear ruling class agenda "favoring management over labor, corporations over corporate critics, affluent whites over low income minorities, officialdom over protestors, the two-party monopoly over leftist third parties, privatization and free market 'reforms' over public sector development, U.S. dominance of the Third World over revolutionary or populist social change, and conservative commentators and columnists over progressive or radical ones."[225]

One indicator of the bias of the media is that in 2001, there were 955 appearances made by corporate representatives on U.S. network nightly newscasts, and only 31 appearances made by labor.[226] Similarly, a survey in 2000 found that when think tanks are interviewed or quoted by the media, ruling class groups are quoted 89 percent of the time, and non-ruling class groups 11 percent. [227] Another study of evening news programs found that workers' issues were featured on only 2 percent of the total airtime.[228]

Although characterized as liberal by members of the ruling class, two-thirds of Washington, D.C. area journalists characterized themselves as center or right on social issues, and 83 percent said that their political views on economic issues was center or right.[229] White women have made some significant gains in the profession, but media professionals remain, "a relatively uniform and well-paid group of mainly white males," primarily from the managerial class.[230]

Media Tactics

Some of the tactics that the media uses to "guide" our attention are described by Parenti as:

- suppression by omission—simply not covering significant news
- attacking the source of alternative information
- using positive and negative labels to direct consumer feelings—the selective use of the label "terrorists" for Arab bombers but not Timothy McVeigh-type white male ones is an all-too-clear example of this)
- questioning the details but not the larger assumptions underlying policy
- accepting uncritical misinformation provided by governmental or corporate sources
- focusing on dramatic, but superficial news
- failing to provide relevant and critical background information and a larger context for information
- claiming to be neutral observers and then creating false balances in their reporting
- not following up on news
- the false framing of news to mislead or misinform consumers[231]

Spin Control

There is a specialized branch of the media—a combination of the corporate information industry and their public relations firms—which puts out propaganda, lies, and false information and advertising to mold citizen's opinions and beliefs about policy issues. Corporate public relations efforts are not new. They began in 1912 with an "Americanization" program, and by 1947 Daniel Bell, an editor of *Fortune* magazine, described that year's free enterprise (and anti-union) campaign as involving "1,600 business periodicals, 577 public relations counselors, 4,000 corporate public relations departments, and more than 6,500 "house organs' with a combined circulation of more than 70 million."

By 1950 these "free enterprise" efforts "inspired" 7 million lines of newspaper advertising stressing free enterprise, 400,000 car cards, and 2.5 billion radio impressions.[232] Often, these campaigns stressed some particular group labeled as threatening to the United States, such as recent immigrants, communists, socialists, anarchists, unions (or, more recently, terrorists), and justified attacks on people's civil liberties, restraints on organizing activities, and greater license and support for business.

Besides putting out false information, the public relations industry has created fake grassroots groups (a half-billion-dollar subspecialty), has pressured news media to withdraw or alter coverage of negative events, has paid scientists to produce counter studies, and has demonized alternative points of view. Using radio programs, magazine and TV advertising, outdoor advertising, news services, films, speakers' bureaus, economic literacy programs, and special reports, they spend over $10 billion a year on manipulating public opinion on a wide range of issues so that the general public will support an agenda favoring the ruling class on economic and foreign policy, and labor, environmental, and social issues. By 1996 there were more people involved in the public relations industry (150,000) than the number of reporters in the U.S. (130,000).[233]

The lies, misinformation, drama, and distractions offered to us by the media and the public relations industry make it difficult for most of us to know what is actually happening in the world. Fortunately, there is an extensive and growing network of alternative and independent media to provide us with information and critical analysis. Some of these are listed in the appendix. They need our support, because an informed citizenry is the foundation for a democratic society.

DISTRACTIONS

Thomas Jefferson, Tom Paine, Walt Whitman, Albert Einstein, Daniel Webster, Andrew Carnegie, Louis Brandeis, John Maynard Keynes, Theodore Roosevelt, Herbert Hoover, Mark Twain, Alexis de Tocqueville, Abraham Lincoln, Emma Goldman, Helen Keller, Adam Smith, Chief Sitting Bull, George Bernard Shaw, W.E.B. Du Bois, Ida Tarbell, President Eisenhower, Malcolm X, John Dewey, and Martin Luther King, Jr.—these are just a few of the most well-known people who have warned us of the dangers to a democratic society of having such a high concentration of wealth and power.

The existence of a ruling class in our country has never been a secret. At the same time, members of the power elite have been aware that if people could see clearly how undemocratic and unfair the system is they would be more likely to get together and try to change it. Members of the power elite don't want the rest of us to notice how much power and control they have accumulated. They have made available, and taken advantage of, many forms of distraction. In addition, there are other dynamics that hold people's attention because of the way the system operates.

For example, if you are fighting for a share of the leftover piece of the economic pie, trying to keep food on the table and a roof over your head, then it is difficult to have the time, attention, and energy to do anything about the social system. People in the U.S. are working more hours per week and more weeks per year for less money now than they were just 30 years ago.

Many other distractions are more systematically developed to focus attention away from the power of the power elite and the wealth of the ruling class.

Wars Overseas

Wars in other countries, initiated or supported by the United States, are a major distraction. Many wars are for the protection of U.S. corporate interests. In addition, when economic circumstances are difficult, and communities are experiencing cutbacks in social services, political and corporate leaders will initiate military excursions to distract people from domestic troubles.

Sometimes foreign excursions are directly related to the political troubles of the president.

When Clinton was embroiled in the Monica Lewinsky scandal he arbitrarily bombed Iraq, the Sudan, and Afghanistan at different times to demonstrate his leadership and divert attention from his personal trials. In full recession, with high levels of unemployment, huge levels of debt, and in a time of crucial elections, President Bush became determined to remove Saddam Hussein from power in Iraq and was able to divert much of our national attention to arms inspections and a set of issues that affect people much less than whether one has a job and how expensive food and housing are.

These wars are often fueled by racism, the perception by many people that other countries should defer to us, that we have the right/ obligation/responsibility to direct the policies of other countries, that the resources found in these countries are best utilized and should be controlled by us, and that lives lost in countries comprised mostly of people of color are not worth as much as U.S. (white) lives. Wars are often justified by racialized fears of invasion or terrorism from darker skinned peoples with different ideologies, different cultures, and different religious beliefs than mainstream (white) U.S. beliefs.

Fear

We are taught to fear crime and violence, fear people of color (if we are white), fear recent immigrants (if we are citizens), fear Jews (if we are non-Jewish), fear young people (if we are older), fear disease such as West Nile virus, ebola, and SARS, fear drugs, fear white sharks and killer bees, fear anthrax, fear Muslims and Arabs, fear our neighbors, and fear people from the other side of town. Fear keeps people looking to the power elite for protection, and putting up with inequality and rollbacks of our civil liberties. Fear can be aroused by portrayal of foreign (usually darker skinned) enemies. But most people's fear is domestic in focus.

Fear in this era has become generalized to a fear of terrorism that, in turn, has become justification for a wide range of restrictive and unconstitutional policies, and allocation of funding, which we are urged to accept because they will supposedly increase our safety.

We are also specifically told by the media to fear crime, particularly violent and property crimes. On the nightly news we are presented with a constant parade of young men of color who are portrayed as dangerous to the rest of us. In particular, this coverage manipulates the racial fears of white people, despite the fact that most interpersonal acts of violence are committed against people of one's own racial/cultural community. White people are more likely to be sexually or physically assaulted by other white people, but

most whites fear people of color because of the misinformation and stereotypes they are presented with.

Corporate crime is not generally covered except in the most large-scale
cases, and even then its impact on ordinary people is minimized. In 1998,
the FBI estimated that robberies and burglaries cost the country about $4 bil-
lion. White collar crimes are not even officially calculated, but the FBI estimates they cost the country hundreds of billions of dollars.[234] The Enron and
MCI scandals, the Savings and Loan bailout, and the cover-up of corporate
fraud through accounting malpractice are examples of ruling class crime that
will cost every person in the U.S. tens of thousands of dollars.[235]

Also in 1998, the FBI reported that 19,000 people were murdered by
other individuals. But it wasn't reported that over 66,000 people died from
work-related diseases and injuries,[236] and tens of thousands of others died
from environmental pollution, corporate malpractice and malfeasance, and
hazardous and contaminated products.[237] We need to ask ourselves who the
biggest criminals are and who should we fear the most.

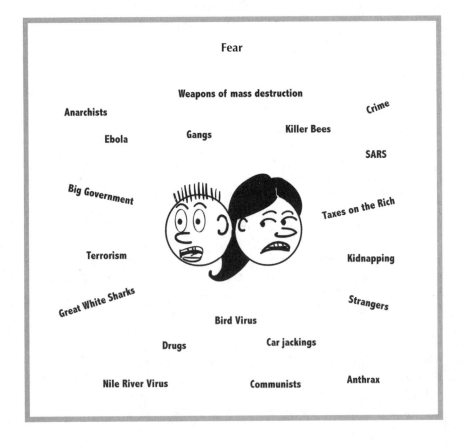

The Cycle of Interpersonal Violence

Another way that we get distracted is by a cycle of interpersonal violence, blame, and scapegoating, all of which keeps our attention on those around us rather than those at the top of the economic pyramid. Our anger at personal violations, disrespect, lack of opportunity, and social injustice is often taken out on those closest to us, such as our children, our partners, our coworkers, friends, and fellow drivers. We turn our pain, anger, and frustrations either outwards towards others, or inwards towards ourselves through high-risk activities, alcohol and other drug abuse, suicide, and other forms of self-destructive behavior. We are directed to do this by those in power. If we are men we are taught that women are the problem, if we are white that people of color are the problem, if we are citizens that recent immigrants are the problem, and if we are adults that young people are the problem. We are fed a constant stream of misinformation, stereotypes, and lies that lead us to direct our attention towards those below us in the pyramid rather than to see the power and wealth of the decision makers who truly influence our life chances. All too often, individuals who are being exploited by the ruling class, who are losing their jobs and seeing their communities destroyed, turn their violence into hate crimes, gay bashing, immigrant bashing, anti-Jewish acts, gang violence, fights, or violence against their partners and children, instead of channeling that anger into work for social justice.

Racism, Sexism, and Homophobia

There is also a social cycle of violence through which we are encouraged to blame and scapegoat and justify violence towards groups of people with little social, political, or economic power. For example, those of us who are white are encouraged to watch people of color in sports and public dramas, such as those involving O.J. Simpson, Clarence Thomas, and Michael Tyson, and to fear people of color as violent, manipulative, dishonest, and dangerous. One function of racism is to keep white people's attention on people of color at the bottom of the economic pyramid and not on the white, male power elite who are doing the real damage to our lives and communities.

Similarly, men are encouraged to blame the women around us for our personal problems, and to keep our attention on women as sexual objects through pornography, prostitution, and advertising, preventing us from working with women to change the power structure.

Homophobia keeps many of us locked into rigid gender roles, and thinking that lesbians, gays, bisexuals, and transgendered people are undermining our families and way of life which makes us unable to see the ways that our families and way of life are destroyed by poverty, corporate crime, lack of jobs, child care, health care, and inadequate public education.

The wealth of our country is so concentrated that what little is left to be divided among those of us at the bottom of the pyramid is not enough to go around. Racism, sexism, and homophobia keep us competitive, blaming and fighting each other, rather than challenging the source of our problems. Racism, sexism, and homophobia are ideal distractions, intentionally used by the power elite to confuse, manipulate, and exploit us.

Anti-Jewish Fears

One way that members of ruling classes have distracted people, both in Europe and in the United States, is by amplifying anti-Jewish stereotypes to portray Jews as the real power holders in society.

The history of anti-Jewish stereotypes goes back to the early Christian period. Negative portrayals of Jews have been consistently present in Western societies for nearly 2,000 years. Although they have never held real economic power in any country except the state of Israel, Jews have often been portrayed as fabulously rich and as ruthless economic exploiters of others. If they had had this much power, they would have been better able to protect themselves from much of the anti-Jewish violence that has been directed at them over the centuries. In reality, there are Jews who are poor, working class, managerial class and members of the ruling class. The largest concentration of people in the ruling class by far is Christian, not Jewish, and even the wealthiest Jews have often been excluded from top levels of decision making.

In Europe and in the U.S., Jews have often been used as a buffer between the owning classes and those who are poor or working class. Jews were prevented from living in white Christian communities but were allowed to live in neighborhoods that were better than those that people of color could live in. They were prevented from entering many elite universities, trades, or occupations, but given better educational and occupational opportunities than people of color, and poor and working-class whites. Therefore, poor and working-class people encounter Jews with a little better economic situation as shopkeepers, teachers, social workers, or landlords, and less often encounter white Christian ruling and managerial class people. In the last forty years, different Asian communities in the U.S. have found themselves in the same buffer location, facing restrictions from those higher up the economic pyramid, and anger and resentment from those further down.

The ruling class has used anti-Jewish propaganda combined with racism and anti-immigrant propaganda to encourage white working- and middle-class people to feel squeezed, to fear that people of color and recent immigrants with less than they will take what they have, and that Jews with more than they will exploit them and also take what they have. Anti-Jewish fears coupled with racism and anti-immigrant fears provide members of the ruling class with further opportunities to escape notice.

Lack of Time

People in the United States have comparatively little leisure time because we work such long hours. In 1999, the average Mexican, Canadian, Australian, and even Japanese worker was on the job approximately 100 fewer hours than the average worker in the U.S. Workers in Brazil and England worked 250 fewer hours, and Germans worked around 500 hours or 12 weeks less.[238] In addition, average commuting time for U.S. workers is now 25.5 minutes.

Longer work hours and longer commute times, more financial stress, and less extended family support means that most people in the U.S. are scrambling for the time to take care of children and the elderly, buy basic necessities, and keep up with the bills. This works extremely well for the ruling class because, as social policy researcher Paul Street has noted, "one does not develop the capacity to criticize US Middle Eastern or Nuclear or Environmental or Criminal Justice policy in a state of perpetual exhaustion and distraction, snatching only small pieces of time from an endless cycle of working, commuting, shopping, and, when possible, sleeping."[239]

Spectator Sports

For men in particular, but increasingly for women, a great deal of our leisure time is spent watching sports. On the weekend and on most evenings we can select from several different sports offerings to keep us occupied. These sports teams are owned by members of the ruling class who buy and sell athletes, many of whom are men of color, to field competitive teams that the rest of us watch, root for, and bet on. The media, advertisers, and team owners make millions of dollars while we sit and watch games that are of little consequence. This means we talk to each other less, and pay less attention to our partners and children. There is nothing wrong with watching professional sports, but for some of us, the time and attention we put into it encroaches on our relationships with family, friends, and community.

Pornography and Prostitution

For men, pornography and prostitution are tremendous distractions. They take up our time and attention, they exploit women we don't know, and distort our relationships with women we do. Pornography is now a $10 billion-a-year industry, and prostitution over $52 billion a year.[240] While women are exploited and abused, and while men are masturbating to pictures of naked women, money is flowing up the pyramid.

Shopping

All of us have to shop for our basic necessities, and it can take considerable time to purchase the food, clothes, and other things that we and our families need. But shopping in and of itself has become a major distraction for women, for men, and increasingly for young people. Many of us now spend substantial time and money browsing stores, catalogues, and the web, often purchasing things we don't need. People in the U.S. now spend billions a year on consumables. Advertisers spend hundreds of millions of dollars a year convincing us that we need more, better, and newer products more often and in larger quantities than ever before.

To give some sense of the outrageousness of these numbers, economist Doug Dowd has calculated that "Americans spend more than $8 billion a year on cosmetics—$2 billion more than the estimated actual total needed to provide basic education for *everyone in the world*, and Americans and Europeans spend $17 billion a year on pet food—$4 billion more than the estimated annual additional total needed to provide basic health and nutrition for *everyone in the world*."[241]

To finance these purchases many of us are increasingly in debt, currently to the tune of nearly $2 trillion,[242] which works out to 109 percent of an average family's total disposable income.[243] This is hugely profitable for those who own the banks and consumer credit companies, not to mention the retail companies, advertisers, and others who try to convince us that it is our patriotic duty to spend more so that the stock market will rise.

Scandal, Corruption, and Drama in the Courtroom

In conjunction with the consolidation of the media into ever larger megacorporations, we are presented with less and less real news, and more and more scandals, corruption, drama in courtrooms, violence and sex. This comes at us through TV, daily newspapers, the Internet, magazines, and books. It is difficult not to become riveted to the stories of O.J. and Nicole, Bill and Monica, Anita and Clarence. But during the period of these distractions our welfare system was destroyed, the prison-industrial complex grew immensely, immigrant rights, affirmative action, and education were cut back, and our communities continued to be devastated by corporate pollution. Whenever we find ourselves focusing our attention on high drama we need to ask ourselves: What social, economic, and political actions are being taken by those in power that they don't want us to look at too carefully?

Alcohol and Other Drugs

The frustration, anger, and pain we feel about what has happened to us personally, what has happened to our friends and families, and what has happened to our communities, lead many of us to turn to drug abuse to numb our pain and lessen our despair. In addition, everywhere we turn, drugs are peddled to us and our children. No wonder that millions of us are addicted to tobacco, alcohol, caffeine, cocaine, heroin, meth, uppers, downers, painkillers, and a whole range of designer drugs. The biggest killers—tobacco and alcohol—are the biggest profit makers and are legally sold in a great variety of stores, including supermarkets and drugstores.

TV and Movies

People in the U.S. spend, on average, four hours a day watching TV, or 1,460 hours a year, while children on average spend even more time, an average of five hours a day.[244] Total U.S. media consumption in 2003 was projected to be over 3,200 hours per person.[245] From cartoons in the morning, through soaps, talk shows, sitcoms, nature shows, and newscasts throughout the day until movies and soft-core pornography in the wee hours, we are sold a lifestyle to aspire to, products to consume, a narrow and one-sided view of the world, fear, misinformation, and justification for continuing the status quo. When you add in the violence, racism, sexism, and homophobia visible throughout the day, it is a potent brew guaranteed to confuse and placate, stimulate but not satisfy, goad, misdirect, and lull us into accepting whatever policies the power elite wants to adopt.

Video Games and Computers

Some of us have moved from watching a TV or movie screen to watching a computer screen (currently in the U.S. at an average rate of about 260 hours a year). Young men and adult men in particular spend inordinate amounts of time playing unrealistic games by themselves (or with virtual partners) often committing acts of (pretend) sexual violence towards women, and lethal violence towards a host of enemies, many of whom are men of color.

New Technological Gadgets

From computers to cell phones, DVDs, CDs, faster and faster computers, handhelds, and wireless, we are presented with a treadmill of technological gadgets which are constantly becoming obsolete, or at least out of style. We must spend time evaluating, purchasing, learning how to use, repairing, and updating these additions to our lives often only to discover that they are not as necessary or as useful (and certainly not as reliable) as we were told they would be. But they are expensive to buy, repair, and subscribe to. In 2001, the average family spent nearly $600 a year just on communications services (Internet, wireless phones, pagers).[246] We know where all of this money ends up.

Legalized Gambling

State lotteries, horse and dog racing, betting on spectator sports, and casinos where people can play poker, blackjack, the slots, and a host of electronic games—legalized gambling takes many forms and is accessible to virtually every adult. Although in some states an individual has a greater chance of being struck by lightning than of winning the lottery, these odds don't deter people from hoping for a chance to strike it big, get out of debt, and have a diversion from their everyday economic reality. Over 70 percent of adults in the U.S. report gambling at least once in the last year, and over 3 million would qualify as problem gamblers.[247] States that implement lotteries to fund education usually see decreases in total spending on education after the lottery begins (perhaps because legislators and voters falsely assume that lottery money is picking up the tab). The largest spenders in state lotteries are the poor, the elderly, high school dropouts, and African Americans. Lotteries are a regressive tax on the poor.

Legalized gambling, in general, leads to increases in personal bankruptcies, broken marriages, suicides, burglary, extortion, loan-sharking, prostitution, and drug abuse. It also decreases the amount of money people spend on local goods and services.[248] Although a percentage of many state lotteries goes to fund education, most of the money collected, as with other forms of gambling, goes to large corporations and the professionals and managers who run them. According to one study, less than 4 percent of state and local educational funds come from lotteries in those states in which lottery money is designated for educational purposes.[249] The multibillion dollar legalized gambling business is another form of diversion, and a source of lucrative profit for the ruling class.[250]

We all need to have fun, relax, hang out with others, and have distractions from the stress of daily life. However, many of us spend too much of our time in activities that, besides distracting us, debilitate us, affect our relationships, consume our time and money, and provide profits to those who own the companies that produce, distribute, and market these goods.

This time could otherwise be spent in connecting with other people, developing our cultural and other creative abilities, doing community service, spending more time with our children, making music and art, gardening, cooking, and organizing for a redistribution of wealth and the development of our communities. The amount of time and money we put into programmed distractions is truly staggering. What might happen if we put some of that time towards developing ourselves, our relationships, and our communities?

The Myth of Equal Opportunity

Another distraction is the myth that if we work hard, or are very clever, smart, or lucky, we can work our way to the top and earn millions. This is the myth that Horatio Alger created in his stories written at the end of the nineteenth century. Alger was a member of the ruling class with a Harvard education. But his stories were about young boys who started at the bottom, penniless, and worked their way into great fortunes. This was actually a quite rare occurrence, as subsequent research showed, but people were nevertheless fascinated by the stories and the possibilities for individual achievement they seemed to foretell.

We are presented with many Horatio Alger stories today. Whether it is political figures who supposedly started out poor and eventually became president, or corporate executives who started with nothing and became rich, we are sold false stories of rags to riches. Very often key information is missing from these stories, information about the financial, educational, or other assets that our "hero" actually started out with.

Starting at the Top

Politicians

George Washington was one of the richest men in America, owning lots of slaves and thousands of acres of land. But even "poor" Abraham Lincoln was a corporate lawyer for railroads, and his wife came from a wealthy southern family. The "common" president, Andrew Jackson, was raised in a well-to-do slave-owning family. Most of the twentieth century U.S. presidents were from the ruling class, including Theodore Roosevelt, William Taft, Franklin Roosevelt, John Kennedy, and George Bush and son. Others who were of more humble origins, such as Herbert Hoover, Jimmy Carter, Ronald Reagan, Lyndon Johnson, and Richard Nixon, used education, family resources, and political connections to become millionaires before or during their presidency.

More recently, Bill Clinton relied on the humble origins story. But by the time Clinton was six and his mother remarried, he lived in affluence. As a teen he was playing golf at the local country club and driving his own car.

These stories of humble origins are used to promote the myth that anyone can become president and that the president is still connected to poor and working-class people's concerns. However, few of our presidents started out poor, and all ended up firmly in the ranks of the ruling class, sharing their interests.

Businessmen

We are also presented with many stories of business success of the poor-boy-becomes-corporate-president variety. According to the report by United for a Fair Economy, "Born on Third Base,"[251] most of our richest business leaders—those who have crossed home plate in wealth—did not start out at the batter's box. They were already on base. Forty-two percent were born on home plate—they inherited the money that put them among the richest people in the country. Another 13 percent were born on second or third base, and 14 percent on first.

Often cited as a rags to riches story, Bill Gates is the son of a corporate lawyer, and he attended an expensive private school and then Harvard University. He did not start off rich, but he enjoyed financial and educational opportunities that most people can only dream of. He also gained his success in an industry that was heavily subsidized by the U.S. government through the defense department, and accumulated wealth from the exploited labor of women of color in computer chip and component assembly factories in the U.S., in East and Southeast Asia, and in the Pacific.

More typical of today's ruling class are men like Warren Buffet, Henry Kravis, and Steve Case,[252] who grew up in wealthy families and started out with significant economic, social, and educational advantages.

Those born in the batter's box were those whose parents did not have great wealth or own a business with more than a few employees. This certainly does not put them among the poor or even working class—although a few of them do come from impoverished backgrounds—but it does mean that they achieved great wealth against immense odds. They are often entrepreneurs, and it is not accidental that many of those who move to the top from far down the economic pyramid are white men who had significant racial and gender bias in their favor.

Most people who are members of the ruling class were born into it. There is certainly some mobility, especially between the ruling and managerial classes. Some people move up and others move down. But few move from the bottom, or even the middle of the pyramid, to the top, and rarely do people fall from the top unless they decide to give up their privileges and give away their money to lead a simple life.

Some members of the power elite start out wealthy, and many others were members of the managerial class, which enabled them to gain the education and connections to move up in power and wealth. They also enjoy the benefits and opportunities that being white and male provide in our society.

When one becomes a member of the power elite one gains access to many ways of accumulating wealth because of the salaries, benefits, stock options, investment options, and general connections to people with wealth that one's power provides. Members of the power elite make decisions affecting millions or even billions of dollars and, not coincidentally, some of that money flows their way. They are not necessarily corrupt (although some are), but opportunities are available to them for building wealth that the rest of us do not have.

Overall, few people move from the bottom or even the middle of the pyramid into the ruling class or power elite. And few of these are white women or people of color. Those who do, succeed partly because they are willing to adopt the values and play by the rules of the system, partly because they are luckier than most of us, and partly because they have some talent, ability, skill, or creative use that the economic system rewards. Our hopes that we will win the lottery, play in the NBA, reach the top of the charts as a performer, or invent the next wildly popular consumer gadget can keep us from getting together with others in our community to work for change in the structure of opportunity.

WHO DECIDES?
WHO BENEFITS? WHO PAYS?:
PUBLIC POLICY ISSUES

Ruling class strategies, distractions, and media spin can make it difficult to sort out public policy issues. Using a class perspective for analysis makes it clearer what the power elite agenda is and how they try to buy public support for it. Not every issue is simple, and most issues have racial, gender, and other factors built into them. The power elite is not united on every issue—even on some economic issues they have differences in strategy, although they mostly agree on basic economic values. There are also different interests among sectors of the general population. But starting with an economic analysis of what part of the pyramid benefits, we can better understand and act on public policy issues.

The power elite only needs the support of some members of the general population of voters to dominate public policy. To do this, power elite strategists almost always package policy issues in a way that appears to benefit some people who are not members of the owning classes, or that relies on emphasizing divisions between groups of people based on race, gender, immigrant status, sexual orientation, or other differences. We have to see through this manipulation or we will be misled into supporting a ruling class agenda.

The questions we should be asking about every issue are:

Who Decides?
The power elite or the general population?
Who Benefits?
The top of the pyramid or the general population?
Who Pays?
The ruling class or the general population?

Let's unravel some of the packaging of public policy issues.

Big Government, Deregulation, and Privatization

The ruling class in general is not against government. They rely on government regulation and government-funded physical and financial infrastructure to provide stability for business, and benefits for their communities. In addition, many industries are subsidized by the federal government, while others are protected from foreign trade. Some corporations are the direct beneficiaries of huge amounts of government spending on defense, prisons, transportation, and war. The ruling class is in favor of huge defense budgets and many are against increased government expenditures on social services unless those services are privatized or contracted out to the private sector for greater profit to them.

The power elite have used the specter of government to scare us into voting against government regulation and public control over social services and social infrastructure. Deregulation of such industries as energy, airlines, finance, and telecommunications has been a disaster for consumers, but of great profit to the ruling class. Privatization of welfare, health care, prisons, and, most recently, education (through vouchers and corporate running of schools), and public utilities such as water and electricity has meant that millions of people don't have their basic needs met. The ruling class has developed new profit centers running welfare programs, providing health care (now a $1 trillion/year industry[253]), building prisons, and taking over schools' and utilities.

The most recent target for privatization has been the Social Security system. It is estimated that if just 2 percent of Social Security taxes were privatized, $86 billion would be channeled through investment firms. Management fees and administrative charges would provide additional millions of dollars of profit to the ruling class.[254] Some members of the ruling class are so extreme in trying to cut back social services and benefits that they are trying to get the consumer price index revised downward so that social security and many other benefits are reduced.[255] In that way, more government money can go into military spending and other more profitable ruling class areas of investment.

Although the ruling class dominates all levels of government, participating in government is still the only way for the majority of us to influence public policy and to protect ourselves, our families, neighborhoods, and communities. Government is not the problem; a ruling class agenda is.

State's Rights

The power elite has long been concerned that they will not have complete freedom to run communities in their interests, as they think best. The federal government has been a vehicle for people, at times, to intervene in the domination and exploitation of local and statewide elites. Again the hypocrisy and opportunism is clear. The power elite is not usually for state's rights when state governments stand up to corporate practices to protect their citizens and their environments. When states regulate business it is not a question of state's rights for them. But when the federal government is questioning discrimination, exploitation, environmental degradation, or other harms to ordinary people, then, and only then, are concerns about state's rights raised.

Members of the power elite raise issues of state's rights and government interference on a selective, case-by-case basis as it suits their interests. We need to look below the rhetoric and find out who benefits from the policies—who is protected and who is made vulnerable.

WHICH SIDE ARE YOU ON?

Most public policy issues have a range of solutions, each of which would affect the ruling and managerial classes differently than they would the rest of the population. To gain some support for policy that primarily benefits members of the ruling class, policy issues have to be portrayed as if they are of benefit to everyone, or at least to some people not in the owning classes.

When a tax bill was proposed in 2000 which gave massive tax cuts to the ruling and managerial classes, there was also a provision that working and middle-class tax payers (ignoring the needs of the poorest 20 percent who make too little to pay taxes) would receive a payment of $300. Another example is the estate tax bill which, by the year 2010, will save each member of the ruling class over $85,000 a year, but people in the bottom 60 percent only $466 (if they owed any estate tax at all, which few do). The claim was made that without this relief, middle-class business owners and family farmers were being unreasonably taxed. In fact, businesses and farms worth over $1 million are quite substantial enterprises and there are other ways to protect them from estate taxes if that is the goal.

Public policy issues can be evaluated by who they benefit—do they contribute to the public good or do they primarily benefit the already wealthy—and who will pay for them. Let's look at a few issues and see how they fall out.

Tax Cuts

Since the ruling class receives most of the income of the country, its members pay a substantial amount of income tax. But the percentage they pay in relation to the rest of us has continually been reduced as they lobby for greater tax cuts. Every tax cut has shifted the tax burden more and more to ordinary working people. Even though these tax cuts have thrown a small morsel of money to the rest of the population so that people would support the legislation, the overall impact of these bills is to enrich the already rich. The top rate that the ruling class pays on its highest earnings has dropped from 91 percent in the 1950s to just under 39 percent in 2003, and the level of income at which that rate kicks in has been increased dramatically.[256]This has shifted a tremendous part of the tax burden to working- and middle-class people.[257]

In addition, most states and local governments have high sales and other non-income based taxes which disproportionately affect the poor and working classes compared to the ruling and managerial classes. In some states poor and working-class people pay about twice the percentage of their income in taxes as that paid by high-income individuals. Federal income tax cuts which favor the rich increase the proportion of total taxes that the rest of the population pays.[258] People in the U.S. paid 21 percent of their income in taxes in 1973 and now pay 28 percent, one-third more than before.[259]

The ruling class has also resisted high corporate taxes because they decrease the distribution of corporate profits to them. In the period 1950 to 1954, corporations paid 76 percent of the total state, local, and federal income taxes collected. By the period 1990 to 1993, they paid just 18 percent of the total.[260] One out of three of the largest corporations—those with over one-quarter billion dollars in assets—paid no federal income tax at all. The result of this slide has been that by the year 2000, individuals were paying 82 percent, and corporations only 10 percent of the total federal income tax (excluding the state and local taxes included in the earlier figures).[261] Compounding this effect is the decline in corporate property tax rates. The share of all property taxes paid by corporations has dropped from 45 percent in 1957 to 16 percent in 1995.[262] The power elite is constantly fighting to

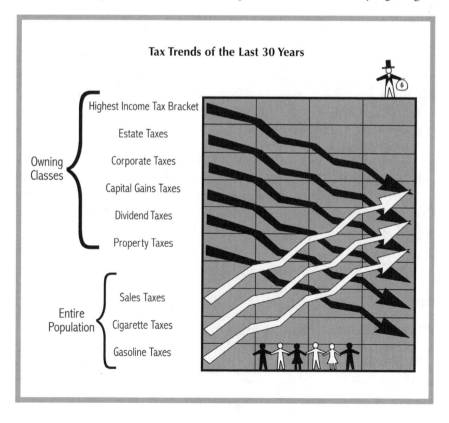

Tax Trends of the Last 30 Years

Owning Classes
- Highest Income Tax Bracket
- Estate Taxes
- Corporate Taxes
- Capital Gains Taxes
- Dividend Taxes
- Property Taxes

Entire Population
- Sales Taxes
- Cigarette Taxes
- Gasoline Taxes

avoid personal and corporate taxes and to shift the tax burden onto the rest of us.[263]

Income tax is a more fair way to raise money than sales taxes, which tend to hit the poor and working class the hardest. Some states don't have income taxes at all, and others have very low taxes, or high sales taxes. The power elite is always pushing to eliminate state income taxes, cap property taxes, and shift the tax burden to poor and working-class people by raising sales taxes and taxes on consumer products such as cigarettes and gasoline.

Estate Taxes

Because of the high levels of exemption on estate taxes ($1 million in 2003 and scheduled to go higher), some of the money that the ruling class has can be passed on to their heirs tax free. The rate for the rest of their estates has been progressively lowered through legislation. Recent legislation proposes to eliminate it entirely. Estate taxes are the main tool the government has to prevent the development of a permanent aristocracy which could preserve its wealth and power forever.

Regulation

Government regulation of industry has been advocated by citizen groups to insure the safety and well-being of people and the environment. Testing of drugs, labeling of food, quality control inspections, safety restrictions like seat belts and air bags, putting limits on prices, challenging false or misleading advertising, ensuring competition in the marketplace—regulation serves a vital function in our society by looking after our interests. Of course, the ruling class wants to eliminate all regulation that constrains them, so that they can pursue greater profits with as few limits and as little liability as possible.

Another way to minimize regulation, lower public standards, and avoid public scrutiny is to decentralize programs from the federal government to the state level. Federally funded programs such as welfare, health care, and child care (e.g. Head Start) are difficult to monitor, set standards for, or change, when every state has its own set of rules and procedures.

Privatization

Public services such as utilities, libraries, the post office, public hospitals, public universities, and public pension plans like Social Security are set up to provide essential services to all people regardless of their race, gender, ability, or economic circumstances. When they are properly supported and supervised, they are the hallmark of an inclusive, caring, and secure society.

The ruling class cannot make money on public services, so they are in favor of privatizing them—or at least privatizing the parts of them that they can make profits on. Bechtel and Monsanto are two transnational corporations which have been buying up water rights and water systems in other countries and more recently, in the U.S., so that they can profit from people's needs for water. This is directly against the interests of the rest of us and has been resisted by many communities both here and in other countries.

Health Care

The ruling class has access to the best medical care that money can buy—and they live longer because of it. However, their excellent care comes at the expense of the millions of people (around 43 million in 2001) without any medical coverage, and many more millions with inadequate coverage. National health care is provided and is successful (better health care and lower costs) in all other major industrialized countries. The power elite has fought against it in this country because of the profits gained from a system of private health care. Increasing privatization of health care in the United States has led to a $1 trillion industry in which the profits of the top five health care providers reached $5 billion in 2000 and the compensation of the top 25 healthcare industry executives was nearly $7 billion in 1995.

Many studies have shown that private health care providers have much higher administrative costs and lower overall quality than public providers. They also ensure that we face fewer people being covered, higher out-of-pocket costs, fewer direct providers, high infant mortality rates, higher health care costs, and more health care money being siphoned off to marketing and administration jobs and into high executive compensation packages than other comparable nations.

Education

As we have noticed, children of the ruling class go to private schools. Members of the ruling class are not interested in expenditures in public education because there is little money to be made there. The move to establish voucher programs, to privatize schools, and to promote consumer products on campuses during school time are efforts to ignore the educational needs of many of our children and establish ways to make more money from those parts of the educational system that can be made into profit centers.

Labor

The power elite has been most united and vehement about controlling workers. They have gone to great lengths to harass, attack, demonize, and destroy the efforts of workers to organize. For example, 25 percent of employers illegally fire at least one worker for union activity during organizing campaigns, 75 percent of employers hire union-busters to fight union organizing, 78 percent of employers force employees to attend one-on-one meetings with their own supervisors against the union, and 51 percent of companies threaten to close the plant if the union wins the election.[264] They have created a climate in which it is difficult for workers to organize, protest, strike, boycott, or sometimes even picket for higher wages and safer working conditions.

The simple fact is that organized workers make more money, enjoy greater job security, and have safer jobs than those who are not organized. Union members earn 26 percent more than their nonunion counterparts, over 75 percent of union workers have health benefits, compared to less than half of nonunion workers, nearly 70 percent of union workers have a pension, compared to only 14 percent of nonunion workers, and the 10 states where unions are strongest have higher earnings, less crime, more civic participation, less poverty, and better schools than the 10 states where union membership is lowest.[265] Strong support for worker's rights benefits all of us who are not members of the ruling class.

The Environment

Even in the face of rising environmental awareness and concern, the power elite has been able to avoid, stall, evade, postpone, or water down environmental regulation in almost every area. This is a growing disaster for our lives, health, and the environment as more and more people get sick, and many die from the direct and indirect effects of toxic chemicals and pollution in our food, our soil, our air, our water, and in the everyday products that we use.

International Solidarity and War

There are belligerent countries in the world and some which are hostile to the United States. However, we are seldom actually under threat of attack, and even in those situations where we are there are many nonviolent or international means to resolving conflict. Most of our incursions into other countries are not about defense, but about ruling class profits and control of natural resources.

Much of the wealth of the ruling class comes from profits created by cheap raw materials, sweatshop labor, and expanding markets abroad. The U.S. government has been used by the ruling class to protect its interests through international financial institutions, through threat and intimidation, and through direct force. The ruling class has never been against sending in troops and risking the lives of our young people to protect its need for profits from oil, minerals, food, and cheap labor. In the last 50 years the U.S. has been involved in armed conflict or risky interference in foreign governments around the world to protect U.S. business interests even though there was no physical threat to our country.

Ordinary people, on the other hand, are usually reluctant to support foreign interventions because they know that most of them are not really about defending our country from attack. They are well aware of the direct risks to family and friends of dying or being injured in combat. Members of the .power elite have used racism to justify our interventions in other countries. Claiming the superiority of white, western culture and leadership, they have claimed that we have the right to exploit the land, people, and other resources of people of color, and the obligation to direct their lives. The loss of lives of people of color in other countries is routinely minimized and valued less than the loss of U.S. lives. Negative stereotypes and deliberately false information about nonwhite people, non-Western culture, non-U.S. political systems, and non-Christian religious beliefs have been used to increase our fears and to justify attacks on other countries.

In spite of these tactics most people in the U.S. are wary of going to war. The power elite has often had to fabricate incidents or situations to convince people that we are under attack and therefore need to protect ourselves. The explosion of the ship Maine, the attack on Pearl Harbor, the Gulf of Tonkin Incident, images of dead babies in incubators in Kuwait, massacres in Serbia, danger to U.S. citizens in Grenada, weapons of mass destruction in Iraq— these events and situations have all been fabricated, intentionally provoked, or wildly exaggerated to develop mass support for U.S. intervention on behalf of the ruling class. It is usually only through alternative media, or many years later when information is released and the war is over, that the real story is revealed.

Immigration

The power elite has always relied on low-paid immigrant labor to work in the fields, factories, and homes of the United States in order to keep wages down, and workers disorganized and fearful. They have tried to control immigration so that those workers they want are allowed in and those they don't want are kept out. They have achieved this through legislation controlling immigration, and by using racism to demonize immigrants so that, whenever necessary, they can marshal public opinion against them. Employers keep wages down by moving work overseas, by preventing workers from organizing, and by pitting immigrant workers against citizen workers. Immigrants have often been on the forefront of efforts to improve wages and working conditions for all workers, and they contribute much more than they receive in public services. Attacks on immigrants' rights are often the first step in attacking the rights of all of us.

Which Side Are You On?

Policy Issue	Benefiting Owning Classes	Benefiting Poor/Working/Middle Classes
Taxes	Tax cuts for the rich No inheritance tax Low capital gains tax Lower top tax brackets Low corporate taxes No dividend tax Flat tax or national sales tax	Progressive taxes—lower on wage earners, higher on the owning classes Inheritance taxes Stock transaction (Tobin) tax Wealth tax No cap of FICA tax
Regulation	Deregulate food, drug, and environmental standards Voluntary or self-regulation	Strict and enforced air, water, food, drug, and occupational health standards
Privatization	Privatize all municipal services, public utilities, social security, education wherever profitable	Public ownership of libraries, utilities, hospitals, schools, health and pension services
Health Care	Privatize all profitable aspects Long-term protection of patents, trademarks, and copyrights Treatment focus	Universal coverage and public administration Public benefit from public funding for research and development Prevention focus
Education	Vouchers Charter schools Private companies running schools Corporate food, products, textbooks, and sponsorships	Community controlled and equitably funded preschool through college in a non-commercial environment for all students
Labor	Nonunion companies Low minimum wage No regulations on wages, benefits, or working conditions Limits on strikes, pickets, and boycotts Substantial unemployment	Ability of workers to form and join unions Ability to strike, picket, and boycott Strict and enforced safety standards Living wages A job for everyone Democratically managed workplaces
Environment	No standards or regulations Voluntary participation Limited liability	Sustainable standards Corporate liability Long-term planning Alternative energy sources Public control
War	Endless, preemptive wars to sustain corporate markets and profits Huge military budget Weapons of mass destruction	Solidarity with people in other countries Peaceful foreign policy Conversion to peace-based economy
Immigration	Regulated so that immigrants can be exploited as needed and will compete with non-immigrant workers	Right to organize Access to education, housing, health care, and other services Freedom from harassment

ASSESSING PUBLIC POLICY ISSUES AND POLITICAL CANDIDATES

Getting Information

Because of power elite control of the media, including textbooks, news sources, "expert" testimony, and academic and scientific research, it is difficult for most of us to have the information we need to make informed choices. However, if we ask a basic question about every policy issue, we can begin to sort out which side we should be on. That basic question is "who benefits more from this, the ruling class or poor and working-class people?" Or, in other words, "who is going to make money and who is going to pay the cost?"

The greatest exploitation in our history has been of the most marginalized groups such as people of color and of women in general. So we also have to ask, "How does this policy affect particular groups such as women, people of color, and low income people?"[266]

There are many good sources for alternative information and analysis. Some of them are listed in the resources section at the back of this book. Many of the websites listed have links to still other sources. We cannot be misled if we think critically about the information we receive from any source, if we compare sources and their class interests, and if we share information about alternatives to a ruling class perspective on current public policy issues.

Questions to Assess Public Policy Issues

Here are some questions to ask yourself when evaluating public policy issues:

1. How is the issue being defined? Who is defining the issue? Who is not part of the discussion?
2. Who is being blamed for the problem? What racial or other fears are being appealed to?
3. What is the core issue?
4. What is the historical context for this issue?

5. What is being proposed as a solution? What would be the actual results of such a proposal? Who would benefit?
6. How would this proposal affect the rich? What would be in their class interests and what would benefit most of the people of the country?
7. How would this proposal affect people of color? How would it affect white people?
8. How would it affect women? Young people? Poor and working people?
9. What are other options for addressing this issue?
10. How are people organizing to address this problem in a more progressive way?
11. What is one thing you could do to support their efforts?

Any public policy issue can be analyzed using these and other questions. They stimulate our critical thinking so we are not misled into colluding with an agenda that benefits a few, and distracts us from the source of our problems.

Questions to Ask Political Candidates

In the current political/economic system just electing good leaders will not change the basic inequalities. But it is important that we elect officials who will challenge those in power, and open doors to community participation and information about how the system works.

It is impossible to tell if political candidates will follow through on what they say during their campaign. There are some clues to use to determine if they are likely to. Below are some questions relating to class which are useful places to start.

a. What is the class background of the candidate?
b. What is their current class and occupation?
c. Who do they profess solidarity with?
d. Who benefits from the policies they advocate?
e. How much do they talk about class?
f. Who finances their campaigns?
g. Have they shown the courage to challenge the ruling class and power elite?
h. Do they have a long-term vision of economic change?
i. Do they make decisions based on the best interests of future generations?
j. Have they shown themselves willing to fight corporate influence and power?
k. Do they listen to and learn from local struggles for economic and social justice?
l. Do they seem to understand and act from an understanding of the interconnections of racism, sexism, and economics?
m. Will they represent the interests of the most disenfranchised groups in the community?
n. Are they willing to work for long-term, structural change in our society?

BEYOND SURVIVAL—
GETTING TOGETHER

Given the present economic system we each must find strategies for surviving in the system. But not all strategies lead to the same results. Some strategies may help us survive in the short-term, but be destructive to us or to those around us in the long-term. Let's look at possible survival strategies and see where they lead us.

Getting Ahead—We all start out as children doing what our parents and teachers tell us to. We want to work hard, stay in school, and succeed. We want to get ahead. However, we soon learn that getting ahead in the present structure means stepping on other people to move up. It can mean isolation, alienation, adopting mean-spirited values, and competing with, rather than cooperating with, others. Getting ahead can come with huge costs to ourselves and to those around us.

In addition, the road to success for many of us is filled with obstacles which become increasingly clear to us as we grow up. Poverty, racism, sexism, homophobia, lack of parental support, lack of role models, inadequate schools, mental or physical disabilities, teasing and bullying, physical and sexual assault, and limited opportunity resulting from the concentration of wealth and resources—all these keep many of us from being able to get ahead. We have to turn to other strategies to make it in the system.

Getting By—Many of us give up trying to get ahead and just try to get by. We adopt an attitude of, "just tell me what to do and I'll do the minimum." We are waiting for the weekend, summer vacation, the end of class, or retirement.

Getting Over—Some of us are committed to getting ahead but know we don't have the resources or opportunity to do it by legitimate means, so we turn to illegitimate ones. We lie, cheat, turn to illegal activities, trying to get over on the system without getting caught.

Getting Around—Some of us don't try to confront the obstacles in our way, but try to get around them by manipulation, seduction, playing the system or the people within it with whatever skills, connections, or resources we can muster for ourselves.

Getting Out—Some of us become so discouraged by the inequality and moral bankruptcy of the current system that we just want to get out. We drop out of our families, out of school, out of community life, or turn to alcohol and other drugs, computer games or other mindless activity, and drop out emotionally.

Getting Back—Some of us are angry at those we perceive to be in the way of our getting ahead. We pick up a gun or some other kind of weapon and try to get back at those in our way—perhaps the people who teased us or those whom we have been trained to scapegoat for our problems, such as our partners, people of color, lesbians, gays, bisexuals and trans people, or recent immigrants.

Getting Together—The only strategy which really helps us, our family, and our communities move forward is getting together with others to work for change. This is how people have always made gains; through organized struggles such as the abolition movement, the movement for women's suffrage, unions, the civil rights movement, the disability rights movement, the lesbian and gay liberation movement, and thousands of others.

On a smaller scale, people have been getting together in workplaces, in schools, in neighborhoods, in religious communities, and many other arenas to gain access to housing, jobs, education, and other resources, and to eliminate exploitation, discrimination, and environmental destruction. Getting together is the only strategy which both helps us get ahead; and helps change the structures of inequality, exploitation, and discrimination which put us behind in the first place. We have a long history of people getting together.

WHAT IS YOUR STRATEGY?

Getting Ahead

Getting By

Getting Over

Getting Around

Getting Out

Getting Back

or

Getting Together

RESISTANCE

The white male dominated ruling class and its power elite have always faced resistance from those marginalized and exploited by them. From Bacon's rebellion to Shay's rebellion, from Harriet Tubman's and Nat Turner's rebellions to the rebellion after the Rodney King verdict in Los Angeles, from Dorr's rebellion to the abolition movement to the suffragist movement—our history is filled with thousands of examples of people who have come together to fight against the control of the ruling class and power elite. Many victories have been won. When the country was started, only rich white men could vote. Today everyone over 18 can vote regardless of gender, race, or wealth (although even now not every vote counts). Slavery and tenant farming have been eliminated and other forms of economic exploitation such as sweat shops are being challenged.

At the beginning of the twentieth century, the U.S. government instituted an income tax, an inheritance tax, child labor laws, The Clayton Antitrust Act, the Federal Trade Commission, the 8-hour work day, and the direct election of U.S. senators because of widespread protest during the populist movement.[267] The working-class protests and organizing of the 1930s produced the 40-hour work week, health insurance, overtime pay, workplace safety provisions, social security, and other social welfare benefits.

However the power elite, operating on behalf of the ruling class, is still the predominant decision maker in our society. We have to ask ourselves, "What do we want?" Many of the struggles in our history have been by one group or another striving for greater inclusion and participation in the unequal and unjust system that has been established by the ruling class. Do we just want a more fair distribution of the small piece of the pie that the ruling class doesn't control? Or do we want to redistribute the entire pie and dismantle the wealth, power, and control that the ruling class has accumulated? According to David Korten, author of *When Corporations Rule the World,* "Because of the systemic nature of the problem, the people who are engaged in campaigns against specific corporate wrongdoing in the end fight a losing battle. You can force some constraint through consumer boycotts or even embarrassment against a specific corporation on specific issues, but you are really fighting against the system.... We have to set our sights on changing the larger rules of the game."[268]

Richard Grossman, cofounder of the Program on Corporations, Law and Democracy, has written, "We're not suggesting that folks work harder to resist each chemical one at a time; each clear cut one at a time; each mass lay-off one at a time; each toxic dump one at a time; each corporate purchase of a law or of an election one at a time. We're advocating citizen authority over the subordinate entity that is the modern, giant corporation."[269]

We will never be a free, democratic, and healthy society as long as there is a power elite and a ruling class. I think that eliminating the tremendous inequalities of wealth and the undemocratic concentration of power in our society should be our goal.

Although our vision may be broad, we will still have to struggle on many local fronts, on many specific issues, for many short-term gains. But if we address short-term situations while educating people about how the larger system works, they will have the understanding and long-term perspective which will keep them in the struggle and sustain them through the ups and downs over the years.

In addition, we will have to learn to work together across our differences, and to support each other's struggles. We will need to continue to hold each other accountable for dealing with racism, sexism, and other systems of power and privilege that interweave with, and serve as the foundations of, the class struggle. Because women and men of color are super-exploited by the ruling class, their struggles have often been in the forefront of efforts to build a more equitable society, and their leadership has been crucial in analyzing how the system works. We will need the participation of many different groups of people around the world to be successful.

We also have to decide on strategies, critically looking at what has worked in the past and might work in the future. Gains for workers, women, people of color, and other marginalized groups have always come through organized and sustained struggle. It has never come from the benevolence of members of the ruling class, or from scapegoating particular members of that class as the problem. One president succeeds another, corporate executives come and go, Supreme Court judges die and are replaced. Through it all, the power elite remains in power. Punishing Enron officials, bureaucrats with their hand in the till, or select corrupt politicians, although necessary, will not make the system more fair—it will simply make members of the power elite more devious.

Nor will we be helped much by regulating corporations, limiting campaign contributions, or other narrowly focused reforms. Although these may be useful strategic campaigns to raise public awareness, nothing less than a

We each need to ask ourselves:

Who am I in solidarity with?

Who am I allied with?

Who benefits from the work I do and the life I lead?

Am I going to be content with a social, political, and economic structure that is exploitative, violent, mean spirited, undemocratic, and devastating to all life? Or am I ready to actively work to change the system?

Do I just want to create the illusion of a safe and secure harbor for myself and my family, or will I reach out and join with others to work for justice and rebuild our communities and our world?

thorough redistribution of wealth and power and the implementation of democratic economic and political decision-making structures will actually move us towards the just and democratic society many of us aspire to.

The ruling class and power elite have differences among them, but they come together in common cause to defend their interests. They are not necessarily more powerful than we are, but they are generally more unified and well organized, more strategic, and they maintain a long-term focus.

When we see that we are engaged in a common struggle with many fronts, our strategies become less competitive and more effective because we understand that we are fighting not just for ourselves and our interest group, but for our neighborhoods, communities, and for all people. We may have different needs and different visions, but none of our needs will be met or our visions realized unless we can overcome our differences, and work together to dismantle the system of ruling class dominance.

Just as some members of the ruling class act in solidarity with those at the bottom of the pyramid, many in the bottom give allegiance to those at the top. We may aspire to be at the top, we may have adopted the individualistic, competitive, and hierarchical values of our current system, or we may just be doing our jobs as workers with buffer zone occupations which end up supporting and collaborating with the status quo.

We each need to ask ourselves: Who am I in solidarity with? Who am I allied with? Who benefits from the work I do and the life I lead? Am I going to be content with a social, political, and economic structure that is exploitative, violent, mean spirited, undemocratic, and devastating to all life? Or am I ready to actively work to change the system? Do I just want to create the illusion of a safe and secure harbor for myself and my family, or will I reach out and join with others to work for justice and rebuild our communities and our world?

There are some days when I am discouraged by the magnitude of the problems we face, and the concentration of wealth and power in the ruling class and power elite. Reading this book may have brought up similar feelings in you of hopelessness or despair about the possibility of change. I have noticed how easy it is for me to feel overwhelmed and to assume that nothing will change, nobody is making a difference and there is little that we can do. But then I think about the organizing and resistance throughout the world and my spirits are raised. I think about the women in the oil fields of Nigeria who are resisting the oil companies, and the people of Cochabamba, Bolivia who have reclaimed their water rights, or the people in the streets of Argentina, and the Zapatistas. And I think about the guerrillas in Colombia, the resistance in Aceh, in Burma, in South Africa, in South Korea, and the international protests against war and globalization led by young people in the last few years. Of course change takes time—but it comes. Of course there are defeats and setbacks, but there are also victories and much to celebrate.

When I am discouraged I also think about ways to renew and take care of myself. Playing with my children, taking a walk with my partner, listening to music, talking with friends—these things renew me. We each need to find ways to enjoy our lives, to connect with others and with the natural world, to be creative, to center ourselves, and to celebrate, celebrate, celebrate.

We are here, we are raising our voices, we are moving forward, we are making a difference, we are raising our children differently, we are linking up with people struggling throughout the world. There is so much to celebrate in our strength, our understanding, our creativity, our diversity, our roots, our connections, and our loving relationships. Our work is yet unfinished. How can we not go forward to create the world we know is possible for us and our children and their children?

Globalize Hope
By Subcomandante Marcos

....Not far from where you are..., a handful of slaves to money are negotiating the ways and means of continuing the crime of globalization.

The difference between them and all of us is not in the pockets of one or the other, although their pockets overflow with money while ours overflow with hope.

No, the difference is not in the wallet, but in the heart. You and we have in our hearts a future to build. They only have the past which they want to repeat eternally. We have hope. They have death. We have liberty, They want to enslave us....

That is what this is all about. It is war. A war against humanity. The globalization of those who are above us is nothing more than a global machine that feeds on blood and defecates in dollars...

This is a world war of the powerful who want to turn the planet into a private club that reserves the right to refuse admission. The exclusive luxury zone where they meet is a microcosm of their project for the planet, a complex of hotels, restaurants, and recreation zones protected by armies and police forces.

All of us are given the option of being inside this zone, but only as servants. Or we can remain outside of the world, outside life. But we have no reason to obey and accept this choice between living as servants or dying. We can build a new path, one where living means life with dignity and freedom. To build this alternative is possible and necessary. It is necessary because on it depends the future of humanity....

Brothers and sisters, there is dissent over the projects of globalization all over the world. Those above, who globalize conformism, cynicism, stupidity, war, destruction and death. And those below who globalize rebellion, hope, creativity, intelligence, imagination, life, memory and the construction of a world that we can all fit in, a world with democracy, liberty and justice.[270]

AFTERWORD

As the evidence in this book makes abundantly clear, we do not live in a democracy, a country run by the people for the people. A few thousand powerful individuals, the power elite—predominately white Christian men—run most of the major institutions in our society for the benefit of the ruling and managerial classes. They make the decisions about our employment and working conditions, our health, the legal system, who votes, whether we go to war, and the state of our neighborhoods and cities. The ruling class and power elite also decide who gets to run for higher political office, who wins, and what the winners can accomplish once in office. It may be tempting to attach the label democracy to some aspects of this, such as voting, but the extreme concentration of wealth and power in the U.S. means that we are a long way from a real democracy even in the narrow arena of electoral politics.

As I write this afterword, the impact of undemocratic wealth and power has been revealed to a shocking extent by the destruction of Hurricane Katrina. The managerial and ruling classes have the transportation, mobility, connections, insurance, education, and skills to minimize the long-term damage to their lives. Many have certainly suffered heart-wrenching losses. But the majority of those dead, ill, stranded, without connections, influence, insurance, or the ability to move and find work are poor, are people of color, are women, are elderly, are people with disabilities, are children.

The coastal vegetation that provides some protection from hurricanes has been severely cut back for ruling class profit. The toxics in the water have been dumped by corporate polluters. The repairs to the levees were slowed to fund pork barrel projects for politicians. The National Guard troops and equipment for emergencies were deployed in Iraq to protect oil company profits. The contracts to provide aid and start the rebuilding are going to the same war profiteers, such as Halliburton and Bechtel, that have been pushing the overseas war drive. At every level of the disaster, class, race, and gender are markers of who benefits, who pays, and who really decides.

Not only do we not have a real political democracy in the U.S. but at the same time the power elite has hypocritically cloaked our foreign policy in a myth of exporting democracy to other countries. We are supposed to ignore the fact that our government has supported military dictatorships throughout the world and has actively worked to overthrow democratically elected governments in Iran, Guatemala, Nicaragua, Greece, Panama, Chile, Venezuela and other countries. We are supposed to ignore the fact that our government's policies have more to do with the control of strategic resources and the elimination of models of real democracy than with a concern for public participation and self-determination in other countries.

The myth of democracy in the U.S. and the good intentions of our foreign policy towards the rest of the world have been amplified by President Bush who speaks of the "world democratic movement" and the "Global democratic revolution" and the "forward strategy of freedom"—all based on non-democratic U.S. military power and invasion of other countries. New ruling class organizations, such as the World Movement for Democracy and the Community of Democracies, as well as older groups, such as the National Endowment for Democracy, are using the mask of democracy to disguise their efforts to undermine the democratic aspirations of many peoples throughout the world.

What does democracy mean? Is it still a useful term? I think we need to embrace the concept of democracy with a much deeper understanding of it. In the simplest sense, democracy means the participation in decision-making by the people affected by those decisions. With some exceptions, if someone is making decisions that affect your life without your participation then that is undemocratic.

It is not surprising that so many people have accepted a watered-down ruling class concept of democracy which is limited to the ability to vote once every four years for one of two hand-picked rich, white, Christian men. We are not educated in democracy and we are not given a daily opportunity to practice democracy. There is not democracy in our families, in our schools, in our workplaces, or in our neighborhoods. Most of us have never experienced a situation in which people come together and make decisions based on mutual respect, full inclusion, and equal participation. If this were truly a democracy, would we have so few opportunities to participate in decision-making?

We have much work to do to redefine the concept of democracy and to restructure the political, economic, cultural, and social institutions in our lives so that participation is widespread, informed, and meaningful. We can each strengthen that work today by asking four questions and beginning to incorporate democratic practice into our daily lives.

Who is not included?
Who is not respected?
Whose voice is not heard?
Whose vote does not count?

Those who are not included cannot be participants. We need to be constantly looking around the room and asking who is affected by what is decided here but is not present? Even if it delays the process, or takes more resources or accommodations, we have an obligation to insure that everyone who has a significant stake in the issue at hand is at the table.

Those who are included are not necessarily respected. Those who are not respected are not able to participate fully. Who is listened to and who is not? How are people, and the cultures, languages, histories, and experiences they bring acknowledged, honored, and visible. What can we do to make sure that everyone is respected and feels respected.

Participating and being acknowledged are not the same as being heard. Often subtle (and sometimes not so subtle) levels of power and privilege prevent the full participation by everyone involved. What are the personal, organizational, or institutional barriers that prevent some voices from being heard while guaranteeing that the interests and needs of those with the most status, wealth, influence, or privilege will be responded to?

Finally we must ask whose vote does not count, or does not count as much as others. (I am using the word vote loosely because there are important and valuable ways to make decisions that don't rely on voting, such as different processes of consensus.) It is a false democracy if everyone is included, respected, and heard, but at the end of the day some people's votes don't count, or count for less than other people's. Of course there are situations, such as in our families, where adolescents and adults have more experience or ability to participate fully than young children. But even in our families, it is vital that we develop age-appropriate processes of participation for everyone.

Let's ask some hard questions about our own democratic practices. If you have children, how much democracy is there in your family? What kinds of discussions, family meetings, skills and experience would have to be developed so that every member of your family, at an age-appropriate level, would be able to participate in family decisions? What difference might this make in your family? In your children's lives? In your own life?

How much democracy is there in your workplace? Have you accepted undemocratic structures at work and yet said that you live in a democracy? What might it be like to work in a worker-managed workplace, or a co-op, or other, less-hierarchical structure? Is there anything you could do to push for more democratic processes where you work?

Why don't we teach about and practice democracy in our classrooms? We have a national government and ruling elite which talks about democracy but dictates educational standards from above, and every level of the hierarchy dictates to those below. Students receive education but don't have real opportunities to practice democracy. This process does not begin to prepare them to live in a democratic society.

Everyday we have an opportunity to practice democracy. We have an opportunity to challenge structures of inequality and structures which exclude, disrespect, silence or undermine the participation of marginalized groups. Everyday we have an opportunity to experiment with forms of participation that build relationships with others, unleash creative problem solving energy within a group, and challenge the false democracy that we are presented with.

Much of the resistance to the ruling class and power elite in the U.S. has come from bottom-up, grassroots, democratic organizing. The civil rights movement, the women's liberation movement, workers' movements, the lesbian/gay/bi/trans liberation, welfare rights, disability rights, anti-globalization, and anti-war movements were all built on people coming together in a variety of democratic processes involving collectives, support groups, direct action groups, meetings, forums, co-ops, consciousness raising groups, councils. The challenge to the myth of democracy promoted by those in power has always been the active practice of democracy by those of us getting together to build a better world. We must not be fooled by ruling class rhetoric. We must deepen and extend the practice of democracy into all the spheres of our lives. Only then will we be able to come together to build a society that is built on democratic participation and that nurtures and sustains the lives of all of its members.

You Call This a Democracy? Not yet, but we each have a role in making it happen.

Paul Kivel

WORKSHOP/CLASSROOM
STUDY GUIDE QUESTIONS

Suggestions for a workshop, class discussion or study group using
You Call This a Democracy?

There are many possible questions and exercises to use to explore the issues of power, wealth, and democracy raised in this book. The curriculum resources listed in the back of the book (pp. 168–218) can provide helpful tools. These issues are not abstract—they impact our everyday lives. As much as possible, help people make the connections to their own situations and the conditions in their communities. Be creative. Get people out into the neighborhoods to see the impact of wealth and class—how it looks and feels. Use videos (see pp. 208–214), exercises, articles, and local speakers (see pp. 215–218) to enhance the discussions. Help people think about what they want to do with the information they've gained from the book.

Where are you in the class system? (pp. xix–xxii) (handout pp. xix–xxii)

Have people read, or group members read out loud, some of the sections in this assessment. Have people break into small groups so that each person can have a few minutes to talk about their current class situation and the situation of their family of origin.

Class Chart (p. xxii) (handout p. xxii)

Pass out copies of this handout and have people discuss the complexities of class. What practical, emotional, and historical issues make it difficult to sort out? Have people discuss the choices or lack of choices that people in different classes have.

What are the costs of having a ruling class? (pp. 4-5) (handout pp. 4-5)

Have people look through the Checklist on pp. 4-5 and talk about what costs they and their communities pay from having a ruling class in the United States. Ask why these costs are not more apparent to people. Ask what costs there are to the rest of the world from the policies and actions of the U.S. ruling class.

The importance of wealth (pp. 32–43) (handout p. 37)

>   Ask the group:

>>   What is the difference between income and wealth?

>>   Why is wealth so important?

>>   Where does wealth come from?

Wealth, race, and gender (pp. 43-47)

>   What are the connections between racism and sexism and the accumulation of wealth? What are specific ways that the ruling class and power elite use racism and sexism to accumulate wealth and power?

The Constitution, corporations and the courts (pp. 48-55)

>   What are some current examples of how the Constitution, corporations, and the courts are used by the ruling class to remain in power?

>   What would need to change in the Constitution, the structure of corporations, or in the function of the courts to democratize our country?

>   Describe current efforts to affect these institutions?

How do they stay in power? (pp. 69-78)

>   How do the ruling class and power elite stay in power? How does this undermine democracy in the U.S.?

>   What is one specific way that your political power has been increased or decreased because of these mechanisms?

How do members of the ruling class increase their wealth? (pp. 79-89) (handout p. 88)

>   What mechanisms does the ruling class use to increase their wealth?

>   What is one form of domestic debt that has affected your life?

How does the ruling class pass on its wealth? (pp. 93-100)

>   What are current ways that the ruling class is trying to change the law to pass on more wealth to their children?

>   How are these efforts being resisted?

Protecting their power (pp. 104-106) (handout p. 105)

What are examples of ways that the ruling class has responded to democratic movements for social justice in your community?

What are ways it has responded to democratic movements in other countries?

Who has provided leadership for these movements for democracy in the U.S. and in other countries?

The ruling class and the buffer zone (pp. 114-119) handout p. 115)

What are the three roles of the buffer zone?

Give examples of organizations that play each role in your community.

How are race and gender played out in the work of the buffer zone?

Philanthropy (pp. 120-124) (handout p. 123)

What are the advantages of philanthropy to the ruling class?

How has philanthropy affected your life and that of your community?

Distractions (pp. 128-140) (handout p. 140)

Name some of the systems that the ruling class uses to keep us distracted?

What are distractions for you and other family members?

How much money do you spend each year on distractions?

Which distractions are most popular in your community?

What are activities that people engage in that are not distractions but that build our communities?

Which of these activities are you and other family members involved in?

Which side are you on? (pp. 144-150) (handout p. 150)

Take a current public policy issue and do a "who benefits, who pays, and who really decides" analysis by class, race, and gender (see p. 150).

Beyond survival—getting together (pp. 153-154) (handout pp. 153-154)

Which strategies have you used to survive in this system?

When have you gotten together with others for change?

What are historical examples of people acting together?

What are current examples from your community?

What information, skills, understanding, and resources do people need to act together?

What are ways that you could implement more democratic processes in your family, work, school, or community life?

What is your next step in doing so?

What is your next step in participating in local or national struggles for social justice and democracy?

Identify persons who have worked for economic justice and democracy who have inspired you?

Give a current example of something that gives you hope for the possibility of a more just and sustainable world.

ENDNOTES

1. Keister, *Wealth in America*.
2. Warren Buffett, interview by Ted Koppel, ABC, July 2003 quoted in Weisbrot, "Labor Day 2003."
3. 1 percent and 20 percent for the managerial class are somewhat arbitrary cut-off points—there are no sharp divides. But there are some significant differences in access to power and in culture that occur around these divisions.
4. Steinem, "The Feminist To-Do List," 51.
5. Hartmann, *Unequal Protection*, 185.
6. Kelly, *The Divine Right of Capital*, 105.
7. The phrase "developed countries" refers to the U.S., countries in western Europe, and Japan. I use the phrase with hesitation because these countries are developed only at the expense of much of the rest of the world which has been exploited to pay for the development. In some sense, they are overdeveloped in relation to how underdeveloped other countries are. Even within these "developed" countries there are huge pockets of poverty and "under" development.
8. See glossary.
9. See glossary.
10. Phillips, *Wealth and Democracy*, 24.
11. This information is drawn from the detailed account in Hartmann, *Unequal Protections*, 45-64.
12. Takaki, *A Different Mirror*, 67.
13. Parenti, *Democracy for the Few*, 55.
14. Exploited aggressively means they are exploited even more than white male workers. People of color and white women are paid, on average, 25 to 40 percent less than white men and are consigned to the lowest paid, most dangerous, and least desirable jobs in our society. Much of the childcare, eldercare, housework, and family maintenance work that women perform is completely unpaid.
15. See the section on anti-Semitism on page 132.
16. This group would also include some members of the managerial class who are in positions of power and decision-making.
17. Income figure is from 2001 from Mishel, et al., *The State of Working America, 2002/2003*, 56. Wealth figure is from The Public Health and Labor Instutites, *Corporate Power and the American Dream*, 77.

18. For a detailed look at how this professional training and screening process works see Schmidt, *Disciplined Minds.*

19. C. Wright Mills, *The Power Elite* and G. William Domhoff, *Who Rules America: Power and Politics in the Year 2000.*

20. The phrase is from Parenti, *Democracy for the Few*, 36.

21. Domhoff, *Who Rules America*, 161-162.

22. Perrucci and Wysong, *The New Class Society*, 59.

23. Dye, *Who's Running America*, 204.

24. Perrucci and Wysong, *The New Class Society*, 94. For a more detailed look at diversity in the power elite see Zweigenhaft and Domhoff, *Diversity in the Power Elite.*

25. Perrucci and Wysong, *The New Class Society*, 2nd ed., 54.

26. Allegra, Donna, "Inconspicuous Assumptions" in Raffo, Susan, *Queerly Classed*, 212.

27. Hartmann, *Unequal Protection*, 201, 204.

28. For more information on the power of loan consortia see Mintz and Schwartz, *The Power Structure of American Business*, 54-56.

29. Ibid., 163.

30. Dye, *Who's Running America*, 39, 41. Perrucci and Wysong, *The New Class Society*, 2nd ed., 124-5.

31. Scott, *Drugs, Oil and War*, 187, and Ruppert, Mike, "The Truth and Lies of 911" (Sherman Oaks, CA: From the Wilderness Publications, 2002).

32. U.S. companies had close business partnerships with German and Japanese companies before and even during World War II. For example, ITT operated factories during the war which built bombers for the German Air Force, and even collected $27 million from the U.S. government because the Allied forces bombed their German factories. Carey, *Taking the Risk Out of Democracy*, 76. IBM provided census machines and punch card technology to Hitler. For more details about IBM see Black, *IBM and the Holocaust.*

33. Phillips, *Wealth and Democracy*, 411-12.

34. Doremus, Paul, et al., *The Myth of the Global Corporation*, 8.

35. Henwood, *WALL Street*, 112. These relations are always in flux. For example, recently, as major oil discoveries have been made in the Gulf of Guinea on the Atlantic coast of Africa, the U.S. has stepped up its economic and political activites there, challenging long-term European interests.

36. More information about most of these groups can be found in Draffan, *The Elite Consensus*, and at the websites of the organizations.

37. Petras and Veltmeyer. *Globalization Unmasked*, 54.

38. United Nations Development Report, UNDP/OUP 2000 quoted in Seabrook, *The No-nonsense Guide to Class, Caste & Hierarchies*, 11.

39. Seabrook, *The No-nonsense Guide to Class, Caste & Hierarchies*, 72.

40. Survey of Consumer Finances, 2001 found at /www.federalreserve.gov/pubs/oss/oss2/2001/bull0103.pdf.

41. Shapiro and Greenstein, "The Widening Income Gulf," 1-10.

42. For current figures see www.aflcio.org/corporateamerica/paywatch.

43. "Want Bigger Returns? Play Politics," *Too Much*, Spring 2001, 3.

44. Perrucci and Wysong, *New Class Society*, 51.

45. A mean average is found by taking the total amount and dividing by the number of individuals in the group. A median average is the midpoint with half the population falling below, and half above, that point.

46. Leondar-Wright, *"Federal Reserve: Racial Wealth Gap Has Grown."* Numbers are from the 2001 Survey of Consumer Finances.

47. Mishel, et al., *The State of Working America, 2002/2003*, 284-5.

48. Wolff, *Top Heavy*, 26. Figures from 1998 Survey of Consumer Finances. Since financial information is not collected uniformly I will occasionally use figures for the top 5 percent or 10 percent of the population, but will stay with 1 percent and 20 percent figures as much as possible.

49. Wolff, *The State of Working America, 2002/2003*, 286.

50. Parenti, *Land of Idols*, 102.

51. Parenti, *Democracy for the Few*, 72.

52. Anderson, *Black Labor White Wealth*, 124, 129, 144, 150.

53. Parenti, *America Besieged*, 68.

54. Kelly, *The Divine Right of Capital*, 33.

55. Hochschild and Machung, *The Second Shift* quoted in Kaufman, *Ideas for Action*, 171.

56. Mies, *Patriarchy and Accumulation on a World Scale*, xi.

57. See Henwood, *WALL Street*, 51 for a fascinating/horrifying list of speculative vehicles.

58. It is also possible to bet on prices going down and to win or lose money on falling prices.

59. Bluestone and Harrison, *The Deindustrialization of America*, 6.

50. See glossary.

61. Dowd, *Capitalism and Its Economics*, 185.

62. Numerous studies show that white people, and white men in particular, receive preference in getting business, housing and other loans, have had access to more educational opportunities than women, and men and women of color, and often receive preferential treatment in job training programs and in hiring and promotion. For more about these benefits see Lipsitz, *The Possessive Investment in Whiteness*.

63. Hundreds were killed and the Black towns destroyed in Tulsa in the middle of 1921 and in Rosewood in early 1923. See Jenkins, *The Real Rosewood*, Volume I and Brophy, *Reconstructing the Dreamland*. The movie "Rosewood" is a fictional account of the events in that town.

64. Mishel, et al., *The State of Working America, 2002/2003*, 283-84.

65. Mies, *Patriarchy and Accumulation on a World Scale*. See also Amott and Mattaei, *Race, Gender, and Work*.

66. Sklar, "Imagine a Country, Reprise," 55.

67. Mehri and Berk, "Stock Option Equity."

68. Abigail Adams and several other women argued for the use of more inclusive phrasing such as persons, people, humans, or men and women, but the writers of the Constitution explicitly used men to refer to men only. Hartmann, *Unequal Protection,* 122.

69. Kellman, *Building Unions,* 12.

70. Nearly three out of four people were or had been indentured servants (short-term property) and another 20 percent were slaves (long-term property). Ibid., 10. Quote ibid., 13.

71. Mitchell and Schoeffel, eds. *Understanding Power,* 315.

72. Parenti, *Democracy for the Few,* 61.

73. Kellman, *Building Unions,* 14-16.

74. Hartmann, *Unequal Protection,* 8.

75. Ibid., 105.

76. Domhoff, *Who Rules America Now?,* 41.

77. Reich, Robert, *The Work of Nations,* 141.

78. The Top 10 were GM, DaimlerChrysler, Ford, Wal-Mart Stores, Mitsui, Itochu, Mitsubishi, Exxon/Mobil, GE, and Toyota. Dowd, *Capitalism and Its Economics,* 173.

79. Including engaging in large amounts of speculation in currencies, commodities and even stocks and bonds.

80. For details see Weatherford, *Indian Givers,* 135-45.

81. Kellman, *Building Unions,* 27-34.

82. "Network analysis has shown that ninety percent of the 800 largest U.S. corporations are interlocked in a continuous network, with any one corporation within four steps of any other corporation in the network." Draffan, *The Elite Consensus,* 5.

83. Dowd, *Capitalism and Its Economics,* 184.

84. Mintz and Schwartz, *The Power Structure of American Business,* 183.

85. Sociologist Michael Useem has labeled this group the inner circle. See Useem, *The Inner Circle.* For graphic illustrations of corporate interlocking directorships visit www.theyrule.org.

86. Domhoff, *Who Rules America?,* 141.

87. Ibid., 145.

88. Shoup, "Behind the Bipartisan Drive Toward War, 36.

89. Korten, *When Corporations Rule the World,* 137.

90. Ibid., 139.

91. Domhoff, *Who Rules America?: Power and Politics,* 156.

92. Carey, *Taking the Risk Out of Democracy,* 92

93. Domhoff, *Who Rules America?: Power and Politics,* 156.

94. Dye, *Top Down Policymaking,* 42.

95. National Council of Nonprofit Associations, "The United States Nonprofit Sector 2001."

96. Perrucci and Wysong, *New Class Society*, 119.

97. Wilayto, Phil, "The Lynde and Harry Bradley Foundation."

98. National Committee for Responsive Philanthropy, *$1 Billion for Ideas*, 32.

99. See glossary.

100. Figures are for 1999.

101. Found at http://www.stmarytx.edu/business/index.php?group=institutes& page=p_pryor.txt

102. ExxonMobil is still contesting even that amount. More details about ExxonMobil's funding of academic research can be found in Zarembo, "Funding Studies to Suit Need," 1.

103. Kelly, *Class War in America*, 50. This book presents a good analysis of the kinds of information found in elite publications.

104. *Sacramento Bee*, March 1, 2001.

105. *Dollars & Sense*, March/April, 2003, 5.

106. Quoted in Dowd, *Capitalism and Its Economics*, 7.

107. Domhoff, *Who Rules America?*, 248.

108. Perrucci and Wysong, *The New Class Society*, 14.

109. Domhoff, *Who Rules America?*, 251.

110. Danaher, *Corporations Are Gonna Get Your Mama*, 62.

111. Dye, *Top Down Policymaking*, 85.

112. Perrucci and Wysong, *New Class Society*, 121.

113. Ibid., 107.

114. Perrucci and Wysong, 2nd ed., 141.

115. Dye, *Top Down Policymaking*, 6.

116. Collins and Yeskel, *Economic Apartheid in America*, 29.

117. For a good history of the early round of corporate participation in setting up regulation at the beginning of the twentieth century see Kolko, *The Triumph of Conservatism*.

118. Parenti, *Democracy for the Few*, 272-3.

119. Perrucci and Wysong, *New Class Society*, 2nd ed., 128.

120. Even the small donations of $200 or less are from wealthy, upper-class, older, white males. Over 80 percent have annual incomes of more than $100,000 and are 45 or older. Dye, *Top Down Policymaking*, 70. By today's standards even a contribution of $1,000 is not much. As one lobbyist says, "So the public perception out there that someone who gives a thousand dollars has influence is laughable. It really is, because that's such chump change today that it doesn't even register on the scale." Makinson, *Speaking Freely*, 84.

121. Moore, *Stupid White Men*, 31. Information available at www.opensecrets.org.

122. Collins and Yeskel, *Economic Apartheid in America*, 70 and *Dollars & Sense*, July-August, 1996.

123. Center for Responsive Politics. Information available at http://www.opensecrets.org/overview/blio.asp?cycle=2002.

124. See glossary. The McCain-Feingold campaign finance law now sets some limits on soft money contributions.

125. Domhoff, *Who Rules America?: Power and Politics,* 221.

126. Public Policy and Education Fund of New York, "Capital Investments, Capital Returns."

127. Phillips, *Wealth and Democracy,* 326.

128. Edney, "Black Voters Ready to 'Get Even' for 2000 Fiasco."

129. Guinier, "Making Every Vote Count."

130. Based on Federal Election Commission data. Available at www.opensecrets.org.

131. U.S. Congress, House Committee on the Budget, "Unnecessary Business Subsidies," 106th Congress, 1st sess., 1999, Serial 106-5, quoted in Perrucci and Wysong, *New Class Society,* 2nd ed., 19.

132. Danaher, *Corporations Are Gonna Get Your Mama,* 28.

133. Andreas, *Addicted to War,* 8-9.

134. Conrad, Joseph, *Heart of Darkness,* quoted in *Z Magazine,* November 2002, 41.

135. Henwood, *WALL Street,* 234.

136. Bond, "Cultivating African Anti-Capitalism," 45.

137. Petras and Veltmeyer, *Globalization Unmasked,* 79.

138. Bond, "Cultivating African Anti-Capitalism," 46.

139. For more details about international debt see Danaher, ed. *50 Years Is Enough.*

140. Bello, et al., *Dark Victory,* 68.

141. Burrows, *The No-Nonsense Guide to the Arms Trade,* 14-15.

142. Ibid., 78.

143. Chomsky, *The Prosperous Few,* 11.

144. Mowery and Rosenberg, *Paths of Innovation,* quoted in Phillips, *Wealth and Democracy,* 247.

145. Holmgren and Holmgren, *Outrageous Fortunes,* ix.

146. Ibid., divided almost equally between Republicans and Democrats.

147. For more information about this process see Chomsky, *Year 501,* chapter 9.

148. Halloran, "What Price U.S. Patrols in the Gulf," 2E.

149. New Alternatives Fund, Inc, Report 4th Quarter, 2002.

150. For more details see Sampson, *The Seven Sisters;* Yergin, *The Prize;* and Spiro; *The Hidden Hand.*

151. I am excluding the tobacco and liquor industries, legal, highly lucrative, and deadly sources of profits to the ruling class. Hundreds of thousands of people in the U.S. die every year from smoking alone.

152. Figure is for 2002 from Corpwatch. Available at www.corpwatch.org/news/PND.jsp?articleid=4790.

153. Engler, "Selling Drugs," 32-5.

154. Statement by U.N. Secretary-General Kofi Annan, 1998, reported at www.oneworld.org/ips2/mar98/drug_trade.html. See also Chomsky, *Understanding Power*, 372 and footnote.

155. Interview with Pulso found at www.narconews.com/pressbriefing21september.html.

156. See Scott, *Drugs, Oil, and War* for details. In addition see McCoy, *The Politics of Heroin*; Scott and Marshall, *Cocaine Politics*; and Haq, *Drugs in South Asia*.

157. See McCoy, *The Politics of Heroin*.

158. Senate Committee on Foreign Relations, Subcommittee on Terrorism, Narcotics and International Operations, report, *Drugs, Law Enforcement and Foreign Policy* (the Kerry report). Washington, DC: U.S. Government Printing Office, 1989.

159. Scott, *Drugs, Oil, and War*, 27-70.

160. Ibid., 71-108 for details and documentation.

161. Henwood, *WALL Street,* 66.

162. For information on the Federal Reserve Bank system see Henwood, *WALL Street*, 92-8, and Greider, *Secrets of the Temple.*

163. These figures and other information on corporate crime are available from *Corporate Crime Reporter* at www.corporatecrimereporter.com/top100.html.

164. Pariser, "American Kleptocracy."

165. Dye, *Top Down Policymaking*, 34 and Zepezauer, *Take the Rich Off Welfare*, 37.

166. Henwood, *WALL Street,* 27.

167. Barlett and Steele, *America: Who Really Pays the Taxes*, 109.

168. Zepezauer, *Take the Rich Off Welfare*, 20.

169. Seabrook, *The No-Nonsense Guide to Class, Caste, and Hierarchies*, 100.

170. Barlett and Steele, *America: Who Stole the Dream*, 215.

171. Quoted in Collins and Yeskel, *Economic Apartheid in America*, 60.

172. Pizzigati, "How Big Will Your Inheritance Be?" 9.

173. Kelly, *The Divine Right of Capital*, 205.

174. Al King, co-chief executive officer of Third Constellation Trust Co as quoted in Gould, Carole, "Saving More Than Memories," *Bloomberg Wealth Manager*, April 2002, 45.

175. Ibid.

176. Phillips, *Wealth and Democracy*, 119.

177. Stanley and Danko. *The Millionaire Next Door*, 145, 165.

178. Perrucci and Wysong, *New Class Society*, 196-99.

179. Quoted in Brooks, *BOBO's in Paradise*, 53.

180. Berube, Allan, "Intellectual Desire" in Susan Raffo, *Queerly Classed*, 57.

181. Schmidt, *Disciplined Minds*, 12.

182. Ibid., 16.

183. Stanley and Danko, *The Millionaire Next Door*, 145.

184. See Kendall, *The Power of Good Deeds* for more details on the role of ruling class women in these activities.

185. There are certainly exceptions to this among ruling class members. As Jamie Johnson, an heir to the Johnson & Johnson pharmaceutical fortune said on the eve of his 21st birthday, "I live in a country that everyone wants to believe is a meritocracy. We want to think that everyone earns what they have. If it makes you feel better, keep telling yourself that... What did I do to earn the kind of money I am going to inherit tonight?" (HBO special "Born Rich" 2003).

186. Perrucci and Wysong, *New Class Society*, 14.

187. Parenti, *Land of Idols*, 106.

188. Domhoff, *Who Rules*, 65.

189. See Mogil, et al., *We Gave Away a Fortune* for stories of people who inherited large amounts of money and then gave most or all of it away.

190. Zepezauer, *Take the Rich Off Welfare*, 32. The Multistate Tax Commission (a nonpartisan coalition of state taxing authorities) estimates that domestic corporate tax shelters rob states of another $12.4 billion a year. Multistate Tax Coalition, "Corporate Tax Sheltering and the Impact on State Corporate Income Tax Revenue Collection."

191. Silverstein, "Trillion-Dollar Hideaway."

192. Lewis, Charles, et al., *The Cheating of America*, 271, 273.

193. Silverstein, "Trillion-Dollar Hideaway."

194. The Government Accounting Office estimated that 64 percent of the losses were due to fraud and corruption.

195. For further information about the S & L scandal see Pizzo, et al., *Inside Job*, and Day, *S & L Hell*.

196. Draffan, *The Elite Consensus*, 27-8.

197. For more information about COINTELPRO see Churchill, et al., *The Cointelpro Papers*.

198. Figures are from *Forbes* magazine's 2002 annual survey.

199. Kendall, *The Power of Good Deeds*, 25.

200. Quoted in *Z Magazine*, November 2002, 39.

201. The *Progressive*, September 1986.

202. Collins and Yeskel, *Economic Apartheid in America*, 4.

203. Ibid., 37.

204. Barlett and Steele, *America: Who Stole the Dream*, 12-13.

205. Soley, "The Invisible Gag," 17.

206. Perrucci and Wysong, *New Class Society*, 53-54.

207. Poppendieck, *Sweet Charity?*, 5-6.

208. Califano Jr., "Too Many Federal Cops."

209. Odendahl, *Charity Begins at Home*, 4.

210. For an excellent case study on this process see Cottin, "George Soros, Imperial Wizard," 1-7. The tax benefits to the ruling class from charitable giving are discussed in the chapter on Preserving Its Wealth.

211. Eisenberg, Pablo, "Foundation Trustee Fees: Uses and Abuses," Washington, DC: Center for Public and Nonprofit Leadership, 2003.

212. Russell Sage Foundation, *Foundation Directory*, 2002 edition. New York: Russell Sage Foundation, 2002.

213. Odendahl, *Charity Begins at Home*, 3.

214. Roelofs, "The Third Sector as a Protective Layer for Capitalism," 16.

215. National Council of Nonprofit Associations, "The United States Nonprofit Sector 2001."

216. Roelofs, "The Third Sector as a Protective Layer for Capitalism," 17.

217. See Cottin, "George Soros, Imperial Wizard," 1-7, and Flounders, "Massacre in Jenin," 8-13.

218. Brandt, "Philanthropists at War."

219. Co-opt means to provide jobs and other resources to a community or its leadership so that they become dependent on and loyal to their funders/supporters and less able or willing to challenge their agenda.

220. Roelofs, Joan, "Foundations and Social Change Organizations." Also see Domhoff, *Who Rules America?*, 131-134. An excellent look at the role of foundations in policy formation can be found in Roelofs, *Foundations and Public Policy*.

221. Roelofs, "The Third Sector as a Protective Layer for Capitalism," 19-23. For more on the role of NGOs in the world see Roelofs, "The Third Sector as a Protective Layer for Capitalism," chapter 8, and Petras and Veltmeyer, *Globalization Unmasked*, 128-38.

222. Brandt, "Philanthropists at War."

223. Ibid.

224. Carey, *Taking the Risk Out of Democracy*, 21.

225. Parenti, "Monopoly Media Manipulation."

226. Howard, "Power Sources."

227. Dolny, "Think Tanks."

228. Perrucci and Wysong, *New Class Society*, 37.

229. Ibid., 159. For more analysis of the role of media and its bias see Herman, *The Myth of the Liberal Media*; Alterman, *What Liberal Media?*; Herman and Chomsky, *Manufacturing Consent*; and Croteau and Hoynes, *By Invitation Only*.

230. Pozner, "Power Shortage for Media Women."

231. Parenti, "Monopoly Media Manipulation."

232. Carey, *Taking the Risk Out of Democracy*, 30.

233. Perrucci and Wysong, *New Class Society*, 170; also in Press, "Spin Cities," 30.

234. Hartmann, *Unequal Protection*, 184-5.

235. More information on corporate crime can be found at www.corporate-crimereporter.org. and in Danaher, *Corporations Are Gonna Get Your Mama.*

236. Cullen, *A Job to Die For,* quoted in *Z Magazine,* November 2002, 61.

237. See the movie "Erin Brockovich" for a case study.

238. Street, "Labor Day Reflections."

239. Ibid. For more on this issue see Schor, *The Overworked American.*

240. Jensen, "Rape is Normal?", or in "Challenging Rape Culture" *Voice Male,* Winter 2003, 8.

241. Dowd, *Capitalism and Its Economics,* 203. (emphasis in the original).

242. Current U.S. Government figures are available at http://www.federalreserve.gov/releases/g19/Current/.

243. Mishel, et al., *The State of Working America, 2002/03,* 295.

244. Dowd, *Capitalism and Its Economics,* 194.

245. Perrucci and Wysong, *New Class Society,* 2nd ed., 263.

246. Ibid., 262.

247. National Council on Problem Gambling. Information available at http://www.gambling.org/pdf/eapa_flyer.pdf.

248. Koughan, "Easy Money."

249. Heberling, "State Lotteries."

250. For more information on the impact of legalized gambling see Goodman, *The Luck Business.*

251. United for a Fair Economy, "Born on Third Base."

252. Second richest person in the U.S. in 2000, Partner in Kohlberg, Kravis, Roberts, and former CEO of AOL/TimeWarner, respectively.

253. Collins and Yeskel, *Economic Apartheid in America,* 78.

254. Perrucci and Wysong, *New Class Society,* 2nd ed., 188. See also Lieberman, "Social Insecurity," 12.

255. Perrucci and Wysong, *New Class Society,* 259.

256. Pizzigati, "America's Revolutionary-in-Chief," 2.

257. Ibid., 11.

258. For details see McIntyre, et al., *Who Pays.*

259. Pizzigati, *Too Much,* Spring, 2003, 11.

260. The Public Health and Labor Institutes, *Corporate Power and the American Dream,* 119. Numbers are from the Bureau of the Census.

261. Perrucci and Wysong, *New Class Society,* 2nd ed., 152. Information is from Office of Management and Budget, "Historical Tables," Budget of the United States Government: Fiscal Year 2002.

262. Hartmann, *Unequal Protection,* 176.

263. Collins and Yeskel, *Economic Apartheid in America,* 101.

264. Information is from Human Rights Watch, *Unfair Advantage;* and Freeman, Richard B. and Joel Rogers, *What Workers Want,* ILR Press, 2002.

265. Information is from U.S. Department of Labor, *Employment and Earnings,* January 2003; Bureau of Labor Statistics, *Employee Benefits in Private Industry,* 2000.

266. The following section on doing an analysis of public policy issues is adapted from my book *Uprooting Racism.*

267. Until that time, having senators elected by state legislatures was a central element of ruling class control of the government.

268. Quoted in Danaher, *Corporations Are Gonna Get Your Mama,* 51-2.

269. Ibid., 198.

270. This is a transcript of a message delivered to the anti-globalization conference in Cancun, Mexico on September 3, 2003 and can be found at www.ezln.org. Subcommandante Marcos is a primary voice of the Zapatista movement which fights for the rights of the people. My thanks to Mary Luckey for bringing this statement to my attention.

GLOSSARY

Average (Mean)—The average when the total amount is divided by the number of individuals. When there is significant inequality in the group then the mean average will be a value above what most individuals have. For example, if you have three people making $9,000, $10,000, and $11,000 and one person making $60,000 then the mean average is $100,000 divided by 4 = $25,000.

Average (Median)—The average at the point where half the individuals are above and half are below the point. In the example above the mean average is $10,500, closer to representing what most (in this case three-fourths) of the individuals make in the sample.

Bailout—When a country, company, or industry goes bankrupt or just loses tremendous amounts of money, a government or financial institution might loan them the money to survive or to prop up their value so that ruling class investors don't lose a lot of money and so that they will remain confident in the financial system. A bailout usually comes with stringent financial controls, high interest, and much ruling class profit.

Bonds—When the federal government, a state or local government, government agency, or a corporation needs money, one way they can raise it is by selling a bond to investors (borrowing money) with a promise to pay a specific interest rate for a set number of years. These bonds can then be bought and sold on the bond market until they reach the date they expire, at which time they are paid off. Or, for various reasons, the issuing body can call them—i.e. pay them off early.

Bonds—tax exempt—Bonds whose interest is exempt from federal and/or state income taxes.

Breton Woods Agreement—A 1944 agreement between the U.S. and European elites to establish the U.S. dollar at a fixed rate to gold to stabilize financial markets and establish the primacy of the U.S.

Buffer zone—Those careers, professions and occupations in society which act as a buffer between the ruling and managerial classes and the people in the bottom of the economic pyramid. The primary functions of these jobs are to take care of people, keep hope alive, and control people.

Capital gains—The amount of money (profit) one makes from selling something after all costs are deducted.

Capital gains tax—When something is bought and held for more than one year, only 15 percent of the profit is counted as income rather than the full amount.

Charitable deduction—Any money or goods given away to a federally certified nonprofit organization can be deducted from one's taxes.

Consumer Protection Agency—The federal agency set up to protect the public from unsafe and unhealthy products.

Corporate welfare—Direct and indirect subsidies paid to corporations—currently estimated to total hundreds of billions of dollars a year.

Dividend—The payout of money or stock that one receives from owning a stock or other investment.

Environmental Protection Agency (EPA)—The federal agency set up to protect the environment.

Estate tax—The amount owed on an estate after a person dies. Currently, a person's entire estate can go to their spouse tax free, and estate taxes are only due on estates over $1.5 million after all deductions and charitable donations.

Family office—A financial business established by a wealthy family to manage the family's wealth.

Federal debt—The amount the federal government owes on the short- and long-term bonds it issues to balance the budget.

Food and Drug Administration (FDA)—The federal agency which regulates the quality and safety of foods and drugs.

Foundation—A federally chartered institution set up to hold and distribute donated money according to the guidelines of its articles of incorporation and by-laws and overseen by its board of directors.

Free Trade Agreement of the Americas (FTAA)—An agreement patterned after NAFTA being pushed by the U.S. power elite to establish a unified trading zone through North, Central, and South America. It would eliminate the ability of national governments to protect local industry, jobs, public services, and the environment.

General Agreement on Tariffs and Trade (GATT)—A multinational agreement in 1947 (and modified in subsequent meetings and agreements) that established general policies on tariffs, and terms of trade between nations. It was highly favorable to the most developed countries because it lowered tariffs and eliminated other barriers to trade, making it difficult for poorer countries to resist multinational predation on their economies.

Gentrification—When owning class people move into a neighborhood or section of a city and, because they can afford to pay more for rent, homes, food, and entertainment, drive up prices and drive out poor and working-class people who had been living there.

Gift tax exclusion—Any individual can give up to $11,000 per year to as many individuals as they like without it being counted against their estate tax deduction.

Grandfather clause—Originally, Southern states passed laws after Reconstruction aimed at preventing newly freed Blacks from voting, which stated that one could only vote if one's grandfather had voted. Today it means activity which is specifically excluded from being covered by a law or regulation.

Gross Domestic Product (GDP)—The sum total of all the goods and services produced by a country in a given year.

Holding company—A financial organization set up by people with wealth to hold and manage assets.

Home mortgage interest—The interest that is due on a home loan. The interest is frontloaded—i.e. the homeowner pays the interest back in the first years and very little on the amount borrowed until the interest is paid off. This interest is deductible on federal and state income tax returns.

Household wealth—A family's total assets minus its total debt.

Income—The total amount of money that an individual or family brings in during a single year from all sources including wages, salaries, tips, interest, dividends, gains from sales, gifts, loan paybacks, and lottery winnings.

Inheritance—The money that a person receives when someone dies, after taxes and charitable contributions are deducted.

International debt—Money owed by one country to another.

International Monetary Fund (IMF)—An organization set up by the U.S. and European power elites in 1944 to stabilize the world economy and provide a framework for post World War II investment, redevelopment, and international trade. It allows countries to borrow to stabilize their balance of trade deficits but imposes very harsh conditions for the borrowing country. It serves as a debt collector for financial institutions in the U.S., Japan, and Western Europe.

Legacy admission—An admission to a private school, college, or university based on being the child or other family member of an alumni.

Liability—The amount by which one can be held legally responsible for the damage or loss resulting from one's actions or the results of one's financial investment.

Managerial class—Defined in this book as the families in the top 20 percent of the wealth pyramid excluding the top 1 percent. The managerial class includes families with incomes above $94,000 and average net worth of $344,000 including net financial wealth of at least $100,000.

Multilateral Agreement on Investments (MAI)—A proposed agreement to regulate international investment by eliminating most forms of restrictions on the flow of money.

National Labor Relations Board (NLRB)—The federal agency established to regulate and supervise labor-management relations.

Net financial worth—The total value of what an individual or family owns minus what they owe in debt excluding housing and personal and household items.

Net worth—The total value of what an individual or family owns minus what they owe.

Nongovernmental organization (NGO)—The general term for nonprofit organizations (not businesses or government agencies) outside the U.S. They are often connected to the United Nations.

North American Free Trade Agreement (NAFTA)—An agreement signed in 1993 by Mexico, Canada, and the U.S. that lowered most tariffs and trade barriers between the countries and established a single trading zone. The agreement superceded local and national laws on trade, labor, and environmental policy.

Occupational Safety and Health Administration (OSHA)—The federal agency which oversees workplace health and safety.

Philanthropy—The web of people, money, and institutions which are privately endowed with tax-exempt contributions, accredited by the federal government as foundations and non-profit organizations with a mandate to work for the public interest.

Political Action Committee (PAC)—A political committee organized for the purpose of raising and spending money to elect and defeat candidates. Most PACs represent business, labor or other special interest groups.

Policy formation group—One of a number of organizations which focus on investigating, discussing and conducting public education on current domestic and international policy issues.

Power elite—Those people in the ruling and managerial classes who hold positions of national decision-making in corporations, the government, think tanks, foundations, philanthropy, policy formation groups, and elite universities. They operate as a network of decision makers.

Public relations—The industry funded by corporations and governments to project a favorable image about their operations or specific projects.

Ruling class—Defined in this book as the families in the top 1 percent in terms of wealth defined as families having incomes starting at about $373,000/year (1999) and net financial worth of at least $2,045,000.

Sibling preference—A private school admissions policy of giving a preference to the brothers and sisters of current or past students.

Soft Money—Any political contribution not going directly to a candidate and therefore not subject to the same limitations as direct contributions.

Stocks—A certificate of ownership sold to investors by corporations to raise money. These are then bought and sold on the various stock markets. The stocks are only worth what someone will pay for them. Some earn dividends and some do not.

Structural Adjustment Plans—The conditions for loans or debt restructuring imposed by the World Bank and IMF. These terms usually call for shifting domestic production to export items, eliminating all trade barriers and other restrictions on transnational corporations, privatizing utilities and services, lifting restrictions on foreign investments, reducing environmental regulations, tightening control over labor organizing, reducing wages and worker safety, and reducing spending for social services.

Tariff—A tax on something imported from another country.

Tax haven—Any locality outside the jurisdiction of the U.S. government where money can be kept or businesses operated protected from taxes, regulation, and liability.

Tax shelter—Any investment that hides or protects money from being taxed.

Think tank—A nonprofit organization specifically set up to do research and disseminate research on public policy issues.

Trilateral Commission—An organization set up in the 1970s consisting of members of the power elites from Europe, Japan, and North America whose purpose was to discuss and advocate for international policy initiatives.

Trust—A legal vehicle for passing on wealth and control of wealth to avoid taxes, establish control, and avoid liability.

Umbrella insurance—An insurance policy to protect a person's wealth which is on top of or in addition to the standard coverage of car and homeowners insurance.

United States Department of Agriculture (USDA)—In charge of regulating meat, poultry, eggs, and dairy products, conserving land, and regulating land use on federal forests and range lands, among many other responsibilities.

Wealth—The total value of what an individual or family owns including land, housing, stocks and bonds, personal items, household items, and financial interests in partnerships, trusts, etc.

World Bank—Originally the International Bank for Reconstruction and Development, it was established in 1944 to oversee post-World War II loans for the reconstruction of Europe. Today it lends money to developing countries (often for costly and inappropriate construction projects, basically financing exports and development projects for transnational corporations) and establishes harsh conditions (structural adjustment plans) for many international loans in conjunction with the WTO.

World Trade Organization (WTO)—Established in 1993 as a more comprehensive successor to GATT. It was supposed to regulate trade but was highly biased towards unrestricted transnational corporate access to resources and markets in every country for every commodity, asset, and public utility. In conjunction with the World Bank, it established terms for international loans which included structural adjustment policies which commanded privatization of public resources and services, elimination of tariffs and other trade barriers, and no restrictions on capital movement. It has the power to settle trade disputes between countries, and to monitor and enforce trade agreements.

BIBLIOGRAPHY

(Books about alternatives to globalization and curricula for teaching about economics and social justice are listed in separate sections at the end of this bibliography.)

Adams, Howard. *Prison of Grass: Canada from a Native Point of View.* Saskatoon: Fifth House Publishers, 1989.

Adamson, Madeline. *This Mighty Dream: Social Protest Movements in the United States.* Boston: Routledge, 1984.

Aguilar-San Juan, Karin, ed. *The State of Asian America: Activism and Resistance in the 1990s.* Boston: South End Press, 1994.

Alaniz, Yolanda and Nellie Wong, eds. *Voices of Color.* Seattle: Red Letter Press, 1999.

Albert, Michael. *The Trajectory of Change: Activist Strategies for Social Transformation.* Boston: South End Press, 2002.

Albrecht, Lisa and Rose M. Brewer, eds. *Bridges of Power: Women's Multicultural Alliances.* Philadelphia and Gabriola Island, BC: New Society Publishers, 1990.

Aldrich, Nelson W. *Old Money: The Mythology of America's Upper Class.* New York: Alfred A. Knopf, 1988.

Alexander, Jacqui M. et al., eds. *Sing, Whisper, Shout, Pray!: Feminist Visions for a Just World.* Berkeley, CA: Edgework Books, 2003.

Alfred, Taiaiake. *Peace, Power, Righteousness: An Indigenous Manifesto.* Oxford: Oxford University Press, 1999.

Alger, Dean. *Megamedia: How Giant Corporations Dominate Mass Media, Distort Competition, and Endanger Democracy.* Lanham, MD: Rowman & Littlefield, 1998.

Allen, Michael Patrick. *The Founding Fortunes: A New Anatomy of the Super-Rich Families in America.* New York: E.P. Dutton, 1987.

Allen, Robert. *Black Awakening in Capitalist America: An Analytic History.* Cambridge, MA: MIT Press, 1970.

Allen, Theodore W. *The Invention of the White Race.* London: Verso, 1994.

Alternman, Eric. *What Liberal Media? The Truth About Bias and the News.* New York: Basic Books, 2003.

Amott, Teresa and Julie Matthaei. *Race, Gender, and Work: A Multicultural Economic History of Women in the United States.* Boston: South End Press, 1991.

Anderson, Claud. *Black Labor White Wealth: The Search for Power and Economic Justice.* Edgewood, MD: Duncan & Duncan, 1994.

Anderson, Sarah and John Cavanagh. *Top 200: The Rise of Corporate Global Power.* Washington, DC: Institute for Policy Studies, 2000.

Anderson, Sarah, et al. *Field Guide to the Global Economy.* New York: New Press, 2000.

Andres, Joel. *Addicted to War: Why the U.S. Can't Kick Militarism.* Oakland: A.K. Press, 2002.

Anthias, Floya, et al. *Racialized Boundaries: Race, Nation, Gender, Colour and Class and the Anti-Racist Struggle.* New York: Routledge, 1992.

Anzaldua, Gloria, ed. *Making Faces, Making Soul, Hacienda Caras: Creative and Critical Perspectives by Women of Color.* San Francisco: Aunt Lute Foundation Books, 1990.

Aptheker, Herbert. *Anti-Racism in U.S. History.* Westport, CT: Praeger, 1993.

Arnove, Robert F. *Philanthropy and Cultural Imperialism: The Foundations at Home and Abroad.* Bloomington, IN: Indiana University Press, 1982.

Aronowitz, Stanley. *How Class Works: Power and Social Movement.* Princeton, NJ: Yale University Press, 2003.

Bagdikian, Ben. *The Media Monopoly.* 5th ed. Boston: Beacon Press, 1997.

Baran, Paul and Paul Sweezy. *Monopoly Capital: An Essay on the American Economic and Social Order.* New York: Monthly Review Press, 1966.

Barlett, Donald L. and James B. Steele. *America: Who Really Pays the Taxes?* New York: Simon & Schuster, 1994.

Barlett, Donald L. and James B. Steele. *America: Who Stole the Dream?* Kansas City: Andrews and McMeel, 1996.

Barndt, Deborah. *Women Working in the NAFTA Food Chain: Women, Food & Globalization.* Toronto: Second Story Press, 1999.

Barnet, Richard J. and John Cavanagh. *Global Dreams: Imperial Corporations and the New World Order.* New York: Simon & Schuster, 1994.

Barrera, Mario. *Race and Class in the Southwest.* North Bend, IN: University of Notre Dame Press, 1979.

Bell, Derrick. *Faces at the Bottom of the Well: The Permanence of Racism.* New York: HarperCollins, 1992.

Bello, Walden F., et al. *Dark Victory: The United States and Global Poverty.* 2nd ed. *Transnational Institute Series.* Oakland: Pluto Press, 1999.

Birnbaum, Jeffrey H. *The Lobbyists: How Influence Peddlers Get Their Way in Washington.* New York: Times Books/Random House, 1992.

Black, Edwin. *IBM and the Holocaust: The Strategic Alliance Between Nazi Germany and America's Most Powerful Corporation.* New York: Crown Publishers, 2001.

Blakely, Edward and Mary Gail Snyder. *Fortress America: Gated Communities in the United States.* Washington, D.C.: Brookings Institution Press, 1997.

Blau, Joel. *Illusions of Prosperity: American Working Families in an Age of Economic Insecurity.* New York: Oxford University Press, 1999.

Blaut, J.M. *The Colonizer's Model of the World: Geographical Diffusionism and Eurocentric History.* New York: Guilford Press, 1993.

Bluestone, Barry and Bennett Harrison. *The Deindustrialization of America.* New York: Basic Books, 1982.

Boggs, James. *Racism and the Class Struggle: Further Pages from a Black Worker's Notebook.* New York: Monthly Review Press, 1970.

Bond, Patrick. "Cultivating African Anti-Capitalism." *Z Magazine,* February 2003.

Brandt, Daniel. "Philanthropists at War." *NameBase NewsLine.* No.15. October-December 1996. Available at http://www.pir.org/news15.html.

Brecher, Jeremy, et al. *Globalization from Below.* Boston: South End Press, 2000.

Brooks, David, *BOBO's in Paradise: The New Upper Class and How They Got There.* New York: Simon and Schuster, 2000.

Brophy, Alfred. *Reconstructing the Dreamland: The Tulsa Race Riot of 1921, Race Reparations, and Reconciliation.* Oxford: Oxford University Press, 2003.

Bulkin, Elly, Minnie Bruce Pratt, and Barbara Smith. *Yours in Struggle: Three Feminist Perspectives on Anti-Semitism and Racism.* Ithaca, NY: Firebrand, 1988.

Burrows, Gideon. *The No-nonsense Guide to the Arms Trade.* London: New Internationalist Publications, 2002.

Califano Jr., Joseph A. "Too Many Federal Cops." *Washington Post.* December 6, 2001.

Carey, Alex. *Taking the Risk Out of Democracy: Corporate Propaganda versus Freedom and Liberty.* Urbana, IL: University of Illinois Press, 1995.

Chang, Grace. *Disposable Domestics: Immigrant Women Workers in the Global Economy.* Boston: South End Press, 2000.

Chang, Robert S. *Disoriented: Asian Americans, Law, and the Nation-State.* New York: New York University Press, 1999.

Chilcote, Ronald H., ed. *The Political Economy of Imperialism: Critical Appraisals.* Lanham, MD: Rowman & Littlefield, 2000.

Chomsky, Noam. *Class Warfare: Interviews with David Barsamian.* Monroe, ME: Common Courage Press, 1996.

Chomsky, Noam. *Keeping the Rabble in Line: Interviews with David Barsamian.* Monroe, ME: Common Courage Press, 1994.

Chomsky, Noam. *Profit Over People: Neoliberalism and Global Order.* New York: Seven Stories Press, 1999.

Chomsky, Noam. *The Prosperous Few and the Restless Many.* Berkeley, CA: Odonian, 1993.

Chomsky, Noam. *Understanding Power: The Indispensable Chomsky.* New York: The New Press, 2002.

Chomsky, Noam. *Year 501.* Boston: South End Press, 1993.

Churchill, Ward. *The Cointelpro Papers: Documents from the FBI's Secret Wars Against Dissent in the United States.* 2nd ed. Boston: South End Press, 2002.

Churchill, Ward. *Indians Are Us?: Culture and Genocide in Native North America.* Monroe, ME: Common Courage Press, 1994.

Clark, Christopher, et al., eds. *Who Built America.* 2nd ed. New York: Pantheon, 2000.

Clawson, Dan, et al. *Money Talks: Corporate PACs and Political Influence.* New York: Basic Books, 1992.

Cockburn, Alexander and Jeffrey St. Cloud. *Whiteout: The C.I.A., Drugs and the Press.* London: Verso, 1998.

Collins, Chuck and Felice Yeskel. *Economic Apartheid in America: A Primer on Economic Inequality & Insecurity.* New York: The New Press, 2000.

Collins, Chuck, et al. *Shifting Fortunes: The Perils of the American Wealth Gap.* Boston: United for a Fair Economy, 1999.

Conley, Dalton. *Being Black, Living in the Red: Race, Wealth, and Social Policy.* Berkeley, CA: University of California Press, 1999.

Cooney, Robert and Helen Michalowski. *The Power of the People: Active Non-Violence in the United States.* Philadelphia: New Society, 1987.

Cose, Ellis. *The Rage of a Privileged Class.* New York: HarperCollins, 1993.

Cottin, Heath. "George Soros, Imperial Wizard: Master-Builder of the New Bribe Sector, Systematically Bilking the World." *CovertAction Quarterly* #74. Fall, 2002.

Creighton, Allan with Paul Kivel. *Helping Teens Stop Violence: A Practical Guide for Counselors, Educators, and Parents.* Alameda, CA: Hunter House, 1992.

Crenshaw, Kimberle, et al., eds. *Critical Race Theory: The Key Writings that Formed the Movement.* New York: The New Press, 1995.

Croteau, David. *Politics and the Class Divide: Working People and the White Middle-Class Left.* Philadelphia: Temple University Press, 1995.

Croteau, David and William Hoynes. *By Invitation Only: How the Media Limit Political Debate.* Monroe, ME: Common Courage Press, 1994.

Cullen, Lisa. *A Job to Die For: Why So Many Americans Are Killed, Injured or Made Ill at Work and What to Do About It.* Monroe, ME: Common Courage Press, 2002.

Currie, Elliott, *Crime and Punishment in America: Why the Solutions to America's Most Stubborn Social Crisis Have Not Worked—and What Will.* New York: Henry Holt and Co., 1998.

Curtis, Mark. *Web of Deceit.* London: Vintage, 2003.

Daly, Herman E. and John B. Cobb, Jr. *Beyond Growth: The Economics of Sustainable Development.* Boston: Beacon Press, 1996.

Danaher, Kevin. *Corporations Are Gonna Get Your Momma.* Monroe, ME: Common Courage Press, 1996.

Danaher, Kevin, et al. *Insurrection: Citizen Challenges to Corporate Power.* New York: Routledge, 2003.

Danaher, Kevin, ed. *50 Years Is Enough: The Case Against the World Bank and the International Monetary Fund.* Boston: South End Press, 1994.

Davis, Angela Y. *Women, Culture, Politics.* New York: Vintage Books, 1989.

Davis, Angela Y. *Women, Race & Class.* New York: Random House, 1981.

Day, Kathleen. *Savings and Loan Hell: The People and the Politics Behind the $1 Trillion Savings and Loan Scandal.* New York: W.W. Norton and Company, 1993.

Derber, Charles. *Corporation Nation.* New York: St. Martin's Press, 1998.

Dobbin, Murray. *The Myth of the Good Corporate Citizen: Democracy Under the Rule of Big Business.* Toronto: Stoddard, 1998.

Dolny, Michael. "Think Tanks: The Rich Get Richer." *Extra!.* May/June 2000. Available at http://www.fair.org/extra/0005/think-tanks-survey.html.

Domhoff, G. William. *State Autonomy or Class Dominance?: Case Studies on Policy Making in America.* Hawthorne, NY: Aldine de Gruyter, 1996.

Domhoff, G. William. *Who Rules America? Power and Politics.* 4th ed. Boston: McGraw Hill, 2002.

Domhoff, G. William. *Who Rules America? Power and Politics in the Year 2000.* Mountain View, CA: Mayfield Publishing Company, 1998.

Doremus, Paul, et al. *The Myth of the Global Corporation,* Princeton, NJ: Princeton University Press, 1998.

Dowd, Douglas. *Capitalism and Its Economics: A Critical History.* London: Pluto Press, 2000.

Dowd, Douglas. *U.S. Capitalist Development Since 1776: Of, By, and For Which People?* Armonk, NY: M.E. Sharpe, 1993.

Dowie, Mark. *Losing Ground: American Environmentalism at the Close of the Twentieth Century.* Cambridge, MA: MIT Press, 1995.

Draffan, George. *The Elite Consensus: When Corporations Wield the Constitution.* New York: The Apex Press, 2003.

Dreier, Peter. "The New Politics of Housing." *Journal of American Planning Association.* Vol. 63 No.1. Winter 1997.

Drinnon, Richard. *The Metaphysics of Indian-Hating and Empire-Building.* Minneapolis: University of Minnesota Press, 1980.

Du Boff, Richard. *Accumulation and Power: An Economic History of the United States.* Armonk, NY: M.E. Sharpe, 1989.

Du Bois, W.E.B. *Black Reconstruction in America: An Essay Toward a History of the Part Which Black Folk Played in the Attempt to Reconstruct Democracy in America, 1860–1880.* New York: Atheneum, 1977.

Dujon, Diane and Ann Withhorn. *For Crying Out Loud: Women's Poverty in the United States.* Boston: South End Press, 1996.

Durning, Alan Thein. *How Much Is Enough: The Consumer Society and the Future of the Earth.* New York: W.W. Norton, 1992.

Dye, Thomas R. *Top Down Policymaking.* New York: Chatham House/Seven Bridges, 2001.

Dye, Thomas R. *Who's Running America: The Bush Restoration.* 7th ed. Upper Saddle River, NJ: Prentice Hall, 2002.

Edney, Hazel Trice. "Black Voters Ready to 'Get Even' for 2000 Fiasco. December 23, 2003. Available at http://blackpressusa.com/news.

Ehrenreich, Barbara. *Fear of Falling: The Inner Life of the Middle Class.* New York: HarperCollins, 1990.

Ehrenreich, Barbara. *Nickel and Dimed: On (Not) Getting by in America.* New York: Metropolitan, 2002.

Engler, Ives. "Selling Drugs: Capitalist healthcare." *Z Magazine.* April 2003.

Enloe, Cynthia. *Bananas, Beaches and Bases: Making Feminist Sense of International Politics.* Berkeley, CA: University of California Press, 1990.

Enloe, Cynthia. *Maneuvers: The International Politics of Militarizing Women's Lives.* Berkeley, CA: University of California Press, 2000.

Ewen, Stuart. *Advertising and the Social Roots of the Consumer Culture.* New York: McGraw-Hill, 1976.

Ezorsky, Gertrude. *Racism and Justice: The Case for Affirmative Action.* Ithaca, NY: Cornell University Press, 1991.

Feagin, Joe R. *Racist America: Roots, Current Realities, & Future Reparations.* New York: Routledge, 2001.

Feagin, Joe R. and Vera Hernan. *White Racism: The Basics.* New York: Routledge, 1995.

Flounders, Sara. "Massacre in Jenin: Human Rights Watch & the Stage-Management of Imperialism." *CovertAction Quarterly* #74. Fall, 2002.

Fones-Wolf, Elizabeth A. *Selling Free Enterprise: The Business Assault on Labor and Liberalism 1945-60.* Urbana, IL: University of Illinois Press, 1994.

Francis, Diane. *Controlling Interest: Who Owns Canada?* Toronto: Macmillan of Canada, 1986.

Frank, Robert. *Luxury Fever: Why Money Fails to Satisfy in an Era of Excess.* New York: Free Press, 1999.

Franklin, Raymond S. *Shadows of Race and Class.* Minneapolis: University of Minnesota Press, 1991.

Freire, Paulo. *Pedagogy of the Oppressed.* New York: Continuum, 1970.

Frye, Marilyn. *The Politics of Reality: Essays in Feminist Theory.* Freedom, CA: Crossing Press, 1983.

Frye, Marilyn. *Willful Virgin: Essays in Feminism.* Freedom, CA: Crossing Press, 1992.

Fussell, Paul. *Class: A Guide Through the American Status System.* New York: Summit Books, 1983.

Gates, Jeff. *Democracy at Risk: Rescuing Main Street from Wall Street.* Cambridge, MA: Perseus Books, 2000.

Gatto, John Taylor. *Dumbing Us Down: The Hidden Curriculum of Compulsory Schooling.* Gabriola Island, BC: New Society, 1992.

Gibson-Graham, J.K. *The End of Capitalism (as We Knew It): A Feminist Critique of Political Economy.* Cambridge, MA: Blackwell Publishers, 1996.

Glassner, Barry. *The Culture of Fear: Why Americans Are Afraid of the Wrong Things.* New York: Basic Books, 1999.

Goldfield, Michael. *The Color of Politics: Race and the Mainsprings of American Politics.* New York: New Press, 1997.

Goodman, Robert. *The Luck Business: The Devastating Consequences and Broken Promises of America's Gambling Explosion.* New York: Free Press, 1995.

Gordon, Linda. *Heroes of Their Own Lives: The Politics and History of Family Violence.* New York: Penguin Books, 1988.

Gramsci, Antonio. *Selections from the Prison Notebooks.* New York: International Publishers, 1971.

Greider, Katharine. *The Big Fix: How the Pharmaceutical Industry Rips Off American Consumers.* (NP):Public Affairs, 2003.

Greider, William. *One World, Ready or Not: The Manic Logic of Global Capitalism.* New York: Simon & Schuster, 1997.

Greider, William. *Secrets of the Temple: How the Federal Reserve Runs the Country.* New York: Simon & Schuster, 1989.

Greider, William. *Who Will Tell the People: The Betrayal of American Democracy.* New York: Simon & Schuster, 1993.

Grossman, Richard and Frank T. Adams. *Taking Care of Business: Citizenship and the Charter of Incorporation.* Cambridge, MA: Charter, Ink., 1995.

Guinier, Lani. "Making Every Vote Count." December 4, 2000. Available at http://www.thenation.com/doc.mhtml?i=20001204&s-guinier.

Guinier, Lani. *The Tyranny of the Majority: Fundamental Fairness and Representative Democracy.* New York: Free Press, 1994.

Hacker, Andrew. *Money: Who Has How Much and Why.* New York: Touchstone, 1997.

Hacker, Andrew. *Two Nations: Black and White, Separate, Hostile, Unequal.* New York: Ballantine, 1992.

Hahnel, Robin. *Panic Rules: Everything You Need to Know About the Global Economy.* Cambridge, MA: South End Press, 1999.

Hall, Peter Dobkin. *Inventing the Nonprofit Sector and Other Essays on Philanthropy, Voluntarism, and Nonprofit Organizations.* Baltimore: John Hopkins University Press, 2002.

Halloran, Richard. "What Price U.S. Patrols in the Gulf." *New York Times.* February 21, 1988.

Hammack, David C., ed. *Making the Nonprofit Sector in the United States: A Reader.* Bloomington, IN: Indiana University Press, 1998.

Hansen, Karen V. and Ilene J. Philipson, eds. *Women, Class, and the Feminist Imagination: A Socialist-Feminist Reader.* Philadelphia: Temple University Press, 1990.

Haq, M. Emdad-ul. *Drugs in South Asia: From the Opium Trade to the Present Day.* New York: St. Martin's, 2000.

Hartman, Chester. *Double Exposure: Poverty and Race in America.* Armonk, NY: M. E. Sharpe, 1997.

Hartmann, Thom. *Unequal Protection: The Rise of Corporate Dominance and the Theft of Human Rights.* New York: Rodale, 2002.

Hawks, John. *For a Good Cause? — How Charitable Institutions Become Powerful Economic Bullies.* Secaucus NJ: Birch Lane Press (Carol Publishing Group), 1997.

Heberling, Michael. "State Lotteries: Advocating a Social Ill for the Social Good." Available at http://www.independent.org/tii/media/pdf/tir64heberling.pdf.

Heintz, James and Nancy Folbre. *The Ultimate Field Guide to the U.S. Economy.* New York: The New Press, 2000.

Hennessy, Rosemary. *Profit and Pleasure: Sexual Identities in Late Capitalism.* New York: Routledge, 2000.

Henwood, Doug. *After the New Economy.* New York: The New Press, 2003

Henwood, Doug. *WALL Street: How It Works and for Whom.* London: Verso, 1998.

Herman, Edward S. *The Myth of the Liberal Media: An Edward Herman Reader.* New York: Peter Lang Publishing, 1999.

Herman, Edward S. and Noam Chomsky. *Manufacturing Consent: The Political Economy of the Mass Media.* New York: Pantheon, 2002.

Herman, Edward S. and Robert W. McChesney. *The Global Media: The New Missionaries of Global Capitalism.* London: Cassell Academic, 1998.

Higham, Charles. *Trading With the Enemy: An Expose of the Nazi-American Money Plot 1933-1949.* New York: Dell, 1984.

Himmelstein, Jerome L. *Looking Good and Doing Good: Corporate Philanthropy and Corporate Power.* Urbana, IN: Indiana University Press, 1997.

Hochschild, Arlie Russell and Anne Machung. *The Second Shift.* New York: Avon Books, 1997.

Hooks, Bell. *Where We Stand: Class Matters.* New York: Routledge, 2000.

Horne, Gerald. *Reversing Discrimination: The Case for Affirmative Action.* New York: International Publishers, 1992.

Howard, Ina. "Power Sources: On Party, Gender, Race and Class, TV News Looks to the Most Powerful Groups." *Extra!,* May-June 2002. Available at http://www.fair.org/extra/0205/power_sources.html.

Hughes, Langston. *The Ways of White Folks.* New York: Vintage Books, 1990.

Human Rights Watch. *Unfair Advantage: Workers' Freedom of Association in the United States Under International Human Rights Standards.* Washington, DC: Human Rights Watch, 2000.

Hurtado, Aida. *The Color of Privilege: Three Blasphemies on Race and Feminism.* Ann Arbor, MI: The University of Michigan Press, 1996.

Jacobs, Harvey, ed. *Who Owns America: Social Conflict Over Property Rights.* Madison, WI: University of Wisconsin Press, 1998.

Jacobson, David, ed. *The Immigration Reader: American in a Multidisciplinary Perspective.* Malden, MA: Blackwell, 1998.

Jaimes, M. Annette, ed. *The State of Native America: Genocide, Colonization, and Resistance.* Boston: South End Press, 1992.

James, Joy. *Resisting State Violence: Radicalism, Gender, and Race in U.S. Culture.* Minneapolis: University of Minnesota Press, 1996.

Jenkins, Lizzie. *The Real Rosewood, Volume I.* (NP): BookEnds Press, 2003.

Jennings, Francis. *The Invasion of America: Indians, Colonialism, and the Cant of Conquest.* New York: Norton, 1975.

Jensen, Derrick. *A Language Older Than Words.* New York: Context, 2000.

Jensen, Derrick. *The Culture of Make Believe.* New York: Context, 2002.

Jensen, Derrick, et al. *Railroads and Clearcuts: Legacy of Congress's 1864 Northern Pacific Railroad Land Grant.* (np): Keokee Co. Pub, 1995.

Jensen, Robert. "Rape is Normal?" *Znet Commentaries.* October 8, 2002. Available at http://www.zmag.org/sustainers/content/2002-10/08jensen.cfm.

Johnson, Allan G. *The Gender Knot: Unraveling Our Patriarchal Legacy.* Philadelphia: Temple University Press, 1997.

Johnson, Allan G. *Privilege, Power, and Difference.* Toronto: Mayfield Publishing, 2001.

Johnston, David Cay. *Perfectly Legal: The Covert Campaign to Rig Our Tax System to Benefit the Super Rich—and Cheat Everybody Else.* (np) Portfolio, 2003.

Jones, Ellis, et al. *The Better World Handbook: From Good Intentions to Everyday Actions.* Gabriola Island, BC: New Society, 2002.

Kadi, Joanna. *Thinking Class: Sketches from a Cultural Worker.* Boston: South End, 1996.

Kaplan, Jeffrey. "The Birth of the White Corporation." *Poverty & Race.* September/October 2003. Vol. 12, No. 5.

Kaufman, Cynthia. *Ideas for Action: Relevant Theory for Radical Change.* Cambridge, MA: South End Press, 2003.

Kaye/Kantrowitz, Melanie. *The Issue Is Power: Essays on Women, Jews, Violence and Resistance.* San Francisco: Aunt Lute Books, 1992.

Keister, Lisa A. *Wealth in America: Trends in Wealth Inequality.* Cambridge, England: Cambridge University Press, 2000.

Kellman, Peter. *Building Unions: Past, Present, and Future.* New York: The Apex Press, 2001.

Kelly, Charles M. *Class War in America: How Economic and Political Conservatives Are Exploiting Low- and Middle-Income Americans.* Santa Barbara, CA: Fithian Press, 2000.

Kelly, Marjorie. *The Divine Right of Capital: Dethroning the Corporate Aristocracy.* San Francisco: Berrett-Koehler, 2001.

Kendall, Diana. *The Power of Good Deeds: Privileged Women and the Social Reproduction of the Upper Class.* Lanham, MD: Rowman & Littlefield, 2002.

Kennickell, Arthur B. *A Rolling Tide: Changes in the Distribution of Wealth in the U.S., 1989-2001.* Washington, DC: Federal Reserve Board, 2003. Available at http://www.federalreserve.gov/pubs/oss/oss2/papers/concentration.2001.9.pdf.

Kerbo, Harold R. *Social Stratification and Inequality.* Boston: McGraw Hill, 2000.

Kimmel, Michael S. and Abby L. Ferber, eds. *Privilege: A Reader.* Boulder, CO: Westview, 2003.

Kivel, Paul. *Men's Work: How to Stop the Violence that Tears Our Lives Apart.* Rev. ed. Center City, MN: Hazelden, 1998.

Kivel, Paul. *Uprooting Racism: How White People Can Work for Racial Justice.* Rev. ed. Gabriola Island, BC: New Society Publishers, 2002.

Kohn, Alfie. *No Contest: The Case Against Competition.* Boston: Houghton Mifflin, 1986.

Kolko, Gabriel. *The Triumph of Conservatism: A Re-interpretation of American History, 1900-1916.* Reissue, New York: Free Press, 1985.

Korten, David. *Globalizing Civil Society: Reclaiming Our Right to Power.* New York: Seven Stories Press, 1998.

Korten, David. *When Corporations Rule the World.* West Hartford, CT: Kumarian Press, 1996.

Koughan, Martin. "Easy Money." *Mother Jones Magazine.* July/August, 1997. Available at http://www.motherjones.com/coinop_congress/easy-money/koughan_jump.html.

Kozol, Jonathan. *Savage Inequalities: Children in America's Schools.* New York: HarperCollins, 1991.

Labrousse, Alain, et al. *The World Geopolitics of Drugs.* Kluwer Academic Publishers, 2002.

Lapham, Lewis. *Money and Class in America.* New York: Weidenfeld and Nicolson, 1988.

Leondar-Wright, Betsy. "Federal Reserve: Racial Wealth Gap Has Grown." March 7, 2003. Article can be found at www.unitedforafaireconomy.org/research/RWG/SCF_Race_2003.html.

Levins-Morales, Aurora. *Medicine Stories: History, Culture, and the Politics of Integrity.* Cambridge, MA: South End Press, 1998.

Lewis, Charles, et al. *The Cheating of America: How Tax Avoidance and Evasion by the Super Rich Are Costing the Country Billions—and What You Can Do About It.* New York: William Morrow, 2001.

Lieberman, Trudy. "Social Insecurity: The Campaign to Take the System Private." *Nation.* January 27, 1997.

Lipsitz, George. *The Possessive Investment in Whiteness: How White People Profit from Identity Politics.* Philadelphia: Temple University Press, 1998.

Lopez, Ian F.H. *White by Law: The Legal Construction of Race.* New York: New York University Press, 1999.

Lorde, Audre. *Sister Outsider: Essays and Speeches.* Freedom, CA: Crossing Press, 1984.

Lowe, Marian and Ruth Hubbard, eds. *Woman's Nature: Rationalizations of Inequality.* New York: Pergamon Press, 1983.

Lowen, James W. *Lies My Teacher Told Me: Everything Your American History Textbook Got Wrong.* New York: New Press, 1995.

Lubbers, Eveline, ed. *Battling Big Business.* Monroe, ME: Common Courage, 2002.

Lundberg, Ferdinand. *The Rich and the Super-Rich.* New York: Bantam, 1968.

Makinson, Larry. *Speaking Freely: Washington Insiders Talk About Money in Politics.* 2nd ed. Washington, DC: Center for Responsive Politics, 2003.

Mantsios, George. "Race, Class and Gender in the U.S." in Rothenburg, Paula S. *Race, Class, and Gender in the United States: An Integrated Study.* 4th edition. New York: St. Martins, 1998.

Marable, Manning. *The Crisis of Color and Democracy: Essays on Race, Class and Power.* Monroe, ME: Common Courage Press, 1992.

Martinez, Elizabeth. *De Colores Means All of Us: Latina Views for a Multi-Colored Century.* Cambridge, MA: South End Press, 1998.

McChesney, Robert. *Corporate Media and the Threat to Democracy.* New York: Seven Stories Press, 1997.

McCoy, Alfred W. *The Politics of Heroin: CIA Complicity in the Global Drug Trade.* Brooklyn, NY: Lawrence Hill, 1991.

McIntosh, Peggy. *White Privilege and Male Privilege: A Personal Account of Coming to See Correspondences Through Work in Women's Studies.* Wellesley, MA: Wellesley College, Center for Research on Women, 1988.

McIntyre, Robert S., et al. *Who Pays: A Distributional Analysis of the Tax System of all Fifty States,* 2nd edition. Washington, DC: The Institute on Taxation & Economic Policy, 2003. Available at http://www.itepnet.org/wp2000/text.pdf.

McKinson, Larry. *Speaking Freely: Washington Insiders Talk About Money in Politics.* Washington, DC: Center for Responsive Politics, 2002.

Mehri, Cyrus and Steven Berk. "Stock Option Equity: Building Democracy While Building Wealth." *Labor & Corporate Governance.* Vol. V, Issue #7.

Meier, Matt and Feliciano Rivera. *The Chicanos: A History of Mexican Americans.* New York: Hill and Wang, 1972.

Memmi, Albert. *The Colonizer and the Colonized.* Translated by Howard Greenfield. Boston: Beacon Press, 1965.

Mies, Maria. *Patriarchy and Accumulation on a World Scale: Women in the International Division of Labour.* London: Zed Books, 1986.

Mies, Maria, et al. *Women: The Last Colony.* London: Zed Books, 1988.

Mills, C. Wright. *The Power Elite.* Oxford: Oxford University Press, 1956.

Mills, Charles Wade. *The Racial Contract.* Ithaca, NY: Cornell University Press, 1999.

Mills, Nicolaus. *Debating Affirmative Action: Race, Gender, Ethnicity, and the Politics of Inclusion.* New York: Delta, 1994.

Mintz, Beth and Michael Schwartz. *The Power Structure of American Business.* Chicago: University of Chicago Press, 1985.

Mishel, Lawrence, et al. *The State of Working America, 1996/1997.* Ithaca, NY: Cornell University Press, 1997.

Mishel, Lawrence, et al. *The State of Working America, 2002/2003.* Ithaca, NY: Cornell University Press, 2003.

Mitchell, Peter R. and John Schoeffel, eds. *Understanding Power: The Indispensable Chomsky.* New York: The New Press, 2002.

Mogil, Christopher, et al. *We Gave Away A Fortune.* Philadelphia: New Society, 1992.

Mokhiber and Weissman. *Corporate Predators: The Hunt for Mega-Profits and the Attack on Democracy.* Monroe, ME: Common Courage, 1999.

Monbiot, George. *The Age of Consent: A Manifesto for a New World Order.* London: Pan Macmillan, 2003.

Monbiot, George. *Captive State: The Corporate Takeover of Britain.* London: Pan Macmillan, 2000.

Moore, Michael. *Stupid White Men…and Other Sorry Excuses for the State of the Nation!* London: Penguin Books, 2001.

Moraga, Cherrie and Gloria Anzaldua, eds. *This Bridge Called My Back: Writings by Radical Women of Color.* New York: Kitchen Table—Women of Color Press, 1981.

Morrison, Toni, ed. *Race-ing Justice, En-gendering Power: Essays on Anita Hill, Clarence Thomas, and the Construction of Social Reality.* New York: Pantheon, 1992.

Multistate Tax Coalition. "Corporate Tax Sheltering and the Impact on State Corporate Income Tax Revenue Collection." July 15, 2003. Available at http://www.mtc.gov/TaxShelterRpt.pdf.

Nace Ted. *Gangs of America: The Rise of Corporate Power and the Disabling of Democracy.* San Francisco: Berrett-Koehler, 2003.

Nader, Ralph, ed. *The Case Against Free Trade: Gatt, Nafta, and the Globalization of Corporate Power.* Berkeley, CA: North Atlantic Books, 1993.

National Committee for Responsive Philanthropy. *$1 Billion for Ideas: Conservative Think Tanks in the 1990s.* Washington, DC: National Committee for Responsive Philanthropy, 1999.

National Council of Nonprofit Associations, "The United States Nonprofit Sector 2001." Washington, DC: National Council of Nonprofit Associations, 2001. Available at http://www.ncna.org/_uploads/documents/live//us.nonprofit.sector.report.pdf.

Nicols, John, et al. *Our Media, Not Theirs: The Democratic Struggle Against Corporate Media.* New York: Seven Stories Press, 2002.

Novick, Michael. *White Lies White Power: The Fight Against White Supremacy and Reactionary Violence.* Monroe, ME: Common Courage Press, 1995.

Odendahl, Teresa. *Charity Begins at Home: Generosity and Self-interest Among the Philanthropic Elite.* New York: Basic Books, 1990.

Okihiro, Gary Y. *Margins and Mainstreams: Asians in American History and Culture.* Seattle: University of Washington Press, 1994.

Oliver, Melvin L. and Thomas M. Shapiro. *Black Wealth/White Wealth: A New Perspective on Racial Inequality.* New York: Routledge, 1995.

Packard, Vance. *The Ultra Rich: How Much Is Too Much?* Boston: Little, Brown and Company, 1989.

Palast, Greg. *The Best Democracy Money Can Buy: An Investigative Reporter Exposes the Truth About Corporate Cons, Globalization and High Finance Fraudsters.* London: Pluto Press, 2002.

Parenti, Michael. *America Besieged.* San Francisco: City Lights Books, 1998.

Parenti, Michael. *Democracy for the Few.* New York: St. Martin's Press, 1988.

Parenti, Michael. *Dirty Truths: Reflections on Politics, Media, Ideology, Conspiracy, Ethnic Life and Class Power.* San Francisco: City Lights Books, 1996.

Parenti, Michael. *History As Mystery.* San Francisco: City Lights Books, 1999.

Parenti, Michael. "Monopoly Media Manipulation." May 2001. Available at http://www.michaelparenti.org/MonopolyMedia.html.

Pariser, Eli. "American Kleptocracy." *MoveOn Bulletin.* July 31, 2002. Available at http://www.moveon.org/moveonbulletin/.

Parker, Richard. *The Myth of the Middle Class: Notes on Affluence and Equality.* New York: Harper Colophon, 1972.

Pateman, Carole. *The Sexual Contract.* Stanford, CA: Stanford University Press, 1988.

Penelope, Julia. *Out of the Class Closet: Lesbians Speak.* Freedom, CA: The Crossing Press, 1994.

Perlo, Victor. *Economics of Racism, I and II.* New York: International Publishers, 1996.

Perucci, Robert and Earl Wysong. *The New Class Society: Goodbye American Dream,* 2nd Edition. Lanham, MD: Roman & Littlefield Publishers, 2003.

Petras, James and Henry Veltmeyer. *Globalization Unmasked: Imperialism in the 21st Century.* London: Zed Books, 2001.

Pharr, Susanne. *In the Time of the Right: Reflections on Liberation.* Berkeley, CA: Chardon Press, 1996.

Phillips, Kevin. *Arrogant Capital: Washington, Wall Street, and the Frustration of American Politics.* New York: Harper Perennial, 1994.

Phillips, Kevin. *Wealth and Democracy: A Political History of the American Rich.* New York: Broadway Books, 2002.

Piven, Frances Fox and Richard A. Cloward. *Poor People's Movements: How They Succeed, Why They Fail.* New York: Vintage, 1979.

Piven, Frances Fox and Richard A. Cloward. *Regulating the Poor: The Functions of Public Welfare.* New York: Vintage Books, 1971.

Pizzigati, Sam. "America's Revolutionary-in-Chief." *Too Much.* (The Apex Press) Spring 2003.

Pizzigati, Sam. "How Big Will Your Inheritance Be?" *Too Much.* (The Apex Press) Winter 2001.

Pizzo, Stephen et al. *Inside Job: The Looting of America's Savings and Loans.* New York: McGraw Hill, 1989.

Poppendieck, Janet. *Sweet Charity?: Emergency Food and the End of Entitlement.* New York: Penguin, 1998.

Pozner, Jennifer. "Power Shortage for Media Women." *EXTRA!* July-August 2001.

Pratt, Minnie Bruce. *Rebellion: Essays 1980–1991.* Ithaca, NY: Firebrand Books, 1991.

Press, Eyal. "Spin Cities." *Nation.* November 18, 1996.

Project Censored. *The Progressive Guide to Alternative Media and Activism: Project Censored.* New York: Seven Stories Press, 1999.

Public Health and Labor Institutes. *Corporate Power and the American Dream.* New York: The Apex Press, 1997.

Public Policy and Education Fund of New York. "Capital Investments, Capital Returns: Corporate Tax Breaks and Campaign Contributions to Governor Pataki and the New York State Legislature, 1999-2001." Albany, NY: Citizen Action New York, March 2002. Available at http://www.citizenactionny.org/taxcuts.pdf.

Raffo, Susan, Ed. *Queerly Classed: Gay Men & Lesbians Write about Class.* Boston: South End Press, 1997.

Rampton, Sheldon and John Stauber. *Trust Us, We're Experts!—How Industry Manipulates Science and Gambles with Your Future.* New York: Tarcher/Putnam, 2001.

Reed, Adolph. *Class Notes: Posing as Politics and Other Thoughts on the American Scene.* New York: The New Press, 2001.

Reich, Robert, *The Work of Nations.* New York: Alfred A. Knopf, 1991.

Richie, Beth E. *Compelled to Crime: The Gender Entrapment of Battered Black Women.* New York: Routledge, 1996.

Ritz, Dean. ed. *Defying Corporations, Defining Democracy: A Book of History and Strategy.* New York: The Apex Press, 2001.

Robinson, Randall. *The Debt: What America Owes to Blacks.* New York: Plume, 2000.

Rodney, Walter. *How Europe Underdeveloped Africa.* Washington, DC: Howard University Press, 1982.

Roediger, David R. *Towards the Abolition of Whiteness.* London: Verso, 1994.

Roediger, David R. *The Wages of Whiteness: Race and the Making of the American Working Class.* London: Verso, 1991.

Roediger, David R. ed. *Black on White: Black Writers on What It Means to Be White.* New York: Schocken Books, 1998.

Roelofs, Joan. *Foundations and Public Policy: The Mask of Pluralism.* Albany, NY: State University of New York, 2003.

Roelofs, Joan. "Foundations and Social Change Organizations: the Mask of Pluralism," *Insurgent Sociologist,* (nd).

Roelofs, Joan. "The Third Sector as a Protective Layer for Capitalism." Monthly Review. September 1995.

Rose, Fred. *Coalitions Across the Class Divide: Lessons from the Labor, Peace, and Environmental Movements.* Ithaca, NY: Cornell University Press, 2000.

Ross Sr., Robert Gaylon. *Who's Who of the Elite: Members of the Bilderbergs, Council on Foreign Relations, & Trilateral Commission.* 3rd rev. edition. Spicewood, TX: RIE, 2002.

Rossides, Daniel. *The American Class System.* Boston: Houghton Mifflin, 1976.

Rothenberg, Paula S. *Race, Class, and Gender in the United States: An Integrated Study.* 4th edition. New York: St. Martin's Press, 1998.

Rubin, Lillian B. *Families on the Fault Line.* New York: HarperCollins, 1994.

Rubin, Lillian B. *Worlds of Pain: Life in the Working Class.* New York: Basic Books, 1976.

Ryan, Mike, et al. *Corporate Strategy, Public Policy and the Fortune 500: How America's Major Corporations Influence Government.* Oxford: Blackwell, 1987.

Ryan, William. *Blaming the Victim.* New York: Pantheon Books, 1971.

Said, Edward. *Covering Islam: How the Media and the Experts Determine How We See the Rest of the World.* New York: Vintage, 1981, 1997.

Said, Edward. *Orientalism.* New York: Random House, 1978.

Schmidt, Jeff. *Disciplined Minds: A Critical Look at Salaried Professionals and the Soul-battering System that Shapes Their Lives.* Lanham, MD: Rowman & Littlefield, 2000.

Schor, Juliet B. *The Overspent American: Upscaling, Downshifting, and the New Consumer.* New York: Basic Books, 1998.

Schor, Juliet B. *The Overworked American: The Unexpected Decline of Leisure.* New York: Basic Books, 1992.

Schwartz, John E. and Thomas J. Volgy. *The Forgotten Americans: Thirty Million Working Poor in the Land of Opportunity.* New York: W.W. Norton, 1992.

Sclar, Elliott D. and Richard C. Leone. *You Don't Always Get What You Pay For: The Economics of Privatization.* Ithaca, NY: Cornell University Press, 2000.

Scott, Peter Dale. *Drugs, Oil, and War: The United States in Afghanistan, Colombia, and Indochina.* Lanham, MD: Rowman & Littlefield, 2003.

Scott, Peter Dale and Jonathan Marshall. *Cocaine Politics: Drugs, Armies, and the CIA in Central America.* Berkeley, CA: University of California Press, 1991.

Seabrook, Jeremy. *The No-nonsense Guide to Class, Caste & Hierarchies.* London: New Internationalist Publications/Verso, 2002.

Sen, Rinku and Kim Klein. *Stir It Up: Lessons in Community Organizing and Advocacy.* San Francisco: Jossey-Bass, 2003.

Sennett, Richard and Jonathan Cobb. *The Hidden Injuries of Class.* New York: Vintage Books, 1972.

Shapiro, Issac and Robert Greenstein. "The Widening Income Gulf." Washington, DC: Center on Budget and Policy Priorities, September 1999.

Shapiro, Thomas A., ed. *Great Divides: Readings in Social Inequality in the U.S.* 2nd edition. Boston: McGraw Hill, 2000.

Shapiro, Thomas M. *The Hidden Cost of Being African American: How Wealth Perpetuates Inequality.* Oxford: Oxford University Press, 2004.

Shoup, Laurence. "Behind the Bipartisan Drive Toward War: The Council on Foreign Relations and the U.S. Invasion of Iraq." *Z Magazine.* March 2003.

Shoup, Lawrence and William Minter. *Imperial Brain Trust: The Council on Foreign Relations and U.S. Foreign Policy.* New York: Monthly Review Press, 1977.

Sivanandan A. *Communities of Resistance: Writing on Black Struggles for Socialism.* London: Verso, 1990.

Silverstein, Ken. "Trillion-Dollar Hideaway." *Mother Jones.* November/December 2000. Available at www.motherjones.com/mother_jones/ND00/offshore.html.

Silverstein, Ken. *Washington on $10 Million a Day: How Lobbyists Plunder the Nation.* Monroe ME: Common Courage Press, 1998.

Sklair, Leslie. *The Transnational Capitalist Class.* Oxford: Blackwell, 2001.

Sklar, Holly. *Chaos or Community? Seeking Solutions, Not Scapegoats for Bad Economics.* Boston: South End Press, 1995.

Sklar, Holly. "Imagine a Country, Reprise." *Z Magazine.* May 2003.

Slater, Philip. *Wealth Addiction.* New York: E.P. Dutton, 1983.

Soley, Lawrence. "The Invisible Gag." *Dollars & Sense.* May/June 2003.

Solomon, Norman and Jeff Cohen. *Wizards of Media Oz: Behind the Curtain of Mainstream News.* Monroe, ME: Common Courage Press, 1997.

Stanley, Thomas J. and William D. Danko. *The Millionaire Next Door: The Surprising Secrets of America's Wealthy.* Atlanta: Longstreet Press, 1996.

Stauber, John and Sheldon Rampton. *Toxic Sludge Is Good for You.* Monroe, ME: Common Courage Press, 1995.

Steinem, Gloria. "The Feminist To-Do List." *Ms. Magazine.* Spring, 2003, 51.

Stout, Linda. *Bridging the Class Divide and Other Lessons for Grassroots Organizing.* Boston: Beacon Press, 1996.

Street, Paul. "Labor Day Reflections: Time as a Democracy Issue." *ZNet Commentaries.* September 3, 2002. Available at http://www.zmag.org/sustainers/content/2002-09/03street.cfm.

Stretton, Hugh. *Economics: A New Introduction.* London: Pluto Press, 1999.

Swerdlow, Amy and Hanna Lessingler, eds. *Class, Race, and Sex.* Boston: G.K. Hall, 1983.

Takaki, Ronald. *A Different Mirror: A History of Multicultural America.* Boston: Little, Brown and Company, 1993.

Takaki, Ronald. *Strangers from a Different Shore: A History of Asian Americans.* New York: Penguin, 1989.

Takaki, Ronald, ed. *From Different Shores: Perspectives on Race and Ethnicity in America.* New York: Oxford University Press, 1987.

Tawney, R.H. *Religion and the Rise of Capitalism.* New York: Harcourt, Brace, 1926.

Teixeira, Ruy and Joel Rogers. *America's Forgotten Majority: Why the White Working Class Still Matters.* New York: Basic Books, 2001.

Tolley, Howard Jr. *Children and War: Political Socialization to International Conflict.* New York: Teachers College Press, 1973.

Torres, Rodolfo D., et al. *Race, Identity, and Citizenship: A Reader.* Malden, MA: Blackwell, 1999.

Tuan, Mia. *Forever Foreigners or Honorary Whites?: The Asian Ethnic Experience Today.* New Brunswick, NJ: Rutgers University Press, 1998.

Tye, Larry. *The Father of Spin: Edward L. Bernays and the Birth of Public Relations.* New York: Crown Publishers, 1998.

United for a Fair Economy. "Born on Third Base: The Sources of Wealth of the 1997 Forbes 400." Boston, MA: United for a Fair Economy, October 1997.

Useem, Michael. *The Inner Circle.* New York: Oxford University Press, 1984.

Vanneman, Reeve and Lynn Weber Cannon. *The American Perception of Class.* Philadelphia: Temple University Press, 1987.

Wagner, David. *What's Love Got to Do with It?: A Critical Look at American Charity.* New York: The New Press, 2000.

Walkowitz, Daniel J. *Working With Class: Social Workers and the Politics of Middle-Class Identity.* Chapel Hill, NC: University of North Carolina Press, 1998.

Ware, Vron. *Beyond the Pale: White Women, Racism and History.* London: Verso, 1992.

Waring, Marilyn. *Counting for Nothing: What Men Value and What Women Are Worth.* Toronto: University of Toronto Press, 1999.

Waring, Marilyn. *If Women Counted: A New Feminist Economics.* San Francisco: HarperCollins, 1988.

Weatherford, Jack. *Indian Givers: How the Indians of the Americas Transformed the World.* New York: Fawcett Columbine, 1988.

Weisbrot, Mark "Labor Day 2003: Nothing to Celebrate." *ZNet Commentary,* August 31, 2003. Available at http://www.zmag.org/sustainers/content/2003-08/31weisbrot.cfm.

Wilayto, Phil. "The Lynde and Harry Bradley Foundation." Available at http://www.mediatransparency.org/funders/bradley_foundation.htm.

Withorn, Ann. *Serving the People: Social Services and Social Change.* New York: Columbia University Press, 1984.

Wolff, Edward N. *Top Heavy: The Increasing Inequality of Wealth in America and What Can Be Done about It.* New York: The New Press, 1996/2002.

Zarembo, Alan. "Funding Studies to Suit Need." *Los Angeles Times.* December 3, 2003.

Zepezauer, Mark and Arthur Naiman. *Take the Rich Off Welfare,* new edition. Tucson, AZ: Odonia Press, 2004.

Zinn, Howard. *The People's History of the United States.* Rev. edition. New York: HarperCollins, 1995.

Zweig, Michael. *The Working Class Majority: America's Best Kept Secret.* Ithaca, NY: Cornell University Press, 2001.

Zweigenhaft, Richard L. and William G. Domhoff. *Blacks in the White Establishment? A Study of Race and Class in America.* New Haven, CT: Yale University Press, 1991.

Zweigenhaft, Richard L. and William G. Domhoff. *Diversity in the Power Elite: Have Women and Minorities Reached the Top?* New Haven, CT: Yale University Press, 1998.

BOOKS ABOUT ALTERNATIVES
TO GLOBALIZATION

Albert, Michael. *The Trajectory of Change: Activist Strategies for Social Transformation.* Cambridge, MA: South End Press, 2002.

Bennholdt-Thomsen, Veronika, et al., eds. *There Is an Alternative: Subsistence and Worldwide Resistance to Corporate Globalization.* London: Zed, 2001.

Brecher, Jeremy, et al., *Globalization from Below.* Boston: South End, 2000.

Brunelle, Dorval. *Alternative to Globalization: A Better World Is Possible.* Montreal: Black Rose Books, 2003.

Burton-Rose, Daniel, et al., eds. *Confronting Capitalism: Dispatches from a Global Movement.* New York: Soft Skull, 2003.

Danaher, Kevin and Roger Burbach, eds. *Globalize This!: The Battle Against the World Trade Organization and Corporate Rule.* Monroe, ME: Common Courage, 2000.

Danaher, Kevin and Jason Mark. *Insurrection: Citizen Challenges to Global Power.* New York: Routledge, 2001.

Fisher, William F. and Thomas Pommah, eds. *Another World Is Possible: Popular Alternatives to Globalization at the World Social Forum.* London: Zed Books, 2003.

The International Forum on Globalization. *Alternatives to Economic Globalization: A Better World Is Possible.* San Francisco: Barrett-Koehler, 2002.

Madeley, John. *A People's World: Alternatives to Economic Globalization.* London: Zed Books, 2004.

Mander, Jerry, et al. *The Case Against the Global Economy: And for a Turn Toward the Local.* San Francisco: Sierra Club Books, 1997.

Mertes, Tom, et al., eds. *The Movement of Movements: A Reader.* London: Verso, 2004.

Nancy A. Naples and Manisha Desai, eds. *Women's Activism and Globalization: Linking Local Struggles and Transnational Politics.* New York: Routledge, 2002.

Neumann, Rachel, et al., eds. *Anti-Capitalism: A Field Guide to the Global Justice Movement.* NY: The New Press, 2004.

Notes from Nowhere. *We Are Everywhere: The Irresistible Rise of Global Anti-Capitalism.* London: Verso, 2003.

Rowbotham, Sheila and Stephanie Linkogle. *Women Resist Globalization: Mobilizing for Livelihood and Rights.* London: Zed Books, 2001.

Shepard, Benjamin and Ronald Hayduk, eds. *From ACT UP to the WTO: Urban Protest and Community Building in the Era of Globalization.* London: Verso, 2002.

Solnit, David, ed. *Globalize Liberation: How to Uproot the System and Build a Better World.* San Francisco: City Lights, 2003.

Wallach, Lori. *Whose Trade Organization? A Field Guide to the World Trade Organization.* 2nd edition. New York: The New Press, 2004.

USEFUL CURRICULA ON CLASS, ECONOMICS, AND SOCIAL JUSTICE

Adams, Maurianne, et al., eds. *Teaching for Diversity and Social Justice: A Source Book.* New York: Routledge, 1997.

American Friends Service Committee. *Coyuntural Analysis: Critical Thinking for Meaningful Action.* Chicago: American Friends Service Committee, 1997. (312-427-2533).

Bigelow, Bill and Norm Diamond. *The Power in Our Hands: A Curriculum on the History of Work and Workers in the United States.* New York: Monthly Review, 1988.

Bigelow, Bill and Bob Peterson, eds. *Rethinking Globalization: Teaching for Justice in an Unjust World.* Milwaukee, WI: Rethinking Schools, 2002. (800-669-4192).

Bigelow, Bill, et al. *Rethinking Our Classrooms: Teaching for Equity and Justice.* (Vols. 1 and 2). Milwaukee, WI: Rethinking Schools, 1994, 2001. (800-669-4192).

Boyd, Andrew. *The Activist Cookbook: Creative Actions for a Fair Economy.* Boston: United for a Fair Economy, 1997/99. (617-423-2148).

Christiansen, Linda. *Reading, Writing and Rising Up: Teaching About Social Justice and the Power of the Written Word.* Milwaukee, WI: Rethinking Schools, 2000.

Derman-Sparks, Louise and the Anti-Bias Curriculum Task Force. *Anti-Bias Curriculum: Tools for Empowering Young Children.* Washington, DC: National Association for the Education of Young Children, 1989. (800-424-2460).

Giecek, Tamara Sober with United for a Fair Economy. *Teaching Economics As if People Mattered.* Boston: United for a Fair Economy, 2000. (617-423-2148).

Hazen, Don and Julie Winokur, eds. *We the Media: A Citizen's Guide to Fighting for Media Democracy.* New York: The New Press, 1997.

Highlander Research and Education Center. *A Very Popular Economic Education Sampler.* New Market, TN: Highlander Research and Education Center, (nd). (423-933-3443).

Kivel, Paul and Allan Creighton. *Making the Peace: A 15-Session Violence Prevention Curriculum for Young People.* Alameda, CA: Hunter House, 1997.

Lee, Enid, et al. *Beyond Heroes and Holidays: A Practical Guide to K-12 Anti-Racist, Multicultural Education and Staff Development.* Washington, DC: Network of Educators on the Americas, 1998. (202-238-2379).

Louie, Miriam Ching with Linda Burnham. *Women's Education in the Global Economy: A Workbook of Actvities, Games, Skits and Strategies for Activists, Organizers, Rebels and Hell Raisers.* Oakland, CA: Women of Color Resource Center, 2000. (510-848-9272).

Martinez, Elizabeth and Doug Norberg. *Viva La Causa: 500 Years of Chicano History.* Albuquerque, NM: Southwest Organizing Project, 1991.

Pelo, Ann and Fran Davidson. *That's Not Fair!: A Teacher's Guide to Activism with Young Children.* St. Paul, MN: Redleaf Press, 2000.

Praxis/Economic Justice Project. *Economics Education: Building a Movement for Global Economic Justice.* Chicago: American Friends Service Committee, 2001. (312-427-2533).

Public Health and Labor Institutes. *Corporate Power and the American Dream.* New York: The Apex Press, 1997.

Rose, Stephen. *Social Stratification Book and Poster.* New York: The New Press, 1999.

SOUL. *Global Justice Training Manual: Political Education Against the War.* Oakland, CA: School of Unity and Liberation, 2003. (510-451-5466).

Teaching for Change. *Putting the* Movement *Back into Civil Rights Teaching: A Teaching Guide for K-12 Classrooms.* Washington, DC: Teaching for Change, 2004.

Vasquez, Hugh, et al. *Making Allies, Making Friends: A Curriculum for Making the Peace in Middle School.* Alameda, CA: Hunter House, 2003.

Wei, Deborah and Rachael Kamel. *Resistance in Paradise: Rethinking 100 Years of U.S. Involvement in the Caribbean and the Pacific.* Philadelphia: American Friends Service Committee, 1998.

VIDEOGRAPHY ON CLASS,
WEALTH, POWER, RESISTANCE
AND SOCIAL JUSTICE

Below is a listing with brief annotations of films about many of the issues raised in this book. Just about every film made deals with issues of class and power, race and gender, whether explicitly or implicitly. Most of these films look directly at these issues, or at least, are excellent tools for discussions about these issues. These films vary tremendously in quality, style, subject, and intent. Use them to provoke your own thinking and to engage in discussions with others about who decides, who benefits, and who pays.

The Adventures of Robin Hood (1938) Classic story of the bandit who redistributed wealth from the rich to the poor.

At Play in the Fields of the Lord (1991) Two U.S. missionary couples in Brazil end up destroying the indigenous people they are trying to save.

Amistad (1997) African captives on the slave ship Amistad free themselves but get caught up in the U.S. legal system.

Antitrust (2000) Computer code writer discovers the superrich head of the company is corrupt and trying to build an empire.

Ballad of Gregorio Cortez (1983) Because of a language misunderstanding a Mexican cowhand kills a white sheriff in self-defense and then tries to elude the law.

Barbarians at the Gate (1993) Tells of the takeover battle for RJR Nabisco and the workings of the tobacco company.

Bastard Out of Carolina (1997) Autobiography of a white girl who struggles out of poverty and child abuse in the south.

Battle of Algiers (1966) Story of the Algerian fight for freedom from French colonial rule in 1954.

Beloved (1998) After Emancipation a slave is still trying to free herself from the effects of slavery.

The Big One (1998) Michael Moore's film about his book promo tour and his encounter with the publishing industry.

Blue Collar (1978) The life of three auto workers trying to improve their lives by robbing the union.

Bob Roberts (1992) Satire about a senatorial race and what the candidate is willing to do to win.

Bopha! (1993) A conservative police officer and his anti-apartheid activist son deal with moral values and family relationships in preliberation South Africa.

Born in Flames (1983) A futuristic story of a women's army that intervenes when women are harassed on the street and challenges state control of the media.

Born on the Fourth of July (1989) A paraplegic veteran returns from Vietnam and becomes an antiwar protestor.

Bowling for Columbine (2002) Michael Moore's look at the roots of violence and the gun industry in the U.S.

Braveheart (1995) Story of thirteenth century Scottish uprising against the British.

Bread and Chocolate (1974) Uneducated Italian immigrant tries to survive in bourgeois Switzerland.

Breaker Morant (1980) Three Australian soldiers are tried for killing prisoners.

Breaking Away (1979) Working class youth compete in bicycle race against local college students while trying to figure out their future.

Broadcast News (1987) A look at network news through the lens of romance.

Bulworth (1998) A politician begins to speak truth about politics and money, sending shock waves through society.

The Burning Season (1994) Brazilian peasants in the Amazon form a union to protect their land.

Cabeza de Vaca (1990) A Spanish sailor is rescued from a shipwreck by Native Americans in Florida, grows to respect their culture, and, subsequently challenges his Spanish rescuers on their behavior.

Cabaret (1972) Cabaret singer in Nazi Germany tries to ignore the rising tide of violence around her.

Casa de los Babys (2003) Six white women wait in a coastal Mexican town to adopt Mexican babies.

Casualties of War (1989) A U.S. soldier in Vietnam brings attention to his buddies' rape and murder of a Vietnamese woman.

Chicken Run (2000) Chickens organize themselves to escape from becoming chicken pies.

The China Syndrome (1979) An executive at a nuclear power plant discovers a concealed accident and tries to sound the alarm.

Chinatown (1974) A detective tries to unravel the roles of the powerful in the complex politics of water in Los Angeles in the early history of the city.

Citizen Ruth (1996) The portrayal of a poor, young, pregnant white woman delivered by the criminal justice system into the hands of anti-abortion and pro-choice forces.

A Civil Action (1998) Lawyer brings case against corporations accused of dumping leukemia-causing toxins among children.

Cradle Will Rock (1999) Depression-era theater project is about to be shut down by right-wing politicians.

Deadly Business (1986) A former criminal becomes a government informant about the dumping of dangerous chemicals.

Deadly Deception: General Electric, Nuclear Weapons, and Our Environment (1991) Documentary about the devastating impact of GE's development and testing of nuclear weapons.

Dodes 'ka-den (1970) Depicts the community life of a group of slum dwellers in Tokyo.

Driving Miss Daisy (1989) Story of the 25-year relationship between an aging Jewish woman living in the South, and the black chauffer she is forced to rely on.

El Norte (1983) Story of a Guatemalan brother and sister, refugees, who make the difficult trip north to succeed in the U.S.

Erin Brockovich (2000) A single mother uncovers a utility company's toxic waste polluting a community's water supply.

Follow Me Home (1997) Four young men of color set out from California to paint a mural on the White House.

Freedom Song (2000) Young Blacks in a small Mississippi town struggle with the impact of participating in the civil rights movement.

Gandhi (1982) The story of Gandhi's life and India's struggle for liberation from England using tactics of non-violent resistance.

Global Village or Global Pillage?: How People Around the World are Challenging Corporate Globalization (1999) This documentary explores the impacts of globalization and uses video clips, interviews, music and comics to show grassroots organizing and transnational solidarity efforts to shape the global economy.

Gosford Park (2001) Drama set at a party in a country house in England in 1932, showing the lives of upstairs guests and downstairs servants.

Grapes of Wrath (1940) The Joad family migrates from dust-bowl Oklahoma to work in the orchards of California.

Harlan County, U.S.A. (1976) Coal miners try to win a United Mine Workers contract in Kentucky.

Heat and Dust (1983) A young bride joins her husband at his post in India and rebels against the caste system.

Hoop Dreams (1994) Documentary about two inner-city basketball stars' lives through high school.

Incident at Oglala: The Leonard Peltier Story (1992) A documentary about the murder of two FBI agents and the trial of Leonard Peltier in the context of recent United States government/Oglala Nation history.

The Insider (1999) Tobacco company executive turns whistle-blower. Newsmen covering the story confront media collusion with the companies.

JFK (1991) A different look at the 1963 assassination of President John F. Kennedy.

Jack and the Beanstalk: The Real Story (2001) Modern day Jack discovers that his family was responsible for the murder of the giant and the theft of his property, and realizes he must take responsibility for it.

Julia (1977) A woman risks her life getting support to a longtime friend working in the resistance in Germany during WWII.

The Killing Floor (1985) A Black sharecropper migrates to Chicago and becomes involved in the labor movement during a period of race riots.

Lagaan (2001) When their taxes are doubled, an Indian village comes together to challenge the local British ruler to a cricket match. A musical set in nineteenth century rural India.

Lakota Woman: Siege at Wounded Knee (1994) Autobiography of Mary Crow Dog and her role in the 1973 American Indian Movement's occupation of Wounded Knee.

Les Miserables (1935, 1978) Classic French story of a man who steals a loaf of bread, is imprisoned, tortured, released, and then pursued by a detective.

Les Miserables (1995) Modern version of Hugo's classic set in WWII Germany with the hero helping a Jewish family escape the Holocaust.

Life or Debt (2002) Documentary about the impact that U.S. foreign and economic policy have on the people of Jamaica contrasted with the impression that tourists receive of the country.

Lone Star (1995) Story of fathers and sons in a border town dealing with race, class, immigration, and family issues.

The Long Walk Home (1989) In defiance of her husband, a well-off white woman in Montgomery, AL decides to support the bus strike to support her Black maid.

Los Olvidados (1950) Story of the harsh lives and the violence of young people living in the slums of Mexico City.

Lumumba (2001) The rise and subsequent CIA supported overthrow of the charismatic popular leader of the Congo.

Malcolm X (1992) The story of Malcolm X's growth from drug dealer to political leader.

Marie (1985) A docudrama about a divorced and battered woman who works her way through school, heads the parole board in Tennessee, and then blows the whistle on her bosses.

Matewan (1987) Coal miners organize and strike during the 1920s.

Milagro Beanfield War (1988) Members of a small New Mexico town organize to oppose land development and save their water rights.

Missing (1982) A conservative U.S. father tries to find out what happened to his son who disappeared during a military coup in a South American country (Chile).

Modern Times (1936) A Charlie Chaplin silent film about life as an assembly line worker.

The Nasty Girl (1990) A docudrama about a bright young German model who uncovers the Nazi collaboration of her fellow townspeople and faces their wrath.

Newsies (1992) Musical about the 1899 New York newsboys' strike against the publisher Joseph Pulitzer.

1900 (1976) The story of two Italian families, one poor and one landowning, during the early years of the twentieth century.

Nine to Five (1980) Three office secretaries kidnap their boss and start running things on their own.

Norma Rae (1979) A poor, uneducated textile worker joins forces with a New York labor organizer to unionize the reluctant workers at a Southern mill.

Northern Lights (1979) A small farmer fights against the government in the Midwest in 1915.

The Organizer (1964) A group of textile workers, led by a professor, strike against unsafe working conditions in nineteenth century Italy.

Panther (1995) A fictionalized account of the Black Panther's fight for community development seen through the eyes of a Vietnam vet turned infiltrator.

Philadelphia (1993) A corporate attorney gets AIDS and is fired, then sues his former law firm for discrimination.

The Quiet American (2003) A story about the growing undercover U.S. military presence in Vietnam in the mid-1950s.

Rabbit Proof Fence (2002) Three young native women are kidnapped by the Australian government and sent to boarding school, but they escape and travel across Australia to return home.

A Raisin in the Sun (1989) The struggles of the members of a black family who face racism and greed when they move into a white neighborhood in the 1950s.

Reds (1981) An account of John Reed's life as an early twentieth century communist who tried to start a communist party in the U.S. and wrote about the Russian Revolution.

The Revolution Will Not Be Televised (2003) An inside look at the U.S. supported 2002 attempted coup in Venezuela.

Roger and Me (1989) Semi-documentary about Michael Moore's attempt to meet with GM's president Roger Smith to talk about the devastating economic impact GM had on Flint, MI when it closed its factories there.

Romero (1989) A biography of the Salvadoran Archbishop who stood up for the poor against the ruling class and military.

Roots (1977) A black man searches for his roots in Africa, revealing many layers of U.S. history.

Rosa Luxemburg (1986) A biography of the life and politics of German Jewish radical Rosa Luxemburg.

Rosewood (1997) The tragic story of a prosperous Black community in Florida destroyed by attacks by neighboring Whites.

The Ruling Class (1972) A satire of the British upper class about an earl who believes he is Jesus Christ.

Salaam Bombay! Story of an Indian child beggar trying to return to his home in the country.

Sally Hemings: An American Scandal (2000) Fictional account of the 38-year relationship between Thomas Jefferson and his young house slave.

Salt of the Earth (1954) Surpressed for 30 years in the U.S., this is the story of a strike in a zinc mine in New Mexico and the anti-Hispanic racial tensions that accompany it.

Salvador (1986) Two U.S. citizens in El Salvador must confront the realities of political violence there.

Sankofa (1993) An African American model on a photo shoot in West Africa is taken back to slave days and vividly experiences the horrors of slavery and the modes of resistance used against it.

School Ties (1992) A story about what happens when private school classmates find out that the football star on campus is Jewish.

Separate But Equal (1991) Dramatization of the 1954 Brown vs. Board of Education Supreme Court decision that outlawed segregated schools.

Silkwood (1983) The story of a nuclear plant worker and activist who was killed while investigating shoddy practices at the plant.

Sounder (1972) The father of a black sharecropping family is jailed for stealing to feed his family in rural Louisiana.

Spartacus (1960) Story of the slave revolt against the Roman Empire led by a gladiator in 73 BCE.

State of Siege (1973) The story of a USAID/CIA employee involved in torture who is killed by guerrillas in Uruguay in the 1960s.

Stonewall (1995) Story of the diverse homosexual and trans community which participated in the uprising at the Stonewall in New York.

Strike (1924) A silent classic about striking factory workers and their fight against Czarist troops in 1912.

This Boy's Life (1993) A young man tries to choose between prep school and hanging with his friends when he and his mother move to a town near Seattle.

Thousand Pieces of Gold (1991) A young Chinese woman is sold to a marriage broker and shipped to the United States to be a prostitute.

Three Kings (1999) At the end of the Gulf War four soldiers go on a secret mission in Iraq and learn about disturbing aspects of U.S. policy in the Middle East.

Titanic (1997) A portrayal of class structure and cross-class romance during the sinking of the famous passenger ship.

Traffic (2000) A complex fictionalized story of the politics and players in the Mexico-U.S. drug trade.

Traffik (1990) Fictionalized story of various people involved in the complicated international heroin trade.

The Triangle Factory Fire Scandal (1979) True story of the Triangle textile factory fire which killed 145 workers and changed worker safety standards.

Viva Zapata! (1952) Biography of Mexican revolutionary Emiliano Zapata.

Wag the Dog (1997) A media company stages a foreign invasion to distract attention from the president's fondling of a Girl Scout.

The War at Home (1996) Story about the long-term effects of the Vietnam War on a vet and his family.

A Woman Called Moses (1978) The story of Harriet Tubman, who bought her freedom as a slave, started the Underground Railroad, and freed hundreds of slaves in an attack at Combahee River.

Z (1969) Semi-documentary about the assassination of a Greek nationalist in the 1960s.

Zoot Suit (1981) A Mexican American is falsely accused of a murder in the 1940s during a time of intense racial conflict.

MAGAZINES

Black Scholar 510-547-6633 or www.theblackscholar.org

Clamor www.clamormagazine.org

Colorlines 510-653-3415 or www.arc.org

Dollars & Sense 617-876-2434 or www.dollarsandsense.org

In Motion Magazine at www.inmotionmagazine.org

In These Times 773-772-0100 or www.inthesetimes.com

Left Business Observer 212-219-0010 or www.leftbusinessobserver.com

Left Turn www.leftturn.org

Mother Jones 415-665-6637 or www.motherjones.com

MS www.msmagazine.com

The Nation 212-209-5400 or www.thenation.com

New Labor Forum 212-827-0200 or www.qcpages.qc.edu/newlaborforum/

Off Our Backs www.offourbacks.org

The Progressive 608-257-4626 or www.progressive.org

Race and Class 44 20 78 37 0041 or www.irr.org/publication/raceandclass/

Rethinking Schools www.rethinkingschools.org

Souls 212-854-7080 or www.columbia.edu

Tikkun 510-664-1200 or www.tikkun.org

Z magazine www.zmag.org

ORGANIZATIONS AND WEBSITES

The Action Center www.corporations.org

AFL/CIO www.aflcio.org/corporateamerica/paywatch

Alternet www.alternet.org

American Friends Service Committee 215-241-7170 www.afsc.org

Applied Research Center 510-465-9577 www.arc.org

Bank Information Center 202-737-7752 www.bicusa.org

Barrons www.barronsmag.com

The Black Commentator www.blackcommentator.com

Break Through: Education for Economic Action 314-862-5773

Campaign Finance Information Center 573-882-2042
www.campaignfinance.org

Center for Economic and Policy Research 202-293-5380 www.cepr.net

Center for Labor Research and Education 512-642-0323
http://laborcenter.berkeley.edu

Center for Popular Economics 413-545-0743 www.populareconomics.org

Center for Public Integrity 202-466-1300 www.publicintegrity.org

Center for Responsive Politics 202-857-0044 www.opensecrets.org or
www.crp.org

Center for Voting and Democracy 301-270-4616 www.fairvote.org

Center on Budget and Policy Priorities 202-408-1080 www.cbpp.org

Columbia Journalism Review 212-854-1881 www.cjr.org

Common Cause 202-833-1200 www.commoncause.org

Common Dreams News Center www.commondreams.org

Corporate Europe Observatory 31-20-612-7023 www.corporateeurope.org

Corpwatch 510-271-8080 www.corpwatch.org

Counterpunch 800-840-3683 www.counterpunch.org

Data Center 510-835-4835-4692 www.datacenter.org

Democracy Now! 212-431-9090 www.democracynow.org

Democracy.org 206-374-2414 www.democracy.org

Economic Policy Institute 202-775-8810 www.epinet.org

Ecumenical Coalition for Economic Justice 416-921-4615

The Emperor's New Clothes www.emperors-clothes.com

Fairness and Accuracy in Reporting 212-633-6700 www.fair.org

Focus on the Global South (FOCUS) 66-2-218-7363 www.focusweb.org

Forbes magazine www.forbes.com

Foreign Affairs magazine www.foreignaffairs.org

Fortune magazine www.fortune.com

The Global Network for Democratic Media 212-246-0202 www.mediachannel.org

Grassroots Policy Project 202-387-2933 www.grassrootspolicy.org

Guerrilla News Netwatch www.guerrillanews.com

Highlander Research and Education Center 423-933-3443 www.hrec.org

Independent Media Center www.indymedia.org

Inequality.org www.inequality.org

Institute for Democracy Studies 212-423-9237 www.idsonline.org

The Institute for Policy Studies 202-234-9382 www.ips-dc.org

The Institute on Taxation and Economic Policy 888-626-2622 www.itepnet.org

Interfaith Center on Corporate Responsibility 212-870-2295 www.iccr.org

International Action Center 212-633-6646 www.iacenter.org

International Council for Adult Education 416-588-1211 www.unesco.org/education

Jews for Racial and Economic Justice 212-647-8966 www.jfrej.org

Just Economics 510-526-8577

Kensington Welfare Rights Union 215-203-1945 www.kwru.org

Labor/Community Strategy Center 213-387-2800 www.thestrategycenter.org

Macrocosm USA, Inc. 805-927-2515 www.macronet.org

Moveon www.moveon.org

National Committee for Responsive Philanthropy 202-387-9177 www.ncrp.org

The New Standard 315-422-1103 http://newstandardnews.net

New York Times www.nytimes.com

No Logo www.nologo.org

Pacifica Radio 510-849-2590 www.pacifica.org

Political Research Associates 617-666-5300 www.publiceye.org

Praxis Project 202-234-5921 www.thepraxisproject.org

Program on Corporations, Law and Democracy (POCLAD) 509-398-1145
    www.poclad.org

Project Censored www.projectcensored.org

Project South: Institute for the Elimination of Poverty and Genocide
    404-622-0602 www.projectsouth.org

Public Citizen 202-588-1000 www.citizen.org

Public Information Network 206-723-4276 www.endgame.org

Public Information Research 210-509-3160 www.namebase.org

Reclaim Democracy 303-402-0105 www.reclaimdemocracy.org

Resource Center of the Americas 800-452-8382 also Jesuit Center/ the
    Moment Project 416-469-1123 www.americas.org

Sanders Research Associates www.sandersresearch.com

School for Unity and Liberation 510-451-5466

Southerners on New Ground 919-667-1362 www.southnewground.org

Taxpayers for Common Sense 202-546-8500 www.bailoutwatch.org

They Rule www.theyrule.net

Tom Paine.Common Sense www.TomPaine.com

TruthOut 213-489-1971 www.truthout.org

United for a Fair Economy 617-423-2148 www.ufe.net

Wall Street Journal www.wsj.org

Worldwatch Institute 202-452-1999 www.worldwatch.org

Yellow Times www.yt.org

INDEX

In this index, f indicates a figure in the text.

FROM THE AUTHOR

Hi, I'm Paul Kivel.

My work is driven by a powerful question: **how can we live and work to sustain community, nurture each other, and create a multi-cultural society based on love, justice, and interdependence with all living things?** I feel strongly that the challenge posed in that question is the most important one we face today.

My Vision of Social Justice

I envision a society where each person is valued regardless of gender, race, cultural background, sexual identity, ability or disability, or access to wealth.

This society would provide adequate shelter, food, education, recreation, health care, security, and well-paying jobs for all. The land would be respected and sustained, and justice and equal opportunity would prevail.

Such a society would value **cooperation** over competition, **community development** over individual achievement, **democratic participation** over hierarchy and control, and **interdependence** over either dependence or independence.

What I Offer
- workshops and trainings
- talks and keynotes
- consulting and individual mentoring

My work covers a wide range of issues, including how to eradicate racism, prevent male violence, avert youth violence, promote progressive parenting, halt homophobia, uproot class and gender discrimination, and promote social justice by helping people get together to form productive alliances.

Resources available from www.paulkivel.com

My website contains many free resources, including articles, exercises, web resource links, and bibliographies and videographies. You can sign up for my newsletter, and send me comments. You'll also find my bookstore, which features workbooks, curriculum guides, and facilitator's manuals. My titles include:

Boys Will Be Men: Raising Our Sons for Courage, Caring & Community

Uprooting Racism: How White People Can Work for Racial Justice

Men's Work: How to Stop the Violence that Tears our Lives Apart

Young Men's Work: Stopping Violence and Building Community (with Allan Creighton)

Young Women's Lives: Building Self-Awareness for Life (with M. Nell Myhand)

Making the Peace: A Violence Prevention Curriculum for Young People (with Allan Creighton)

Helping Teens Stop Violence

For further information and resources, I invite you to contact me at: pkivel@mindspring.com.